1·86

Religious Organization and
Religious Experience

Association of Social Anthropologists
A Series of Monographs

A.S.A. MONOGRAPH 21

Religious Organization and Religious Experience

edited by

J. Davis

Reader in Social Anthropology,
The University of Kent at Canterbury

1982

 ACADEMIC PRESS

A Subsidiary of Harcourt Brace Jovanovich, Publishers
London   New York
Paris   San Diego   San Francisco   São Paulo
Sydney   Tokyo   Toronto

ACADEMIC PRESS INC. (LONDON) LTD.
24/28 Oval Road
London NW1

United States Edition published by
ACADEMIC PRESS INC.
111 Fifth Avenue
New York, New York 10003

British Library Cataloguing in Publication Data

Religious organization and religious experience.
—(A.S.A. monographs; 21)
1. Religions
I. Davis, J.   II. Series
306'.06   BL80.2

ISBN 0-12-206580-8
LCCN 810831

Typeset by Permanent Typesetting & Printing Co., Ltd.
Printed by Whitstable Litho Ltd., Whitstable, Kent

Contributors

Bourdillon, M.F.C., Department of Sociology, University of Zimbabwe, P.O. Box MP 167, Mount Pleasant, Salisbury, Zimbabwe.

Bowes, A.M., Department of Sociology, University of Stirling, Stirling, FK9 4LA, UK.

Christian, W.A., Jnr., 34 Victoria, Somerville, Mass. 02144, USA.

Davis, J., Eliot College, The University, Canterbury, Kent CT2 7NS, UK.

Eades, J.S., Darwin College, The University, Canterbury, Kent CT2 7NS, UK.

Fuller, C.J., Department of Social Anthropology, London School of Economics, Houghton St., London WC2A 2AE, UK.

Kiernan, J.P., Department of African Studies, University of Natal, King George V Avenue, Durban, S. Africa.

Lienhardt, R.G., Institute of Social Anthropology, 51 Banbury Rd., Oxford OX2 6PF, UK.

Mardin, S., Department of Social Sciences, Bogaziçi Universitesi, P.K. 2, Bebek, Istanbul, Turkey.

Ruel, M.J., Clare College, Cambridge, UK.

Southwold, M., Department of Anthropology, University of Manchester, Roscoe Building, Brunswick St., Manchester M13 9PL, UK.

Swanston, H.F.G., Eliot College, The University, Canterbury, Kent CT2 7NS, UK.

Trexler, R.C., Department of History, S.U.N.Y., Binghamton, N.Y. 13901, USA.

Preface

The contributors to this volume were invited to present papers to the 1981 ASA conference which would illuminate the contrast between organized and community religions: what are the differences in the day-to-day experience of being a Christian, a Buddhist, a Jew and of being a Dinka or a Nuer? The fact that the former terms indicate a person who belongs to a religion, the latter, a person who belongs to a people is already some indication of the kinds of problem addressed here. But why do some religions proselytize and others not? Why are some more hierarchical and bureaucratic than others, and what consequence does that have for their practitioners? To what extent is experience in fact controlled in the organized religions?

As anthropologists study more complex and civilized societies they find new kinds of problem, as well as terms and concepts used by other kinds of scholar. They have to adapt tried techniques of investigation to different kinds of field. The contributors who include historians and a theologian have each chosen a topic which illustrates some of these themes, and which explicitly or implicitly demonstrates the adaptations of method they are constrained to make. The essays remain nonetheless recognizably anthropological — devoted to a scrupulous investigation of institutions and culture which is then translated, is made accessible to readers who lack the experiences and assumptions of those whose practices are described.

The Association wishes to thank the Esperanza Trust and the Spalding Trust for grants which made it possible for Professor Mardin and Dr Christian to attend the conference. Professor Trexler's own University (State University of New York) made a grant to him: to each of these institutions thanks are due for generosity which made the conference, and this derived book, so successful. The excellent index to the book has been compiled by Mr John Goy.

January 1982   J. Davis

For Professor Sir Raymond Firth, to remind him of the affection and respect his fellow members have for the Life President of the Association of Social Anthropologists; and to celebrate his eightieth birthday.

Contents

Introduction

J.Davis

It is of course always a matter of judgement where to draw boundaries in social matters (say, between communities) as in intellectual ones (say, between kinds of religion). Given that, the writers whose papers are included in this volume have concurred that there are marked differences in the nature of religious experience between community religions and others. In general terms, the classic anthropological studies of religion have concerned those cases where the (roughly defined) boundaries of religious practice coincide with the (roughly defined) boundaries of political and economic institutions and of language. If the contributors here concern themselves with religions where there is no such coincidence of boundary, that is because anthropologists increasingly study societies where such relative simplicity is lacking; and because they think that religious experience, the ordinary everyday experience of living with a particular divinity, with particular questions and answers about life, death, misfortune, happiness — religious experience is quite different in the two cases.

The classic studies of religion have shown that the language which shapes peoples' notions of divinity, the practices of their religion, the questions and answers which are important to them, is typically fairly closely related to the daily experience of family, political, and economic life. But in the more complex religions those elements of religious discourse have to serve for peoples of sometimes very different social orders: urban, industrial Christians, for example, use the language of sheep herding, about which they are quite likely to have rather different ideas from Abraham. These religions, moreover, are typically organized, and the language of religion is related to the discourse of experts within an organization: religious experience is more specialized and more controlled in these cases because the idioms of (say) a pious old woman in a Spanish village are related to (although not exclusively nor directly derived from) an esoteric discourse in Rome. In contrast to community religions, organized ones are characterized by religious experts who talk to each other, who hold office and who are to some degree arbiters of truth.

The existence of such specialists carries a number of consequences. For example, all the members of the religion make a distinction between specialists and non-specialists; and the distinction may be marked by ritual, residential, or hereditary segregations. In many cases esoteric religious knowledge generates an exoterics, a simpler and sometimes less exigent form of doctrine and practice, more adapted to the simplicity and even heterodoxy of the non-experts, allowing greater speculation and broader practice than may be proper for learned or otherwise distinguished persons. A universalizing religion seems always to contain such room for local communities to colour-in the broad outlines of their religion. Indeed, Southwold suggests that when an elite priesthood needs to eat, it will quite likely tolerate the doctrinal vagaries of farmers; and he argues that the contempt and differentiation which leads the present-day Sinhalese middle classes to distinguish village Buddhism from true Buddhism is not traditional: it has rather more to do with absorption by English-speakers of the western Buddhist scholars' notion that educated people must necessarily know more truth than uneducated ones.

The distinction between expert and non-expert, which is the basis of religious organization, entails another distinction between the more expert and the less so. The community of experts is thus an arena in which men may strive to differentiate themselves. That is so whatever the kind of organization they belong to. The spirit mediums discussed here by Bourdillon scarcely constitute an organization at all, but they compete in terms of the hierarchical position of their spirits, as well as of the numbers of their followers. Mardin describes the ways Said Nursi sought to make his mark in the various arenas offered by the Ottoman state and the fluid, uncentralized religious institutions: a man with the signs of a religious vocation makes his career in academic dispute, in mosque politics, as a peacemaker among tribesmen and between tribesmen and townsmen, even between the state and dangerously strong religious orders. The growth and importance of Said Nursi's movement however is probably related to his relative insuccess in imperial politics: lodged in Istambul with the bird-keeper, his *Entführung* or dismissal was probably a pre-condition of the ultimate development of a potentially pan-Islamic movement of revival, of the communion of hearts. A comparison of Said Nursi with Swanston's account of Luther suggests interesting differences, which may be related to what Mardin calls "the close conjunction of religion and politics" in Islam, and their relative disjunction in the Roman church: Luther's academic and theological struggle — verbally at least scarcely less violent than Said

Nursi's — did not lead him to an attack on the university system nor on Caesar's affairs.

A third distinction necessarily made in organized religions is between co-religionists, whether expert or not, and others. When the boundaries of polity, economy, religion, language coincide, the issue is not important. It is universalizing religions which require criteria of inclusion and exclusion. It is the experts who control definitions of membership : these are extremely variable and, as Ruel argues so forcefully, it is a "monumental peculiarity" of Christianity to include belief among the criteria. Similarly, the scrupulous rules devised to establish whether inspiration is divine or devilish, described by Christian for early modern Spain, have parallels only in the attempts by lay bureaucracies, based on western models, to reform Tamilnadu Hinduism. The more usual tests are performance of rituals (while may include liturgical performance of creeds) and observance of laws. The central irony of Bowes' contribution is that Israelis who make a declaration of atheism do so in a system in which belief is not really a central issue : of great importance to the kibbutzniks of Goshen, unbelief is not really a marker in the wider Israeli society. Israeli atheists are perforce Jewish atheists, a point which Kibbutzniks recognize when they insist that Christian women who marry in to Goshen should convert to Judaism before they can become atheists.

Again, the distinction between members and non-members entails the formulation of an attitude towards the non-members. In extremely loosely organized religions, Bourdillon's work suggests, there are possibilities of movement between mutually tolerant systems of spirit mediumship; and the tolerance of Sinhalese Buddhists to non-Buddhists seems absolute. Proselytization is another matter: it requires an organizational commitment to the urgency of persuasion, even though — as a comparison of the papers by Trexler and Lienhardt shows quite clearly — the doctrines of conversion may change significantly. It is usually helpful to have a colonizing state to support the mission, and for the mission to have a territorial basis which corresponds to that of the intended converts. Part of the success of the conversion of New Spain in the 16th century, as Trexler points out, results from the fact that missionaries and Aztecs shared roughly similar notions of ritual space, and could conduct their warfare on a commonly defined ground. The mission to the Dinka came up against Dinka contempt for settlements, and the missionaries described themselves as ill-organized to cope with transhumant pastoralists. Lienhardt thinks it is difficult to convert people from a religion which is in important respects similar to the one you wish to convert them to; and that most Dinka converts were attracted by the availability of knowledge of a technical, administrative and political kind, rather than by the essential importances of the Christian message: without such knowledge, Dinka realized, they would have found it even more difficult to survive in a modern state of a not particularly protective kind. Trexler does not provide directly parallel information: it is hard to know at this distance with what response the youth of New Spain greeted the news, for example, that they would be the first of their kind in heaven. Trexler thinks, however, that the attractions of legitimate spiritual paternity, of spouses, of property (which were on offer because the Church and the colonizing state had combined to deprive young men of traditional access to these goods) were more important than the remoter attractions of salvation.

Lienhardt's discussion of parallax is crucial to the discussion of conversion, and has, indeed, a wider significance: it could be used fruitfully of any attempt to convert people from one way of thought to another — in development programmes, for example, or in centrally directed programmes to introduce political ideologies and systems to local populations. Lienhardt uses the word to refer to the ways images shift in meaning as the user shifts position. In this case the shift from Roman Catholic Italian to Dinka creates shifts in meaning and understanding. It is not simply that the Italians created for themselves a touching illusion when they so eagerly discovered that Dinka knew about *il Demonio, paradiso, inferno*; but rather that Dinka were, or are, using Dinka words which in the mission have one sense and, when spoken in other contexts, have a more specifically Dinka set of referents: "going ahead", as a version of "progress"; even "What".

Language is crucial, not only because parallax can permit an easy accomodation of differences. Any organization creates an esoteric discourse, which shapes and even stimulates experience. Two other papers suggest ways in which language and organization are associated. Christian shows how Ignatius Loyola in effect created a language for the analysis of emotional movements, for the interpretation of apparently unreasonable or inexplicable accessions of tears, of contentment. The handbooks of emotional analysis not only gave meaning to sudden and otherwise unaccountable emotion, but showed how to cultivate tears, by spiritual exercise. Neither private nor public weeping are now so currently accepted as signs of contrition granted, and they occur less often. But this is a clear case of a realm of theological discourse creating a kind of religious experience.

Swanston's paper on Luther makes a rather different point. In relatively highly organized religions, where the language of divinity is used with unusual precision, there may be a fit between the structure and the language of the organization so tight that a change in one has consequences for the other. To some extent Ruel suggests this point when he remarks that disagreement over the inclusion of the word *filioque* in the creeds led to the organizational differentiation of eastern and western churches. Swanston puts the point rather more elaborately and very strikingly: the essence of

Luther's inspiration, of his conversion, and his salvation too, is grammatical — a change from the active to the passive voice. Luther's perception was that it is not man's efforts to achieve, but God's willingness to give, which makes men wise, just, faithful: and his colleagues immediately realized that this change of voice "thrust against the entire structure" of the Church and of the orderliness created in the world by the theology and philosophy of the previous millennium or so. Luther had to fight to maintain the disruptive consequences of his work when less combative followers tried to suggest there was room for accomodation between a Lutheran grammar of divinity and a Roman organization.

The westerner's ideal image of bureaucracy includes a heavy emphasis on writing: it is the organization's ability to create records, to make rules and to remember what they are which makes it so formidable. That is no doubt so also for religious organizations, especially when the religious elite is property-owning or tax-exacting. But, on the evidence presented here, by Swanston, Fuller, and Southwold, it is mistaken to think of sacred texts in those terms: they do not contribute particularly to such hegemony as God's bureaucrats may achieve. In the first place, it is characteristic of sacred texts that they are not precise prescriptions of practice or belief: they are richly redundant, demanding interpretation. In some cases, people do not read them much, but wrap them up and venerate them. Written in relatively inaccessible language, they may be valued more for what they are thought to contain than for what they actually say. As these words are written, it should be said, a British parliamentarian is attempting to get access to some of the rules of the Department of Social Security: there is a temptation to draw a parallel between the rules for the provision of state benefits and, for instance, the rules for invoking the true presence of Siva in his emblematic penis: secret, in an inaccessible language, with little correspondence between what is written and what is done, publication might cause acute embarassment to all parties. But it is only at a superficial level that such parallels exist: for sacred texts are unrevisable, are attributed to a supernatural or inspired agency. The existence of a text and its sacredness is enough, and it scarcely matters in normal times what it actually says.

Nevertheless, a wrapped revelation can also become the object of formal bureaucratic treatment. Fuller describes how the Hindu Religious and Charitable Endowments Commission has insisted that temple practice should be consistent with the prescriptions of the texts — the 28 fundamental Āgamas and the various manuals, all in Sanskrit. Apart from the difficulties of training the priests in such a vast and arcane literature, the texts do not in fact prescribe the correct performance of worship. Like Southwold, Fuller accounts for the intrusion of positivist bureaucracy into religious matters by referring to western influences which lead state officials to set up objective scrutinies of religious activity: it is (is it not?), so clearly in the public interest that religion should be efficacious, in accordance with the principles as revealed, and as unwrapped. The diffusion of religious texts in vernaculars is usually associated with reform or reformation. Mardin says that Said Nursi's teaching, made available nowadays through a movement-owned Californian printing house, "may have been able to legitimise modern science for many Turks". And Luther's German bible, the publications of the French Indology Institute at Pondicherry, and of the western scholar-converts to Buddhism are all associated in broad terms with western modernizing influences. Publication of the revelation allows discussion and interpretation of its meaning by new kinds of expert. So it seems that sacred texts are not necessarily part of the instruments of control by organizations: it depends on who reads them, if anyone does.

The state bureaucracies which, in India, attempt to regulate religion need objective criteria to be able to measure the extent to which religious organizations serve the public spiritual interest. Religious concern with interior states is not always consistent with the positivism inherent in, for example, the government's confidence that "rituals performed correctly are necessarily efficacious". Uncertainties attend that word "correctly", and it is not clear that outward performance is always efficacious. It is easy to exaggerate the inaccessibility of inner states; but it remains the case that organizations are uncomfortable with them, and that people find it easier to be sceptical abut them. Although they recognize the distinction in principle, Sinhalese villagers say it is difficult to distinguish particular cases of meditation from nodding-off. The men who interrogated Francisco Ortiz, Christian says, could not claim authority to dispute his interior certainties about the divine source of his contentment. The awkwardness, from an organization's point of view, of private states is further shown in the publishing history of Juan de Avila's manual *Audi Filia*: in later editions the sections on autodiagnosis of the sources of inspiration were replaced with a note to consult an approved expert.

The Weberian opposition between bureaucracy and charisma is resisted by some of the contributors. Kiernan argues that the distinction does not aid analysis of Zulu Zionist churches. They are highly organized internally, and have a system of transfers between congregations which, in its bureaucratic details, resembles a pass law. The congregations also have charismatic prophets, legitimate mavericks and healers whose conventionalized role, among others, is to control and limit the abuse of authority by the ordained clergy. Kiernan's argument that authority and charisma are interdependent confirms the doubts expressed on this score by sociologists, who have noted the importance of charisma in formal western bureaucracies. But the religious organizations studied here are not like Post Offices. On the one hand, they display a greater variety of kinds of organization than Post Offices do. Bourdillon's spirit mediums operate with a very fluid and negotiable hierarchy; while the highly structured Church militant of New Spain allows mobility only in tightly prescribed paths. Fuller describes the organization of temples with a priesthood which inherits its particular roles and offices; and Mardin's description of Said Nursi's institutional adventures reveals his ability to exploit the differences of competing schools and orders in a system which has no over-arching authority. On the other hand it is clear that religious organizations, of whatever kind, are not simply administrative bodies applying a set of rules to the performance of routine tasks. They have to accomodate human creativity; even the most formally hierarchised and hegemonic church must live in expectation of divine inspiration. They thus belong to a category which is in important respects different from the ideal typical Post Office, and which includes also, perhaps, universities and Arts Councils, some publishing and broadcasting organizations, *conservatoires* and the like: they are all concerned to some degree with the administration of creativity, and with the control of experience which is considered, at any rate in the post-romantic West, perhaps to a lesser extent in the devotionalist East, to be intrinsically personal and interior.

Eades's paper, which is unfortunately the sole representative of post-structuralism in this volume, suggests some of the possible ways in which exterior events — in this case music — might become interior experiences. More apparently abstracted from social reality than the other papers, it is nevertheless a forceful argument that such paths are fundamentally social: symbols, codes, under-codes are social constructions in large measure; and it would be possible in the future — no-one has done so here — to examine the ways in which social constructions, at this level of intimacy, are controlled by identifiable organizations whose personnel and procedures may be studied more concretely.

Writers sometimes distinguish among the universalizing religions according to the immediacy with which individual practitioners communicate with divinity, and the intrusiveness of human mediators in what is conceived as a most personal relation with an almighty. That is undoubtedly a form of differences among religions; but the discussions do not take account of the fact that such distinctions are made within a field which is already relatively homogeneous, and that the religious experience of a Christian, Muslim, Jew, Buddhist, Hindu is, as these papers demonstrate, qualitatively different from that of practitioners of community religions. That is because the language of divinity is not derived from the language of everyday experience, but from the esoteric discourse of experts organized in many different ways and degrees, but confronting similar issues — issues of inclusion and exclusion, of differentiation within the arena created by the organisation, of language and texts, of the assessment and control of interior states. These are among the common

J. Davis

characteristics of organized and universalizing religions, and they are distinctive, uncharacteristic of those community religions traditionally studied by anthropologists.

Christians as Believers

Malcolm Ruel

The argument of my paper is summed up in an early observation of Wilfred Cantwell Smith:

> The peculiarity of the place given to belief in Christian history is a monumental matter, whose importance and relative uniqueness must be appreciated. So characteristic has it been that unsuspecting Westerners have... been liable to ask about a religious group other than their own as well, 'What do they believe?' as though this were the primary question, and certainly were a legitimate one (1978, p. 180. But see also Smith, 1977, 1979, discussed below).

"Unsuspecting Westerners" must of course include unsuspecting western anthropologists who, as many texts will show (e.g. Evans-Pritchard, 1937, p. 21), give primacy to what people "believe" without fully declaring what that word means, nor recognizing, it would seem, just how rooted the concept is in our own cultural religious tradition, Christian and post-Christian, and thus how loaded any statement concerning "belief" easily becomes.

This then is one reason why an anthropologist may be excused if he moves so far from his last as to attempt, however incompetently, to sketch in outline the monumental peculiarity of Christian "belief". At a time when anthropology has turned more and more to give an account of the cognitive aspects of culture it is as well for us to be aware of the complexity of the concepts that we draw from our own culture, which have a history and contextual compulsion of their own which often ill-match the ideas and actions they are used to interpret. The need for critical reflexion becomes even greater when, as in the case of "believing", there has been a radical shift in the use of a term whilst something of its force has been retained. "Believing" in the sense of being committed to some definable set of values has become secularized, detached from Christian believing but not demoted

9

as a concept, so that in a post-Christian, secular culture the phrase "I believe..." (e.g. in the title of Forster's essay, 1939) still gives promise of a personal statement of some significance, a declaration of moral identity.

There is here another reason why it is appropriate for an anthropologist to attempt the task of ethnographic placing, for it is part of the anthropologist's trade to look hard and long at certain key concepts and to explore how use and meaning, context and idea, are constantly engaged in an interplay in which concepts link situations while situations qualify (and thus help to define) concepts. Now "belief" is essentially a word that relates and defines: it relates people, situations and ideas; but in its turn, as I shall argue, it is also in very important ways defined by the context of its use. In this, function and meaning come almost (but never entirely) to coincide; consider, for example, the phrase "the community of believers" that runs like a thematic passacaglia through Hans Küng's *The Church* (1968). If only to keep for some short time the philosophers at bay (to whom the cognitive promise contained in the word "belief" comes, as it were, as a gift from heaven) let us assert resolutely, at least for the present, that the (Christian) concept of belief is as it does and proceed to consider it situationally and behaviourally.

I

To narrow somewhat the vastness of the topic, four periods have been selected from the history of the church in which to discuss the idea of belief and how it is involved in any definition, corporate or personal, of Christian identity. They are: (1) the critical, initial phase in which Christians, the Nazarene sect, emerged as a distinctive religious movement, a community of believers; (2) the immediately succeeding period leading to the Council of Nicaea (325) that witnessed both the developing formal organization of the Church and the establishment of orthodox creeds, sanctioned by the Church councils; (3) the Reformation and in particular Luther's reformulation of what it means to believe (i.e. to have faith); and finally, since we cannot leave ourselves out, (4) the present period, which might be characterized in both Christian and secular contexts as belief diffused — "beyond belief" in the phrase of one (diffusely) believing anthropologist. In this section I use the word "belief" only with its Christian reference and where at all possible I keep to this one word, assuming a sufficient continuity and overlap in meaning between "faith" and "belief" to allow "belief" to do duty for both, except where there is a particular need to distinguish them. This usage has the advantage of permitting a single word correspondence between *belief* in English, *pistis* in Greek and the root *'mn* in Hebrew; this does not imply that these words have (collectively) the same meaning nor that they have (singly) a constant meaning, only that their range of meaning is historically and semantically continuous. (On this issue my usage is radically at variance with that of Wilfred Cantwell Smith, see Section III below.)

The detailed scholarly writings on the terminology of belief, *pistis*, in the New Testament books make it possible to offer a number of summary points. (I rely chiefly on Bultmann and Weiser, 1961; Hatch, 1917: Michel, 1975; and Moule, unpublished.) In its various forms, *pistis* (belief), *pisteuo* (believe), *pistos* (faithful, trustworthy), *apistia* (unbelief), form a key and much used set of terms in the New Testament. The meaning of the word-group does not (with some qualification) depart from its general meaning, or set of meanings, in Greek, but its New Testament use also carries certain connotations derived from that fact that *pisteuo*, to believe, was the term consistently used to translate the Hebrew *he²min*, from the root *'mn* (meaning to be true, reliable or faithful) in the Septuagint. One needs here to distinguish between the meanings of words and the religious ideas they express, for although the two may coincide, they do not always do so, and changes in meaning follow often from the development of pre-existing ideas. Thus both the original Greek use of *pisteuo* and the Hebrew term *'mn* express centrally the notion of trust or confidence. Originally the Greek word-group "denoted conduct that honoured an agreement or bond. It had a social orientation, and its use indicated misconduct by implication" (Michel, 1975, p. 594). In classical Greek literature *pistis* means the trust that a man may place in other men, or gods; credibility, credit in business, guarantee, proof or something to be trusted. Similarly, *pisteuo* means to trust something or someone (ibid.). The word acquired a religious use at an early date, when to "believe" (*pisteuo*) the gods or an oracle expressed on the one hand confidence in them (their veracity or ability to promote welfare) and on the other obedience to them, an acknowledgement of their power to determine human fate. The Hebrew term *'mn* denotes even more directly a quality of relationship: it was used of the reliability or trustworthiness of a servant, a witness, a messenger, or a prophet, but it also served to characterize the relationship between God and his people, reciprocally trusted and trusting, bound by covenant to each other (Michel, 1975, pp. 595-6). In the New Testament the word *pistis* and its related forms still carry the ideas of trust and confidence. In a citation that rings reverberatively through the theology of the centuries, Paul refers to the belief (*pistis*) that Abraham had in God's promise that he would become "the father of many nations" (the story is told in Genesis 15) as an exemplar for the kind of belief (*pistis*) shared by the early Christians. As the belief (i.e. trust) of Abraham was reckoned as righteousness for him, so "Faith is to be reckoned as righteousness to us also, who believe in Him Who raised from the dead our Lord Jesus Christ, who was delivered to death for our sins and raised again to secure our justification" (Romans 4:13-25 Phillips).

Yet in spite of this continuity between the Hebrew and the Greek, the Old and the New Testament, the word *pistis* does come to acquire a special twist in the apostolic writings of the New Testament. One might say that it acquires a technical use. Thus the verb *pisteuo*, to believe, is often used in the sense of to be converted, to become a Christian: "they heard the message and believed" is a formula that repeatedly occurs in the narrative of the expanding church in the Acts of the Apostles; Paul writes of "when we first believed" (Romans 13:11) in the sense of "when we were first converted"; and there are other examples. Similarly, the nominal form "believers" (either *hoi pisteuontes*, "those believing", or *hoi pistoi*, "those of the belief") refers to the converted, the "brothers" or the "saints" as they are also called. We should note that the word "Christian" is itself rarely used (three times in the New Testament) and then always in the context of what others — the people the Christians called unbelievers — were calling them. Finally, the noun *pistis* denotes the "belief" held collectively by the early Christians as a common conviction, a shared confidence that both distinguished and united them as a community. Paul lists these identifying features explicitly and succinctly in Ephesians 4:4-5 in which the central elements are "one Lord, one belief, one baptism".

We need to look more closely at the substance of this shared belief in the last sense above, for it is in relation to this that the concept gains added depth and range. Essentially what these early converts believed was what theologians have come to call (using another technical term) the *kerygma* or proclamation of the Christian message (Bultmann and Weiser, 1961, p. 69; Michel, 1975, pp. 601, 605; Hatch, 1917, pp. 33-4). Now this does not mean just the teaching *of* Jesus, but rather the teaching *about* Jesus, and the crucial fact about Jesus, which summed up all the rest, was his resurrection: this fact is expressed clearly in the passage from Paul, quoted above, and throughout the epistles (and we should recall that these are the earliest Christian documents that we have; the gospels were written later). Christian *belief* now begins to part company from Hebrew *trust*. Both refer to a relationship — the confidence that people have in God, and in the case of the Christians in God through Christ — but for Christians there is the added confidence or conviction about an event (the resurrection and all that that signifies) that had actually taken place. The belief is not just open-ended, oriented to what God may or can do: it is rooted firmly in what God has done, which to deny is to deny the Word of God, that is, the action of God in the world. (On this point see especially Bultmann and Weiser, 1961, p. 82 *et seq.*) This development was to have enormous consequences for the later use of the concept for it is but a short step from *belief* as accepting as a fact (i.e. the event of the resurrection) to *belief* as asserting as a proposition. A distinction made frequently today is between "belief in" (trust in) and "belief that" (propositional belief). The distinction may clear our minds today but it confuses history, for the point about Christian belief, reiterated by theologians (e.g. Lampe, 1976: Moule, unpublished), is that it was both at once.[1]

The creeds, which we must now consider, both reflect and perpetuate this particular notion of Christian belief, that concerns a complex person-event, not least in their reiterated verbal formula: "I believe in — who did—": Person + Event, the two reciprocally defining (Lampe, 1976). Yet if the kernel of the creeds is the recognition of this person-event, their history is one of growing elaboration and formalization, a development that takes place in relation to the developing organization of the Christian body: the shared conviction of a scattered community of Christians becomes the confirmed orthodoxy of the conciliar church.

Brief credal phrases are common in the New Testament and there are occasional longer summaries (as in the passage by Paul) when the writer evidently felt something more explicit was required. In either case they serve as summary statements of the teaching or *kerygma* concerning Christ. The formulary phrase, *Kurios Iesous*, "Jesus [is] Lord", is common and there are many variants. It is clear moreover that such phrases served as conventional declarations of religious allegiance of a symbolic kind. Thus Paul: "If with your mouth you confess *Kurios Iesous* and believe in your heart that God has raised him from the dead, you will be saved" (Romans 10:9) and in another passage (1 Corinthians 12:3) Paul contrasts this confessional formula of affirmation with its opposite, that of denial or denunciation (*Kurios Iesous* v. *Anathema Iesous*, "Cursed be Jesus"), declaring that only the former can be spoken by the Holy Spirit, i.e. that a Christian should be unable to deny Christ. There is some evidence that suspected members of the Christian sect were tested by being asked to make just such a formal denial (Lampe, 1976, p. 54; Kelly, 1972, p. 15) and in the gospels the story of Peter's thrice denial of Christ assumes its significance against the importance of thus "confessing Christ" in the early church (and indeed thereafter). Belief in this context becomes then a badge, a symbol, something that is explicitly affirmed where the act of affirmation has its own functional value.

Such formulary statements were not however creeds in the usual sense of extended declarations of belief. These were to develop in the period up to the fourth century. They emerged in the first place in the context of baptism and then, it would seem, began to be used as statements of the received teaching first for regional congregations and then, in a more self-consciously developed form, as the conciliar creeds prepared for and affirmed by councils representing the whole church or large sections of it. The fact that the earliest creeds were baptismal (on this all authorities are agreed) leads us to note the important post-Easter development of this rite, which acts as a ritual counterpart to the "believing" we have already spoken of as denoting conversion. Jesus's religious career was initiated by baptism from St. John the Baptist but he himself did not baptize people and (except in the case of Jesus) the baptism of St. John was specifically a "baptism of repentance" (i.e. a cleansing rite) and not an initiation. (St. John's message was similarly one of repentance, not of belief.) From the time of the early church, however, baptism came to be used to mark the transition to membership that is so characteristic of Christianity and which in this clear-cut, boundary-marking way is absent from all other world religions. Baptism and belief have parallels in other ways too, for baptism re-enacts symbolically the basic postulate of the belief: as Christ died and rose again so too (it is held) the person being baptized dies and rises again "in Christ". Baptism acts therefore not only as a rite of passage for individual Christians but also as the act by which the church, identified with the risen Christ, is perpetually re-constituted. For it should be understood that the church, although pre-figured in Christ's life, was not in fact founded until after his death and resurrection by those who "believed", i.e. accepted the *kerygma*. (On this point see Küng, 1968, pp. 70-79.) "Belief" here has theologically and sociologically a critical function in establishing the organic relationship between Christ, the risen Lord, and the church as the community who believe in his resurrection and in this way perpetuate it. Hence the importance of conversion (believing) as a break, a passage from the old life to the new life, a kind of resurrection, comparable for the community of believers to the passage through the Red Sea for the Israelites (the Old Testament analogue for Christian baptism). All this is implicit in Paul's "one Lord, one belief, one baptism".

In their relation to baptism the earliest creeds had a dual function: first, and as part of the ritual, candidates were required to respond affirmatively to certain questions about their belief put to them; second, and by extension of the first, statements of belief in the form of a condensed, continuous declaration were used for the instruction of the candidate. (Here and throughout my account of the creeds I rely heavily on Kelly, 1972.) It was the latter form that was to be adopted by the later conciliar creeds but it would seem that even before that happened their use was influenced by the recognition that the received teaching they embodied should be uniform, subject to what Irenaeus in the second century defined as a common "rule of truth", and such credal declarations grew in length and elaborateness because of this. Emerging as "a by-product of the Church's fully developed catechetical system" (Kelly, 1972, p. 64) such creeds were in fact ancillary to the interrogatory baptismal creeds. Thus, a fourth century treatise recalls and comments on the questions asked at baptism that date in this form from at least the second century:

You were questioned, "Dost thou believe in God the Father almighty?" You said, "I believe", and were immersed, that is were buried. Again you were asked, "Dost thou believe in our Lord Jesus Christ and His cross?" You said, "I believe", and were immersed. Thus you were buried along with Christ; for he who is buried along with Christ rises again with Him. A third time you were asked, "Dost thou believe also in the Holy Spirit?" You said, "I believe", and a third time were immersed, so that your threefold confession wiped out the manifold failings of your earlier life (*De Sacramentis* 2, 7 quoted Kelly, 1972, p. 37).

The triadic structure of this interrogatory form was carried over into the declaratory baptismal creeds and thence all the later creeds.

The baptismal creeds summarized the received teaching, but their local use in the widely scattered Christian communities, headed as each was by their bishop, was subject to variation and reformulation. By the end of the third century there is evidence of certain baptismal creeds being cited to test the acceptability of the teaching of a local community, which is to say the teaching of the bishop. There was here a shift in the use of creeds which was critical. It was no longer the catechumen's belief that was at issue (and thus individual membership of the Christian community) but rather the orthodoxy of the bishop (and thus his and his congregation's valid membership of the Christian body). The major, decisive step was taken with the Council of Nicaea (325) when the assembled bishops were asked to accept a statement of teaching, which was set out in the form of a declaratory creed. (This was not the "Nicene creed" of the prayer books but it laid the basis for it.) A major preoccupation in the drafting of this statement was to exclude the teaching of Arius and his followers who (as it happened) had themselves drawn up a creed-like summary of their position (Kelly, 1972, p. 206). Two hundred and eighteen out of 220 bishops attending the Council did sign their acceptance and an indication of the change in function of this the first of the conciliar creeds is the fact that the document drawn up states not only what is the received belief, but also what is not: *anathema* is pronounced on those who hold certain propositions (i.e. those held by Arius and his supporters). "Belief" now comes to define, not merely the Christian from the non-Christian (the believer from the non-believer), but the true Christian from the false (the true believer from the heretic). Moreover, the latter function assumes an organized authority: bishops in council and not just in their sees.

Two important circumstances are associated with the Council of Nicaea (Kelly, 1972; Chadwick, 1967). The first is the patronage of Constantine, who had recently adopted the Christian cause and who was concerned to bring the scattered Christian communities into some kind of common organization. Nicaea was the first of the church councils and its establishment of an overall church authority is evidenced not only by the bishops' formal acceptance of the creed but also by their agreement to a number of other liturgical and disciplinary measures (the latter concerning not least the actions of bishops). The second circumstance has already been mentioned: the teachings of Arius who, in emphasizing the absolute perfection of the Godhead, was led to accord a lower, unequal place to Christ. The Council of Nicaea did not resolve the Arian controversy (nor indeed the underlying issue of how to interpret a trinitarian God) and the fluctuating fortunes of the Arian and anti-Arian (or Nicene) camps dominated the church until the Council and creed of Constantinople (381) formulated what was to become the basic doctrine of the Trinity. Any account of this period (e.g. Chadwick, 1967, Chapter 9) makes it clear that, whatever the merits of the intellectual issue, community loyalties and identities were also very closely involved: the major cleavage between Greek East and Latin West; the dominance of certain key bishoprics and their sees; the fortunes of individual bishops who were promoted or ousted according to their spiritual (and human) loyalties; the relationship of the church to the foundering Roman empire; all have a part to play in the story. Out of this time and out of this general debate also (but not directly out of Arianism) emerged the one doctrinal and credal point that separates the Roman from the Orthodox churches, the West from the East. This concerns the phrase *filioque*, "from the Son", which found its way into the Western creeds after the Constantinopolitan creed and has been consistently rejected by the Eastern churches. The issue bears, like Arianism, on the relative status of God the Father and the Son: the Western church, concerned for their equality of status, has come to hold that the Holy Spirit emanates equally "from the Father *and from the Son*" whilst the Orthodox churches hold that the phrase both is an interpolation and makes little theological sense (cf. Ware, 1964, pp. 58-60). In all these issues belief as doctrine has become embedded in the authority-structure of the church.

The conciliar creeds did not replace the baptismal creeds, nor were they intended to do so. The so-called "Athanasian" creed (composed in Latin and unrecognized as a statement of belief in the East) is really a hymn that uses the credal form (and, uniquely, embodies the anathemas also) to make an act of worship. The Apostles' creed entered the liturgical tradition by a later and yet different route; I return to it below. Such developments in the credal form were paralleled by an ever-extending use of creeds in the liturgy. Always important in baptism, creeds were later adopted for general use in the eucharist, first in the East (from at least the sixth century) and later in the West (formally, from the early eleventh century; Jungmann, 1951, pp. 295-8). The Orthodox, Roman, Anglican and (in lesser measure) Nonconformist churches all continue to give central place to the singing or saying of the creed in their services. The point to make here is that this performance of the creeds is as complex, symbolic and condensed an act of ritual as any other liturgical act and is consequently as much subject to the categories developed, for example, by Turner (1967) for the analysis of ritual symbolism. (On the variable meaning of the creed for different persons saying it see the chapter on the creeds in Doctrine Commission of the Church of England, 1976.)

The historical account of the creeds sketched above is that of modern scholarship but for a great many years a different, more popular account of their origins was current. These stories have all the marks of a Malinowskian mythological charter and, as such, tell us something about the central place of the creeds in the on-going life of the church. Two stories stand out, one relating to the Latin term for the creed, *symbolum*, the other to the "Apostles' Creed".

The Latin *symbolum* is the same word as the Greek *symbolon*, with the general sense of a mark, sign or token. Putting aside a number of fanciful etymologies for the word as it is applied to the creed (and we should recall that *pistis* like *symbolon* was used in Hellenistic Greek to refer to a warrant, token of trust or laissez-passer), Kelly reaches the conclusion that the Latin *symbolum* in the sense of "creed" originally referred to the baptismal interrogations — the ritual act that identified the newly admitted member of the Christian community (1972, pp. 56-58). However, from at least the fourth century more dramatic interpretations of the word held currency. Thus Rufinus, in an account written in that century, which was to be adopted by many others later, dwells at length on the derivation of the word from the idea of a token or password.

> The Apostles realised, he says, that there were Jews going about pretending to be apostles of Christ, and it was important to have some token by which the preacher who was armed with the authentic apostolic doctrine might be recognised. The situation was analogous, he says, to one which often arises in civil wars, when the rival partisans might make the most disastrous mistakes of identity were it not that the opposing commanders hand out distinguishing emblems, or passwords (*symbola distincta*), to their supporters: thus, if there are doubts about anyone, he is asked for his token (*interrogatus symbolum*), and at once betrays whether he is friend or foe (Kelly, 1972, p. 54).

Geoffrey Lampe in his own brief but still authoritative account of the creeds rehearses this story from Rufinus and, accepting its tenor rather than its historical accuracy, uses it to confirm the significance of the *symbolum*, the creed, as in origin "a sign of recognition" that differentiated the early Christians from their Jewish neighbours (1976, pp. 52-3).

The second story probably also derives its later widespread acceptance from Rufinus' telling of it, although as he narrates it it is already ancient tradition. It concerns the origin specifically of the Apostles' Creed and it held sway for something like a thousand years before coming under any serious criticism in the mid 15th century. Scholars are in doubt about the actual origin of the present text of the Apostles' Creed. The likeliest place of origin is somewhere north of the Alps, possibly southwest France in the late sixth or seventh centuries; by the ninth century its use had become widespread in the Western church and it was then, it would seem, that it was adopted in the Roman baptismal rite (Kelly, 1972, Chapter 13). The popular account is, however, much simpler, which is that on the day of Pentecost when the disciples were gathered and the Holy Spirit came upon them they then collectively composed the creed, each adding one phrase:

> Peter said 'I believe in God the Father almighty... maker of heaven and earth'...Andrew said 'and in Jesus Christ His Son...our only Lord'... James said 'who was conceived by the Holy Spirit... born of the Virgin Mary'... John said 'suffered under Pontius Pilate... was crucified, dead and buried'...etc. (From a series of sermons, *De symbolo*, probably of the eighth century, quoted by Kelly, 1973, p. 3.)

The story has enormous appeal, for it represents as a collective act that which distinguishes Christians as a community, and it does so on the very occasion, the day of Pentecost, when the community first came together and consciously assumed their mission as the church.

There is no simple formula to describe what happened at the Reformation; the processes that are distinguished by that term were already in train before the period usually covered by it and they certainly continued beyond it. In describing the nature and effects of the Reformation it becomes necessary to resort to the term "faith" which, although by no means new, acquired an extra dimension of significance that gave it (like the *pisteuo* word-group before it) a quasi-technical use. Deriving from the Latin *fides* (itself cognate with the Greek *pistis*, which it normally translated in the Bible), "faith" carries by semantic origin very much the same range of meanings as did originally "belief"/*pistis*, that is, trust or confidence; and, as alternative translations of the Bible show, the two words in English often serve as synonyms, with "faith" becoming religiously the more specialized (see OED under "Belief"); the fact that "faith" has no verbal form has also produced the asymmetrical situation in which the verb "to believe" is often matched with the noun "faith". This linguistic variation is more confusing however than the broad semantic situation would seem to warrant. Augustine in his treatise on the creed, *De Fide et Symbolo*, uses the term faith/*fides* precisely in the sense of orthodox belief as it is expressed in the creeds, "the Catholic faith" as the received teaching of the church. We may contrast this sense with the meaning the word more readily has in many Protestant writings, where what is at issue is less the substance of belief (although that is not unimportant) than how such belief (often expressed as the Gospel or the Word) has been subjectively appropriated. The difference between "faith" in the two senses — "the Catholic faith" and a person's own "faith" — is thus less a matter of the difference between church authority and individual reason (which anyway much exercised medieval theologians) than of the difference between belief as declaration and belief as commitment. This extra dimension to the notion of belief had organizational implications but its immediate thrust was psychological.

Luther's role in helping to effect this shift was crucial but complex. Some would see Luther as simply re-expressing the personal commitment already implicit in the Pauline explication of belief (and Paul's Epistles were of vital importance in Luther's own spiritual biography); others would see his account of belief as an appeal ultimately to unreason, a faith that is given by God's grace, no-one can know how. But however one interprets Luther's life and work, a characteristic theme of both is his stress on the inward totality of Christian belief, the faith of the believer. Thus his so-momentous reaction to the spurious hawking of indulgences (the very first of the Ninety-Five Theses sets the tone by insisting that when "Jesus Christ said 'Repent...', he meant that the whole life of believers should be one of penitence"); thus his contrast between the (external) Theology of Glory (that of the Church to date) and the (inwardly experienced) Theology of the Cross (Luther's own preferred theology); thus his distinction between law, a matter of outward performance, and the Gospel, Word or Grace, that works inwardly (the point is made by one of the Heidelberg theses: "The law says 'Do this' and it is never done. Grace says 'Believe this' and everything is done"); and thus, not least, the governing principle of justification by faith, which while proffering intellectually an objective view of God's grace in fact locates faith in the intensity and totality of a person's experience of it. (On these various points see Rupp, 1975; von Loewenich, 1976; Rupp and Drewery, 1970.) Luther stands in history not only as a thinker and writer but also as a paradigm of the person who achieves a fully realized belief only after an intense inward struggle, who possesses belief by being possessed by it: such is the "faith" that comes from without but signifies a subjective transition from disorganized doubt to clarity, conviction and a certain kind of personal freedom.

Two recent representations of Luther that have something of this paradigmatic aura provide a useful bridge to the present. Erikson's psychoanalytic study (1959) grants all of Luther's theological importance (e.g. p. 250) but focuses especially on the concern Luther showed in his own biographical struggle with the intensity and expressiveness of the experience of belief. The title of the key chapter in the book, "The meaning of 'meaning it' ", states the issue succinctly: as Erikson writes, "To Luther, the preaching and the praying man, the measure in depth of the perceived presence of the Word was the reaction with a total affect which leaves no doubt that one 'means it' " (1959, p. 203). But, Erikson goes on to point out, what Luther had to fight to secure, comes to us as the easy convention of our age:

[Luther's] formulations, once revolutionary, are the commonplaces of today's pulpits. They are the bases of that most inflated of all oratorical currency, credal protestations in church and lecture hall, in political propaganda and oral advertisement: the protestation, made to order of the occasion, that truth is only that which one means with one's whole being, and lives every moment. We, the heirs of Protestantism, have made convention and pretence out of the very sound of meaning it... (ibid).

John Osborne's play (1961), which is based on Erikson's study, points a different but related message. If — to paraphrase Erikson — we are all sincere believers now, Osborne's *Luther* hints that we should beware of being too convinced, too secure in our righteous convictions. The point is made most clearly in the two final scenes, most notably when "Martin" admits to his longstanding friend and advisor (Staupitz) that his delay under interrogation at the Diet of Worms (when his career and even his life were in jeopardy and he is said by tradition to have declared "Here I stand. I can do no other") was in fact the result of his uncertainty, of his doubt. Left alone on the stage, he confesses "Oh Lord, I believe. I do believe. Only help my unbelief."

In our age we seem then to believe in belief, but with not too exclusive a conviction. This note of diffuse belief is struck quite remarkably by two books that are in their separate ways both revealing and authoritative. *The Culture of Unbelief* publishes "studies and proceedings from the First International Symposium on Belief held in Rome, March 22-27, 1969 " under the sponsorship, amongst others, of the Vatican Secretariat for Non-believers, which was set up following Vatican II. The Symposium gathered a highly distinguished group of social scientists, mainly sociologists, specializing in the study of religion, without regard to their personal religious position, together with and including a number of notable churchmen. It was not, however, the intention of the Symposium to produce "dialogue" — we are told that "in a number of cases the organizers would have been hard put to identify a participant as either a 'believer' or a 'non-believer' " — but rather that of "study in preparation for dialogue" (Caporale and Grumelli, 1971, p. ix). One must break off at this point to comment on the crucial word "unbelief". The idea itself is as old as its positive counterpart "belief": *apistia* means lack of trust, non-confidence in its general sense and specifically lack of trust in God or non-belief in Christ in a religious context. Thus the remark of Osborne's Luther quoted above recalls the outburst of the father of the convulsed boy in Mark 9:24, "Immediately the father of the child cried out and said, 'I believe; help my unbelief!' " There is then nothing new, or especially contemporary, in the idea of unbelief, although it has no doubt a contemporary twist. Pope Paul in his address to the Symposium certainly knew what he meant — the rejection of the Christian religion (see p. 302, op. cit.). Yet one of the features of the Symposium is the very indeterminate value that the terms "belief" and "unbelief" come to acquire in it. Berger in his foreword refers to this "ambiguity in the definition of the problem" and notes the "rather remarkable" fact that "the theoretical position papers, each in its own way, tend to deny the very existence of the phenomenon under scrutiny [i.e. unbelief]" (ibid. p. xiii). The remark covers papers by both Luckmann and Parsons but is nowhere so pertinent as in its reference to Bellah's paper, "The historical background of unbelief". Starting with an account of the Greek concept, the paper sets "belief" in an institutional, church context and associates it with "an effort to maintain authority" on the part of the church, "part of a whole hierarchical way of thinking about social control" (p. 44). Belief (which in Bellah's discussion has become very rapidly intellectualized, a matter of doctrine and dogma) is thus distinguished from religion, the former tied to an institutional (church) structure, the latter more diffusely present in shared values. Against then this narrowly defined, historical view of "belief" Bellah contrasts what he sees as an "emergent religion of humanity" (p. 50). Nevertheless, by the end of the paper he is so carried away in his enthusiasm for the latter that all distinctions have disappeared and Christians and non-Christians, belief and religion, the Church and humanity are all rolling together in a single glorious banner:

> The modern world is as alive with religious possibility as any epoch in human history. It is no longer possible to divide mankind into believers and non-believers. All believe something and the lukewarm and those of little faith are to be found inside as well as outside the churches... Christians, along with other men, are called to build the boundaryless community, the body of man identified with the body of Christ, although all men are free to symbolize it in their own way (p. 52).

There *can* be no unbelief in such a world and the word "believe" has become so generalized as to have lost most of its content. Like Forster's "What I believe", it is a muffled (but not so muted) cry.

Christian Believing (1976), as a book, is an altogether less grandiose affair. It is the report of the Doctrine Commission of the Church of England, who were asked by the Archbishop of Canterbury to examine "the nature of the Christian faith and its expression in holy scripture and creeds". The very striking thing about the report is its lack of dogmatism, tolerance of even opposed views, concern to respect both tradition and the right to criticize and re-evaluate it. The emphasis once again is on existential belief, *believing* as the adventure of faith rather than *belief* as a body of doctrine. The most singular feature of the report is, however, the fact that over half of it consists of eight individual essays by members of the Commission, each in effect outlining his personal view of the nature of the

Christian faith. The implication throughout is that each "believer" must find his own way, respecting traditional truths but respecting also other people's right to hold different views from his own. Belief as doctrine has *almost* become the honest opinion of anyone who declares himself to be a Christian.

There is both continuity and change in the notion of belief that I have sketched above at four phases of its history: trust become conviction about an event (the "Christ-event" of history); become an initiatory declaration; become a corporately declared orthodoxy; become an inwardly organizing experience; become values common to all men (even though different). Yet throughout the concept remains central to Christianity, which is clear from the way it reflects so much of the Church's organizational and intellectual history. Moreover much of the word's meaning in non-Christian use can only be drawn from the particular significance that it has acquired in Christianity — else why attach any importance at all to having or not having beliefs? In the remainder of this chapter I write Belief with a capital letter to signify this multi-layered, complex yet condensed range of use and meaning that the concept has acquired in this its long career in Christianity.

II

Negative demonstrations are always difficult and usually lengthy and for this reason I argue the comparative case only summarily. I find little evidence that there is anything equivalent to Christian Belief in other world religions although there are other comparable organizing or nodal concepts. The contrast is greatest with Judaism (as one would expect, historically and sociologically), the similarities (as one would also expect) closest with Islam. The teaching of the law, the *Torah*, stands at the centre of Judaism in a way functionally comparable — but with different practical implications — to Belief in Christianity; and there are comparable differences in the identity-markers of the two religions. With Islam the parallel is closer: the first of the "five pillars" of Islam — witness to God and his prophet — comes close to being a credo; there is some concern for orthodoxy of belief and there are even formal creeds (although the ordinary Muslim is unlikely to know them). Islam — submission to the one God — can be identified with having belief, *iman*; a Muslim is also a believer, *mu'min*. Yet, as these words' shared root with the Hebrew *'mn* testifies, their reference is essentially to the quality of a relationship, that of keeping faith, having trust. Correspondingly, it is less the content of belief that has become alaborated in Islam than the duties of relationship: the practice of ritual, the following of Islamic custom, the observance of Islamic law.

Gombrich, writing about Buddhism, struggles awkwardly for two pages to find an equivalent to the verb "to believe" or "to believe in" before moving directly to the term ("best not translated at all") *dharma* (1971, p. 60). For Hinduism the parallels are even more indirect and fragmented.

The absence of any self-conscious credal or doctrinal component forms a commonplace observation of most, if not all, traditional or community religions. Should one attempt to distinguish for them, as one can perhaps for other world religions, any organizing concept, comparable to that of Belief in Christianity? I can answer only for the two cultures I know at first-hand, and in both cases I find the question relevant and revealing. For Banyang the idea of truth (*tetup*) has a central significance, in part as an attribute of God but more particularly as a touchstone in people's relationships, where the possibility of duplicity is obsessively elaborated by Banyang witchcraft beliefs. On a less cognitive level, the Kuria category of *inyangi*, which I am forced to translate summarily as "ritual", although it means something less, and more, serves also as touchstone ordering their own relationships (kin and generational) so as to accord with what Kuria see as the natural principles of growth. Both concepts have content but also operate functionally in the organization and determination of relationships.

III

The arguments advanced by two writers, Rodney Needham in *Belief, Language and Experience* (1972) and Wilfred Cantwell Smith in *Belief and History* (1977) and *Faith and Belief* (1979), bear directly upon my socio-historical discussion of the notion of belief and my conclusions regarding its comparative use.

The central argument of Needham's book is that "... the notion of belief is not appropriate to an empirical philosophy of mind or to an exact account of human motives and conduct. Belief is not a discriminable experience, it does not constitute a natural resemblance among men, and it does not belong to 'the common behaviour of mankind' " (1972, p. 188). None of this is in contradiction to my own argument and I would want to endorse a number of his ancillary points, e.g. "Anything that we might please to say, and which in common speech is usually hung on to the handy peg of 'belief', will be better said by recourse to some other word; and if we are clear about what we want to say, we shall find that it can be said clearly only by another word" (p. 229). However, my account of the situation would be different from his, giving more centrality to the particular (though vastly complex) historical and cultural circumstances associated with the notion of Belief in Christianity. It is true that Needham recognizes something of this (and for a few pages my account of *pistis* and *'mn* looks very like his: we are in fact relying on the same basic authors) but Needham's discussion concerning the specifically Christian concept is quite considerably briefer than his discussion of the concept as treated by philosophers.

Moreover, although Needham writes of the need to treat concepts (or words) in the context of their use (e.g. p. 186), contextual considerations are notably lacking in his accounts of the way key words or concepts such as belief have been used. This applies in large issues as in small. Thus he makes much point of Evans-Pritchard's remark that "Nuer religion is ultimately an interior state" but this is one of the final sentences of a conclusion in which it is clear that Evans-Pritchard is identifying Nuer apprehension of God (Spirit) with his own:

> Though prayer and sacrifice are exterior actions, Nuer religion is ultimately an interior state. This state is externalized in rites which we can observe, but their meaning depends finally on an awareness of God and that men are dependent on him and must be resigned to his will (1965, p. 322).

Yet in drawing to a conclusion his discussion of the status of Nuer belief, Needham is able to summarize his enquiry thus: "We have been trying to determine how we can understand the interior state of an alien people with regard to their god" (p. 30). The shift in meaning is quite radical: "the interior state of an alien people with regard to their god" is not what *Nuer Religion* is about, and whether we accept Evans-Pritchard's identification of God and *Kwoth* or not, it constitutes a contextual fact of some considerable significance. Again, the contrast Needham makes much of between Evans-Pritchard's remark on the absence in the Nuer language of a word for belief and Crazzolara's recording of one (found also in Kiggen's dictionary) would seem similarly to depend upon the underplaying of obvious differences in the aims and circumstances of the respective writers. It is wholly characteristic that Needham notes in passing (in a paragraph that is worth perusing as a whole):

> The opening words of the Christian confession of faith, the Creed, define the "interior state" of the adherent by the declaration, "I believe in God..." (p. 20),

but on what grounds does he make this assertion and what is its sense as it stands? The acontextual, naive view of what is happening when the creeds are said is matched by the much truncated account of Christian "belief" that stops with the New Testament and, except for a few airy waves ("centuries of dogmatic strife, theological explication, and the arduous ingenuities of translators... accretions and giddy twists of sense"), gives no account of the later development of that notion, either in its theological or practical context.

This, of course, is to imply that Needham might do something that he is not doing and clearly does not want to do: to look specifically and contextually at his subject. If Needham ends by destroying categories, he starts by assuming that categories of this kind (i.e. universally valid classifying concepts) are really what count and that "belief" is such a category. His question, "Is belief an experience?" is treated by him as a general issue, and the conclusions that he reaches follow logically from the way he has posed the question. He would, I am sure, be unsatisfied by the answer that I would be tempted to give — that it was for Luther. (It was no doubt for many others as well; certainly for Evans-Pritchard, but probably for few Nuer.) My final point would be that in searching for what is common to all humanity one may well lose sight of what is highly significant for some people. Christian Belief is no less real and, in that sense, true, if it is shown to be rooted in the particularities of a certain history and culture. But I agree that, just as we should not assume that we are all Christians, neither should we assume (*pace* Bellah) that we are all believers.

The two recent books by Smith, *Belief and History* and *Faith and Belief*, develop a position already sketched in his earlier *The Meaning and End of Religion*, originally published in 1962. In that book he specializes the concept of "faith" to denote personal response to transcendent qualities, making this personal faith the critical, underlying feature of all religion. The central argument of the book is that such a quality of faith can be found within the major religions of the world but that it is expressed in different ways by them. Christian belief (which in this earlier book is the same as what I have called Belief) is only one expression of faith. Smith's two later books develop this position yet further. The word "belief" he now limits in his main argument to its modern propositional sense ("the holding of certain ideas" 1979, p. 12) and he distinguishes this very sharply from "faith", "the fundamental religious category" (p. 5), "an engagement... the search for conceptual clarification of man's relation to transcendence... that human quality that has been expressed in, has been elicited, nurtured, and shaped by, the religious traditions of the world" (p. 6). He seeks to show (as in the *Meaning and End of Religion*) that other world religions, Buddhism, Islam and Hinduism, can all be interpreted as expressions of faith, and goes on, inversely, to argue that belief in the propositional sense plays no or little part in them. So too in Christianity, where it is faith rather than (propositional) belief that is the most important quality. (This modification to his earlier line of argument he notes in 1977, p. 39.) Thus in *Belief and History* Smith documents the changing meaning of the verb "to believe" from the end of the middle ages to the present time, where the sense has shifted from "recognizing what is true" to "proposing what is in doubt" which he describes, together with other meaning shifts, as "the drift away from faith". Furthermore, he argues somewhat startlingly that the concept of "belief" is not scriptural (the noun appears only once in the 1611 Authorized Version of the Bible whereas "faith" appears 233 times), that "believe" is used primarily because the noun "faith" lacks a verb, and (in the later book) that the correct translation of "credo" is not "I believe". But all this depends on the limited meaning he is adducing for "belief".

There are many insights that Smith provides, not least in the historical discussion of the changing meaning of the word "belief" and in his comparative comments on other world religions. On two points, however, his argument poses very grave difficulties. First, his extreme specialization of the terms "faith" and "belief", defined so as to have no overlap with each other, runs counter to almost all usage up until now. "Belief" is left as a quasi-intellectual presuppositional residue to a "faith" that has become so subjectivist and general that it is very difficult to give the word any real content. It is true that this specialization is in line with what has occurred from the Reformation ownwards, but it clean outruns anything that has gone before (cf. Wiebe, 1979; also above p. 18 ff). Second, the meaning of both words is intrinsic to Smith's argument but his use of them moves between his own defined sense (which has normative implications) and a much wider, historically variable sense in his more descriptive passages so that one is never quite sure where they stand with regard to each other.

There is much in Smith's two books that supports my present case yet overall his conclusion is very different from mine. He is arguing for "faith" precisely what Needham denies for "belief", that it is a universal experience distinctive of all religions (at least, of all world religions). Yet, to use Smith's own avowal, it is a highly engaged argument, depending upon prior persuasion as to the meaningfulness of faith, and, it would seem, an equally engaged rejection of belief as an important interpretative category. My own impression is of a humane and scholarly heir to the Protestant tradition surveying the world religions with a sharp and sympathetic eye as, for example, a Buddhist might look at the same religions from a different angle, concerned with their underlying behavioural code, their *dharma*. As any language can with effort and ingenuity be stretched to describe any situation (although not always exactly) so can the key terms of a religion be similarly exercised, but they are not always the most appropriate terms to use, and in the stretching they lose something of their own distinctiveness. So with Smith's "faith" and "belief": "faith" seems overstretched and "belief" (the modern sense of belief) has been detached and disowned. It is surely very difficult to talk about the idea of Christian Belief without both of them, referring though they may to different aspects of it, which change in emphasis through time and for different bodies of Christians.

IV

Clearly it is not possible, nor even desirable, to limit the word "belief" to its specifically Christian use. Yet at the same time we should be clear that it has a Christian use and that this use must affect its connotations in contexts other than Christian. It is surely plain naive to pluck the word from the linguistic planisphere (the OED Guide to the Galaxy conveniently at hand) and to use it then as though it were a given, something that just happened to be around, which had incidentally been made some use of by Christians. Let me be clear: in ordinary speech there are many uses of the word "believe" that are straightforward and unambiguous. On the whole these have a relatively weak set of connotations, implying usually (of oneself) presupposition or expectation, or (of others) assumption. There are advantages, as Needham indicates, in avoiding "believe" altogether, but the word is current English and in this its weak sense it is not likely to be misunderstood. It is when the word is given a strong sense that it may well mislead: for example, when it forms part of a definition or categorization or is used in posing a problem. Here I would argue that it is almost impossible not to draw on connotations from its Christian use. Moreover, these connotations, contextually transposed, create false assumptions that then lead to fallacies. I speak of these contextually transposed assumptions as "shadow fallacies" and for the non-Christian use of the term "belief" identify four:

(1) That belief is central to all religions in the same way as it is to Christianity. That this is a fallacy is the major argument of my paper and Sections I and II of the paper are concerned with its demonstration. It is, however, very easy for a Western writer to slip from talking about religion to talking about Christianity, and back again, without clear distinction. For example, Needham in considering spiritual commitment as a possible criterion of religious belief (1972, p. 86-89) appears to do just this: he moves from a specifically Christian view of belief as commitment to Christ (ibid, p. 86), then argues that other people can be similarly "committed" to particular enterprises or persons (pp. 87-88) and then concludes that there is no discriminable difference between religious and non-religious commitment (ibid, p. 88). But it is not commitment *per se* that identifies Christianity but commitment to Christ: Christianity cannot be treated as a type-case of religious commitment; it is a specific case of a particular commitment to a single historical person. The same fallacy can be detected I think in a somewhat different way in Martin Southwold's thoughtful paper on "Religious belief". Much of Southwold's critical commentary is highly relevant to any discussion of religion but why focus the discussion on the

nature of belief? And does not the framing of the question thus itself determine the kind of answer that will be obtained? Namely, that "basic religious tenets are 1) empirically indeterminate 2) axiomatic 3) symbolic, and 4) collective" (1979, p. 633). Christian Belief is historically and conceptually more precise in its references than this, but take belief (the shadow idea) to apply to other religions (as one might take Judaic *torah* or a shadow extension of it) and one may well find the correspondence to be indeterminate and indirect (symbolic).

(2) That the belief of a person or a people forms the ground of his or their behaviour and can be cited therefore as a sufficient explanation for it. For an example of this fallacy I would draw on my own teaching experience. Along no doubt with many others, I regularly set my first-year students in social anthropology an essay on Zande witchcraft usually in the first few weeks of the course. One topic I commonly use runs: since Zande oracles must often give false answers, why then do Azande continue to believe in witchcraft? and, all being well, the essay that is returned duly rehearses Evans-Pritchard's situational analysis of Zande reasoning. But, not infrequently, all is not well and my (I think now misguided) weak use of "believe" is turned into a strong use: the evidence in the book for individual Zande scepticism is ignored, as is much else, to present Azande with such unalterable firmness of conviction as would make a Calvinist jealous. Nor does the matter stop there, for make belief fundamental to the behaviour of a person or a people and the issue in relation to others is then relativized. That is what Azande believe: finish: there can be no further discussion of the substance of their belief in terms that do not bracket it off as something to do with *them* (rather than their experience of the world) and thus hinder its discussion in comparative terms (i.e. what we too experience of the world). The insidiousness of this process of relativization must be emphasized. "We all have our beliefs: all peoples have their beliefs." It is a way of setting people into cultural compartments.

(3) That belief is fundamentally an interior state, a psychological condition. The fallacy once again is to transpose what some have emphasized as the inwardness of Christian belief (faith) to the non-Christian context and use of the word. I would argue that Needham does just this, to the enormous detriment of his discussion, in adopting Evans-Pritchard's assertion concerning Nuer religion and generalizing it to all belief. Yet as Alan Ryan points out (1973), over-insistence on the privacy of what goes on in people's minds distracts from the primary task of construing the sense or reality of what it is they believe, and it is one of the skills of anthropology to do precisely this by contextual explication. Is the meaning of words interior to the words? That belief was a psychological state for Luther does not imply that it must be a psychological state for everyone, or even that it was *only* that for Luther. It does not make much

sense to call the belief subscribed to by the Council of Nicaea a psychological state. Southwold's criticism of Leach on the "inner psychological" aspect of belief is here much to the point (1979, p. 631). We should recall that the notion of "belief" gains much of its significance in Christianity from the first person use of the verb: I believe... But anthropologists necessarily use the verb in the third person: Azande believe... To assume that *our* presentation of their belief carries the same force as though *they* said "We believe..." is to misunderstand the semantic conjugation of the verb and to transpose Christian assumptions unwarrantably (cf. Southwold, 1979, p. 630; Smith, 1977 p. 52 et seq.).

(4) That the determination of belief is more important than the determination of the status of what it is that is the object of the belief. In Christianity to be a believer is to acknowledge an allegiance and to declare an identity: the person does not always have to be clear about the full content of his belief. The same circumstance transposed to non-Christian religions makes much less sense. To say that a people "believe" in this, that or other abstraction (witchcraft, God, spirits of the ancestors, humanism) tends to bracket off ideas that they hold about the world from the world itself, treating their "beliefs" as peculiar to them, a badge of their distinctiveness, and all knowledge of the world our privileged monopoly. The shadow cast by the Christian respect-for-belief obscures what really it is that people see or think they see. If we are to converse with each other (and I assume that social anthropology is a kind of conversation between cultures) we need fewer such shadows, cast by the contextual transposition of inappropriate categories, and a clearer, steadier gaze on to the world we share. Or, at least, a clearer admission as to what we think, or assume or presuppose, or understand about the world we share.

Acknowledgements

This paper owes much to friends and colleagues, not least from my own College, who have advised on background reading and commented on an earlier draft.

Notes

1. Bultmann has suggested that this specifically Christian sense of the word belief/*pistis* is associated with a particular, and in some ways unorthodox, linguistic construction, *pistis eis* or *pisteuoeis* + Accusative (instead of *pisteuo* + *lis* Dative): "belief in" or (as one might say, using an archaic construction in English) "belief on" (1961, pp. 68-69; of Michel, 1975, p. 599). Bultmann sees this construction in particular as gaining currency from its use as "missionary

parlance" expressing acceptance of the person–event, the *kerygma* of Christ's life and resurrection (ibid., pp. 48-49, 59, 69). But this interpretation is contentious, for at this period the Verb + Dative construction of classical Greek was already giving way to a Preposition + Accusative construction (with either *eis* or *en*) and the forms *pistis eis/en* are found with no apparent discrimination of meaning *either* between the alternative prepositions *or* between this construction and the earlier, orthodox Dative construction (Browning, 1969, p. 42; Moule, unpublished, 7; Hatch, 1917, p. 46).

References

Bellah, R.N., 1970: *Beyond Belief*. New York (Harper and Row).
Browning, R., 1969: *Medieval and Modern Greek*. London (Hutchinson).
Bultmann, R. and Weiser, A., 1961: *Faith*. Bible Key Words from G. Kittel's *Theologishes Wörterbuch zum Neuen Testament*. London (Adam and Charles Black).
Caporale, R. and Grumelli, A. (eds.) 1971: *The Culture of Unbelief*. Berkeley (University of California Press).
Chadwick, H., 1967: *The Early Church*. The Pelican History of the Church Vol. 1. Harmondsworth (Penguin Books).
Chadwick, O., 1972: *The Reformation*. The Pelican History of the Church Vol. 3. Harmondworth (Penguin Books).
Doctrine Commission of the Church of England, 1976: *Christian Believing*. London (SPCK).
Epstein, I., 1959: *Judaism*. Harmondsworth (Penguin Books).
Erikson, E.H., 1959: *Young Man Luther*. London (Faber and Faber).
Evans-Pritchard, E.E., 1937: *Witchcraft, Oracles and Magic among the Azande*. Oxford (Clarendon).
Forster, E.M., 1939: *What I believe*. Hogarth Sixpenny Pamphlets 1. London (Hogarth Press).
Gombrich, R.F., 1971: *Precept and Practice*. Oxford (Clarendon).
Guillaume, A., 1956: *Islam*. Harmondsworth (Penguin Books).
Hatch, W.H.P., 1917: *The Pauline Idea of Faith*. Harvard Theological Studies Vol. 2. Cambridge, Mass. (Harvard University Press).
Jungmann, J.A., 1959: *The Mass of the Roman Rite*. Trans. from the German by F.A. Brunner and C.K. Riepe. London (Burns and Oates).
Kelly, J.N.D., 1972: *Early Christian Creeds*. London (Longman). (3rd edition).
Küng, H., 1968: *The Church*. Translated from the German by R. and R. Ockenden. London (Burns and Oates).
Lampe, G.W.H., 1976: The origins of the creeds. In *Christian Believing*, Doctrine Commission of the Church of England. London (SPCK).
Loewenich, W. von., 1976: *Luther's Theology of the Cross*. Belfast (Christian Journals Ltd).
Michel, O., 1975: Faith, Persuade, Belief, Unbelief. In *The New International Dictionary of New Testament Theology*, ed. C. Brown. Exeter (Paternoster Press).
Moule, C.F.D., unpublished: Belief and trust in the New Testament vocabulary. Paper given to the Cambridge 'D' Society, manuscript.
Needham, R., 1972: *Belief, Language and Experience*. Oxford (Blackwell).

Nock, A.D., 1933: *Conversion*. Oxford (Clarendon Press).

Osborne, J., 1961: *Luther*. London (Faber and Faber).

Ruel, M., 1965a: Religion and society among the Kuria of East Africa. *Africa* **35**, 295-306.

Ruel, M., 1965b: Witchcraft, morality and doubt. *Odu* University of Ife *Journal of Africa Studies* **2**, 3-26.

Ruel, M., 1970: Were-animals and the introverted witch. In *Witchcraft Confessions and Accusations* (M. Douglas, ed.). London (Tavistock).

Rupp, E.G., 1975: Luther and the German Reformation to 1529. In *The Reformation* (G.R. Elton, ed.). The New Cambridge Modern History Vol. 2. Cambridge (Cambridge University Press).

Rupp, E.G. and Drewery, B., 1970: *Martin Luther*. Documents of Modern History series. London (Edward Arnold).

Ryan, A., 1973: By-ways of belief. Review of Needham (1972). *New Society*, 11th January.

Smith, W.C., 1978 (1962). *The Meaning and End of Religion*. London (SPCK).

Smith, W.C., 1977: *Belief and History*. Charlottesville (University Press Virginia).

Smith, W.C., 1979: *Faith and Belief*. Princeton, N.J. (Princeton University Press).

Southwold, M., 1979: Religious belief. *Man* **14** (4) December.

Turner, V., 1967: *The Forest of Symbols*. Ithaca (Cornell University Press).

Ware, T., 1964: *The Orthodox Church*. Harmondsworth (Penguin).

Wiebe, D., 1979: The role of "belief" in the study of religion. *Numen* **26** (2), 234-249.

Atheism in a Religious Society:
the culture of unbelief in an Israeli kibbutz

Alison M. Bowes

Introduction

Atheism in the kibbutzim of the Kibbutz Artzi Hashomer Hatzair federation[1] has its roots in the rejection of a particular religious tradition, Judaism, and takes on a special character because that tradition is not only concerned with cosmological beliefs, but also with the history, character and customs of the Jewish people, and forms a background to, and in some respects a justification for, the very existence of the Israeli State. In becoming atheists, the pioneers of Hashomer Hatzair did not reject the religious tradition *in toto*, but attempted to purge it of its superhuman elements, whilst retaining many of its historical and customary features by adapting them to the purposes of a secular political ideology and community, the kibbutz. For them, traditional religious belief was a relic of the *shtetl* (the Jewish community of Eastern Europe),[2] which had been created by the anti-Semitic environment in which it existed as a restricted and unnatural community.

We can define atheism as the pioneers of Hashomer Hatzair did, as unbelief in the existence of God.[3] Luckmann (1971, p. 36) argues that unbelief as a social fact is "constituted by institutional definition": it can only appear where religious specialists exist to define the limits of belief. Those who stand beyond those limits are labelled, and in some cases (such as Hashomer Hatzair) regard themselves as, unbelievers. It is crucial to the present argument that Hashomer Hatzair kibbutz unbelief was thematized in opposition to Judaism rather than any other religion (cf. Glock, 1971). Members of Hashomer Hatzair cannot be classified as religous "nones" (Vernon, 1968) because whilst they explicitly rejected one set of beliefs, they constructed an alternative set which relied for its legitimacy on their self-labelling as *Jewish* unbelievers, and which drew much from the old religious tradition.

Hashomer Hatzair kibbutzniks today continue to reject religious Judaism, represented in Israel by powerful religious institutions which use their power to extend the coincidence of religious and state law. Over the years, domination of the state by religious agencies has increased (Leslie, 1971; Frankel, 1980), and as Judaism has changed, so has kibbutz unbelief and the strategies of non-conformity it comprises.

Today, Jewish religion affects the social relations and social activities of Jews in Israel in three main areas, the regulation of everyday life, collective festivals and rites of passage. The kibbutz "culture of unbelief" (Caporale and Grumelli, 1971) offers counterpoints to religious observance and operates in three main ways: firstly, kibbutzniks may resort to inaction, although this is practicable only to a limited extent; secondly, they may transform religious observance; thirdly, they may reinterpret tradition, whilst retaining many of its ancient forms. Whether they ignore, transform or reinterpret, they must do so within the legal and customary framework of Israel.

The kibbutz culture of unbelief consists of a set of negative attitudes towards traditional religion which are subject to constant exposure, examination and reaffirmation in social action. The kibbutz world view is a combination of the culture of unbelief and Socialist Zionism, the fundamentals of which are that the Jews must attain, firstly, rebirth as a nation through migration to their traditional homeland, secondly, the creation of a proletariat through the experience of manual labour and, thirdly, the establishment of a socialist way of life.[4] Each element of the world view informs the other, as both have the same roots, that is, the Jewish people's historical record as presented in the ancient writings and as embodied in the religious tradition.

Historical background of kibbutz unbelief

The pioneers of Hashomer Hatzair, who settled in Palestine after World War I, did not believe in the Jewish God, and they did not worship. They rejected traditional religious observance (e.g. *kashrut*,[5] Sabbath observances, sexual taboos). As the movement developed, traditional Jewish festivals were reinterpreted, and the pioneers tried to revive the ancient associations of the festivals with the agricultural year in Palestine (Schauss, 1962), thus tying them to contemporary kibbutz life. They did not use all the traditional festivals, but concentrated mainly on those marking historical events. These could be readily stripped of their supernatural elements and used as affirmations of Zionism, offering it an extra historical justification to complement the class analysis of Socialist Zionism. The pioneers' world view differed most markedly from tradition in the areas of everyday life and rites of passage, where religious prescriptions were simply ignored.

The observer can easily be misled by the vehemence of the early pioneers' self-declared atheism[6] to conceive of their unbelief as the antithesis of Jewish religious belief. There were, however, strong correspondences between the two, as the old tradition was being used selectively to construct the new. Spiro gives an example of how this could be done. Referring to traditional religious beliefs, he states

> Concretely, Jahweh redeemed Israel from Egypt, and, after a long struggle with a harsh desert environment, and with their own "stubbornness", he brought them to the land of "milk and honey" which, however, was acquired only through conquest. The Exodus, Sinai and the Conquest of the Land comprise, jointly, the symbols of the nuclear, historical experience of Judaism. This set of symbols implies (a) that suffering can be overcome in this world, for (b) the world is potentially good, but that (c) to overcome suffering and to make the world good requires struggle. (Spiro, 1979a, p. 326)

To use the same set of symbols as a component in their unbelief was for the pioneers relatively straightforward. They needed only to transfer the responsibility for human history from Jahweh to themselves. The Exodus, Sinai and the Conquest of the Land could then be treated as historical lessons. The ethico-philosophical implications for Zionist Socialist struggle were (a) that the centuries-old suffering of the Jews could be overcome through Zionism, (b) that a Socialist society was possible and desirable and (c) that they would have to fight for their own liberation.

Kibbutzim of Hashomer Hatzair were very firmly part of the wider Zionist movement, seeing themselves as revolutionary cells, prototypes of the new Jewish society and political campaigning units carrying the Socialist message to the whole of the Zionist movement.

Early on in the Yishuv, the Zionist establishment was somewhat suspicious of the "communist" kibbutzim and their rejection of so much traditional Jewish culture (Kanovsky, 1966). Gradually, however, the establishment came to recognise the economic and military value of kibbutz settlement (Kanovsky, 1966; Stern, 1965; Darin Drabkin, 1962), and by the Second World War, all the kibbutz movements[7] were heavily involved in the higher echelons of government (Davis, 1977). Political and military representation of kibbutzniks in the governing bodies of the Yishuv in its later years and the State until the mid-1970s (election of Begin's Likud government) was extensive, out of all proportion to the actual number of kibbutzniks in the population (Davis, 1977; Shur, 1972). The influence of kibbutzniks was to be accentuated by the massive immigration of Oriental Jews in the early years of the State: government policy in this period was essentially kibbutz policy, biased towards agriculture and rural settlement (Cohen, 1970).

Despite their influence and respectability, kibbutzniks, the vast majority of whom were atheist or agnostic, did not achieve, perhaps did not even attempt to ensure a secular state. Whilst they voiced opposition to some of the requirements of the religious parties which held the balance of power in the Knesset (the Israeli Parliament), their opposition was neither enthusiastic nor effective, and they were therefore indirectly instrumental in ensuring that religious power and influence in the State of Israel would be strong.[8]

As a result, religious tradition is today entrenched in Israeli law: the legal definition of Jewishness is a religious one, i.e. a person must either have a Jewish mother or have undergone conversion to Judaism in his or her own right (Frankel, 1980); there is no civil marriage, so all marriages must be religious (i.e. Jewish, Moslem, Christian or Druze) and both parties to a marriage must be of the same religion; Jews who wish to divorce must go through a religious divorce ceremony (described by Rein, 1980); some Jews (Cohens, Levis) are forbidden to marry divorcees (Frankel, 1980); Jewish men incapable of fathering children may not marry at all (Hazleton, 1977); circumcision is virtually compulsory for all baby boys (Tamarin, 1973); almost all food sold is kosher; in most areas, there is no public transport on the Sabbath (i.e. Friday evening to Saturday evening); and there are many more examples.

Religion has both the power of the law and the power of custom behind it, and both have increased considerably since 1948. Two major events stimulated strong religious revivals. The June War (1967) took the Israeli army into the West Bank, Gaza, Sinai and, most significantly, Jerusalem. Excitement at the victory brought about a resurgence of feelings of Jewish identity, particularly amongst the young; on reaching the Western Wall for the first time, soldiers reported that they suddenly felt Jewish, rather than simply Israeli (Near, 1970). The Yom Kippur War (1973) was by contrast seen as a defeat, and a sign that Jewry was again threatened and vulnerable. It also led to religious revivalism, including the formation in 1974 of Gush Emunim (the Bloc of the Faithful), which campaigned for what it saw as the divinely sanctioned right of Jews to settle on the West Bank, and, indeed, in all of Biblical Palestine (Frankel, 1980). It should be noted that my fieldwork in Kibbutz Goshen[9] came after both wars, but before the election of Begin's government.

Rituals of unbelief in Kibbutz Goshen

The regulation of everyday life

The religious influences on the daily life of kibbutzniks of Goshen can be attributed entirely to the pressures of the wider, religiously dominated society. Nearly all purchased food is kosher, because few alternatives are available (Tamarin, 1973), but the kibbutz does not keep a kosher kitchen, e.g. the same utensils are used for the preparation and consumption (often together) of both meat and dairy foods. The Sabbath is a day for staying at home, there being no public transport, but is not necessarily a day of rest. On Friday evenings, when the Sabbath begins,[10] kibbutzniks eat a hot meal (instead of the normal weekday salads), but no traditional ceremony is attached to this. The meal is a special occasion, but only because it is the one meal in the week which can be eaten at one's leisure.[11]

None of the traditional pollution taboos regarding the body is observed on Goshen. Children share bedrooms and showers until they are about eleven years old: their segregation after puberty is a result of practical movement experience rather than religious principle. Women of Goshen go to the *mikvah* (ritual bath) perhaps once in their lives, before their marriages (rabbis will refuse the ceremony to a woman who is not ritually pure[12]), i.e. when they have no choice. Finally, kibbutzniks do not observe the sexual taboos of traditional Judaism.

Thus in their everyday lives, kibbutzniks ignore traditional observance as far as they can, expressing their unbelief by inaction, simply omitting to do as the religious tradition prescribes. We cannot in this area identify a set of alternative *practices* which would counterpoint traditional observance.

Collective festivals

By contrast, the culture of unbelief does provide active alternatives to traditional observance of collective festivals. The annual cycle of collective festivals celebrated in Goshen divides neatly into two categories. The first comprises the national Israeli festivals of Holocaust Day, Remembrance Day, Independence Day, and May Day. The second consists of the traditional Jewish festivals of Rosh Hashana, Succot, Hannukah, Tu Bishvat (also called Rosh Hashana Lailanot), Purim, Pesach and Shavuot (also called Hag Habikkurim).[13]

National Festivals. National festivals on Goshen are celebrated without religious referent. For observant Jews, Israel may be a sacred community, but for kibbutzniks it is the goal and fulfilment of a secular Zionism. The festivals which celebrate nationalism and socialism derive mainly from the modern Zionist tradition, and kibbutzniks can comfortably celebrate them to accord with their own wholly secular philosophy. Despite this, their celebration is not free of conflict, engendered both by internal division and by the influence of developments in the wider society. National festivals can be seen as social dramas in Turner's (1957) sense, occasions of heightened social activity, when underlying conflicts are exposed.

For example, on Holocaust Day in 1975, many members of Goshen refused to participate in the ceremony, stating that as North Africans, it was not their concern. At the ceremony, a kibbutz pioneer and a member of the second generation of Goshen were to give formal speeches on the Holocaust. The young man made what was considered a very inflammatory speech (saying in effect that it was time to forget the Holocaust), setting off a heated discussion in what had been intended as a purely formal ceremony.[14]

The May Day celebrations show how the environment of the kibbutz can affect its celebration of national festivals. May Day is less important for the kibbutz movement generally since Israel's relationship with the USSR deteriorated in the 1950s. Hashomer Hatzair had looked to the USSR as a model socialist state, and had celebrated May Day accordingly (Spiro (1970) tells us that Kiryat Yedidim also celebrated the anniversaries of the Russian Revolution. In 1975 on Goshen, there was little ceremony on May Day, save a banner in the dining hall reading "Long live May Day: festival of friendship for all workers", a coffee evening, and a day's outing to the cotton fields.

The changes in the celebrations of May Day (and the Russian Revolution), indicate that national festivals in the kibbutz are affected by broad changes in Zionism and Israeli politics. Also, the variable participation in and disruption of the ceremony on Holocaust Day are in indicative of current ideological strain regarding the importance of the Holocaust, as well as of social tensions internal to Goshen. Despite the changes they have undergone, and the conflicts they expose, the national festivals retain their broad ideological fit with both kibbutz belief and national belief. They are, for the kibbutz, true and direct expressions of Socialist Zionism.

Tradition-based festivals. Examination of the celebrations of all the tradition-based festivals observed on Goshen shows certain recurrent behaviour patterns. Firstly, participation in the ceremonies was markedly unenthusiastic, in contrast to the Zionist festivals: for example, in 1975, no members willing to organise Shavuot (Pentecost) could be found, and the Secretary was obliged to take charge, a task outside his normal duties. To provide entertainment for the festival, he press-ganged a group of volunteer workers from abroad (outsiders: see Bowes (1980) for a full account). At the ceremony itself, people complained that it had been badly organized. Secondly, norms of behaviour were flouted, apparently deliberately: there was usually some form of entertainment, designed to be listened to, but invariably, the audience would be engaged in conversation, sometimes so animated that the entertainment was barely audible.[15] At some festivals, there were slide-shows: the most extreme form of inattention here was reading a newspaper, and otherwise, people would talk among themselves about how boring the slides were, as they were the same every year. Such inattention was not characteristic of kibbutzniks on all public occasions: they were quite capable of attending to films, lectures, political speeches and so on: their behaviour at the festival celebrations was quite distinctive. Thirdly, people had very confused conceptions about what the ceremonies meant, either traditionally or in their reinterpreted forms. For example, at Succot (Tabernacles), the citron[16], myrtle, willow and palm were prominently displayed. In the Diaspora from one area and from one period to another, several traditional meanings had been given to these four symbols (Schauss, 1962). Children of Goshen were told by their school teacher in 1975 that they symbolized all the possible kinds of Jews in the world. Otherwise, the meanings, if any, given to the symbols by members of Goshen varied according to the knowledge and background of the individual concerned. The first generation of children of Goshen knew nothing beyond the fact that these symbols were associated with Succot, because they had never been taught anything else.

A second example of the prevailing confusion, is a typical account of the meaning of a whole festival, Hannukah (Lights), given by a member of Goshen's first generation of children. She said

> Several things, including the Maccabees, are mixed up with it. And once, the temple was destroyed; there was only enough oil left to burn for one day and it burned for eight days. That was a miracle. In the kibbutz, it is a children's festival. My son loves it.

She admitted that this was all she knew, and apologized for what she saw as the inadequacy of her account (Fishman (1973) describes the full traditional significance of Hannukah). This confusion is in some ways not particularly surprising: anthropologists (e.g. Leach, 1968) have shown that adherents of a religion are not necessarily experts in the interpretation of its symbols. In the kibbutz, however, we are not concerned with a "folk" religion, but with anti-religion, and the confusion about meaning can be understood as a component of the culture of unbelief.

These observations are not unique to Goshen. Spiro (1970) reports that members of Kiryat Yedidim were dissatisfied with their festival celebrations. There was little enthusiasm, e.g. the choir would not rehearse for Pesach (Passover) until publicly shamed, the Rosh Hashana (New Year) entertainment was unenthusiastically received. One of his informants "complained that the old had been abolished, but that nothing new had been added to take its place" (Spiro, 1970, p. 147). In enacting the festivals in ways which eliminated their traditional religious content, the kibbutzniks of Kiryat Yedidim and Goshen were very much aware that there was something missing. For the maintenance of their unbelief, it was important that they reminded themselves from time to time that they had rejected one system of meaning and replaced it with another. The unsatisfactory experiences of their festivals can be seen as reminders that the kibbutz is a society which has attempted to be atheistic in a religious environment. The "anti-ritual" of the festivals is sustained both by this religious environment and by the kibbutzniks' own reaffirmation of their alternative beliefs in their everyday lives and in the national festivals. We have to assume (with e.g. Turner, 1968, 1969) that all ritual is meaningful, and we must accept that the meaningfulness of the kibbutz festivals is that *inter alia*, they help maintain a critical attitude towards the Jewish religion (cf. Bocock, 1974).

The data from Goshen also allow changes in the culture of unbelief to be ascertained, as each generation of the kibbutz had a different view of the festivals. When asked about the meanings of the ceremonies, pioneers (and immigrant members) would give accounts distinctive to their countries of origin, omitting any supernatural elements. The first generation of children of Goshen knew little of the traditional meanings of the festivals, whereas the second generation of children were learning about tradition at school. This variety reflects historical changes in the environment of the culture of unbelief. The ideas of the pioneers of Goshen corresponded with the old culture of unbelief of Hashomer Hatzair in the Yishuv, when institutionalized Jewish religion had little power. The first generation of children, born in the late 1940s to the early 1950s before institutionalized religion was well entrenched, were educated by pioneers into the old culture of unbelief. By the 1970s, the institutions of religion had considerable legal and customary power. In the kibbutz movement, the counterpart to the religious revivals after the wars of 1967 and 1973 was a resurgence of interest in "historical and cultural roots" (Frankel, 1980, p. 182), which included modification of the educational curriculum to include material on tradition. Thus as religion was strengthened, the culture of unbelief was elaborated.[17]

Rites of passage

In carrying out certain rites of passage, kibbutzniks of Goshen have no alternative but to participate in religious ritual as prescribed by religious authority. Possibilities for developing "anti-rituals" are limited, and kibbutzniks cannot resort to inaction as they could in everyday life. The rites are therefore incorporated into the culture of unbelief, albeit in a strenuous fashion which lays bare some of the ambiguities which lie at its heart. All the rites of passage celebrated on Goshen are rooted in the religious tradition: some are marked with non-religious ceremonial and some with religious ceremonial.

Non-religious ceremonial. At the traditional *bar mitzvah*, a boy becomes a man, part of the religious congregation of Jews. In Hashomer Hatzair, the boy's *bar mitzvah* has been transformed into a ceremony of enrolment into the Youth Movement (the junior branch of the kibbutz movement) for boys and girls. The ceremony on Goshen is purely political, Zionist and Socialist, and takes place when the children are 12 or 13 years old.[18]

Funerals and memorial ceremonies on Goshen are marked by non-religious ritual. This is possible because the kibbutz has its own burial ground, over which the religious authorities and the Orthodox burial societies have no control. Funeral practices vary between kibbutzim and even between funerals on the same kibbutz (Criden and Gelb, 1974). Some kibbutzim (including Goshen) follow the traditional practice of holding memorial ceremonies for the dead, but these again may contain no religious referents at all (as on Goshen). According to Criden and Gelb, the kibbutzim have as yet no established ceremonial practice to mark death, and they note that this is a source of unease for many kibbutzniks. During my fieldwork, there was one death on Goshen, of the old mother of one of the veteran members. A non-religious ceremony was held in the kibbutz cemetery, and the weekly film show was cancelled as a mark of respect. There was no evidence of the kind of unease to which Criden and Gelb refer, but Goshen is a young kibbutz, which has so far faced few deaths. Some members have been killed in the wars, and they were given military funerals, but otherwise the only deaths until 1976 were of aged parents of members, essentially marginal to the community. Goshen is therefore not the case from which to make generalizations regarding deaths, funerals and memorials on kibbutzim.

Religious ceremonial. All male babies in Goshen are circumcised; this marks them, in the terms defined by institutionalized religion, as Jews. All Jewish Israelis are subject to very strong pressures regarding circumcision (Tamarin, 1973), and the vast majority, including kibbutzniks, have the operation done by the *mohel* (religious circumciser) with religious ceremony (described by Zborowski and Herzog, 1962). The kibbutzniks of Goshen justify the practice by saying they do not wish their sons to be singled out for ridicule, to be different from other Israeli boys, with whom they are certain to come into contact when they enter the army at the age of about 18. As Tamarin shows, even if the boys did escape circumcision as babies, they would almost certainly be "persuaded" by the army to undergo the operation, as are for example newly arrived immigrants who are uncircumcised. And of course, an uncircumcised Jewish male could not be married.

In the practice of circumcision, the kibbutzniks conform because they have no effective choice, justifying their conformity by referring to the community of Israelis to which, as Zionists, they wish to belong: they say "we do it because we must". There was at least one other justification for circumcision on Goshen: when pressed on the subject, a member of the second generation stated that at least the Jews were better than the Arabs, who carried out circumcision on teenage boys.[19] Also, very occasionally, people would comment on "complexes" which boys develop about circumcision, but they would not enter into public discussion of these.

The material on circumcision is difficult to interpret fully, not least because of people's general unwillingness to comment upon it. It is worth noting that this is one of the areas in which, for the kibbutzniks, the separation of national and religious identity (see note 8) is particularly difficult. They try to justify circumcision in national terms, whilst knowing that it is in fact a very important sign of membership of the religious community.

In marriages (and divorces) kibbutzniks again go through a religious ceremony. Spiro (1970) asserts that in Kiryat Yedidim, marriage signified little because the couple would already be living together, their union recognized by the whole community.[20] Criden and Gelb mention the use of stand-ins if one of the couple happened to be away when the rabbi came to perform the ceremony, noting that "the rabbi wouldn't know the difference" (1974, p. 141). On Goshen, marriage is highly valued (Bowes, 1978) and meaningful: the ceremony is a true rite of passage, marking the transition from cohabitation to an intended permanent alliance. It is almost unheard of for a couple to have children without getting married first, and few girls are already pregnant on their wedding days (despite Criden and Gelb's assertions to the contrary). Jewish marriages are celebrated on the kibbutz with a party, to which the whole community is invited: the ceremony itself may be performed on the kibbutz or in town, depending on the wishes of the couple concerned. Some kibbutzniks expressed distaste at the rabbi coming to the kibbutz, and there were some inconclusive moves to prevent this during my fieldwork.

It is certainly the case that in the early days of the kibbutz movement, many kibbutz "marriages" were not marked by any traditional ceremony, but simply by a couple announcing their intention to live together. There has therefore been a change of practice, attributable again I think to the increasing preeminence of religion in the society as a whole. As the wider society turns to the forms and content of traditional religion, so the kibbutz has taken up its forms, in this case, the traditional wedding ceremony. If kibbutzniks wish to be married, there is a sense in which they have no opportunity to establish any alternative kind of ritual: since they recognize the ceremony as a rite of passage, and they value very highly the state of being married (cf. Bowes, 1978), the marriage ceremony is meaningful to them.

Some kibbutzniks have taken part in campaigns for civil marriage in Israel. Were such a campaign to be successful, it is likely that the kibbutz culture of unbelief would be weakened. Kibbutzniks opting for civil marriage could arrange their own, secular ceremonies, and would lose one of their existing opportunities to air their unbelief by ignoring the traditional symbolism of the religious marriage ceremony and the traditional observances enjoined upon a married couple.

In 1975–6, three male members of Goshen married non-Jewish foreign women. These weddings took place abroad. When they returned to Goshen after their marriages, the three women, who had originally come to the kibbutz as volunteer workers, started conversion school: they were to become Jews. This is, on the surface, an unexpected development: they were married, their marriages were recognized both by the state (Ghilan, 1974), and by the atheistic community they were entering. We have to remember that one factor which qualifies a person as a Jew is having a Jewish mother. Therefore, if these girls converted, their children would automatically be Jewish.[21] But this is still an insufficient explanation; as one of the women herself pointed out, the children could be allowed to decide for themselves whether to convert. She and the others, however, opted to go to the conversion course, and gain the status of Jew for themselves, in response to considerable pressure from the kibbutzniks of Goshen.

There is an obvious ambiguity here. As an atheistic community, the kibbutz apparently requires new members to undergo ritual initiation into a religion to which it does not subscribe. This can, however, be explained if we remind ourselves again that the kibbutz uses the religious tradition of *Judaism* to secular ends and confers upon it secular meaning. All the members of Goshen knew something about the things in which they did not believe, even if, as we saw, their knowledge might be rather limited and confused. This knowledge is essential to them if they are to maintain a thriving culture of unbelief. The conversion process which the brides of Goshen undertook involved learning about the Torah and about the observances which a good Jew must follow. We can regard the conversions as a kind of cultural initiation: as far as Goshen was concerned, the women were being taught how to be Jews in a culture of unbelief which took traditional Jewish religion as its point of departure. They were taking on the cultural baggage needed by kibbutzniks who founded their way of life on traditional religion by explicitly rejecting it. Immediately before and immediately after their conversion course, the women were given lessons in Hebrew and instruction in movement tenets in the kibbutz.

Conculsion

The culture of unbelief in kibbutzim of Hashomer Hatzair has a distinctive character firstly because of the strength of institutionalized Judaism in the State of Israel, and secondly, because of the nature of the religious tradition itself which contains an historical base for the Zionist enterprise. It has arisen partly because religion intrudes willy nilly into the daily life of the kibbutz community, and partly because kibbutz ideology draws to a large extent on the same tradition as that of the religious institutions. Kibbutzim of Hashomer Hatzair have attempted to reject tradition and maintain it at the same time.

The culture of unbelief is a complex of ideas and actions which facilitate the testing, celebration and affirmation of Jewish atheism. It operates in three ways. First, some aspects of the religious tradition are simply ignored: these are the everyday observances required of the religious, and the religious meanings which may be accorded the Zionist festivals. Secondly, tradition may be transformed, as in the *bar mitzvah*, funeral and memorial ceremonies, in which it is possible because the religious authorities have neither formal nor informal control over what is done within the community. Thirdly, there are areas in which the kibbutz can neither ignore nor transform tradition, for various reasons. These are first, traditional festivals and conversions, in which the kibbutz uses the tradition to its own ends, and second, marriages, divorces and circumcisions, in which religious ceremonies are compulsory, legally so in the cases of marriage and divorce, and customarily so in the case of circumcisions.

The culture of unbelief is undoubtedly most elaborate and most strongly expressed in its third operative mode, when kibbutzniks make direct use of traditional ceremonies. We find that marriage, divorce and circumcision are treated as true rites of passage, marking changes of status recognized on the kibbutz. The statuses do not have the same meaning as they do for the observant, e.g. marriage on the kibbutz follows rather than precedes cohabitation, circumcision makes a boy an Israeli rather than a Jew, Jews may marry non-Jews and do so, and so on. So here, tradition is being used unaltered in form, but altered in meaning (both maintained and rejected), and we find expressions of basic contradictions in the culture of unbelief, e.g. the complaints about the rabbi coming to the kibbutz for the marriage ceremonies, the "complexes" about circumcision, the incomplete acceptance of the non-Jewish wives of Goshen, who were pressured to convert to Judaism. Conversion itself was treated by the kibbutz as a kind of cultural initiation, which would make the converts accomplished Jewish atheists.

Those traditional festivals which the kibbutz selects for reinterpretation give us the clearest expressions of inherent contradiction. The festivals are reinterpreted in that they are divested of their traditional supernatural elements and their ancient agricultural associations are revived: both processes are further examples of the way the kibbutz simultaneously rejects and uses tradition. In the explanatory and evaluative interpretations of the ceremonies given by the kibbutzniks, and in their conduct at the celebrations, we find further dimensions of the culture of unbelief, in particular, self-declared ignorance of their meaning, criticisms of their organization and complaints of disorderly behaviour (in which, nevertheless, the complainants themselves take part without compunction).

It is reasonable to conclude that the culture of unbelief is important both for the integration of the Hashomer Hatzair kibbutz into Israeli society, and also for the kibbutz's own integrity and autonomy as a community following a distinctive way of life. Through the culture of unbelief, the kibbutz demonstrates that it is a Jewish community which belongs to the nation of Zion, by drawing on the ancient religious tradition, but at the same time, it affirms that it is a community of atheists who reject tradition. The fundamental message of the culture of unbelief is therefore that the kibbutz is a *Jewish* atheist community, Judaism giving it its national, Zionist dimension, and atheism its community, Socialist dimension. In keeping with this formulation, the culture of unbelief is generated and maintained, as I have argued, by both intra- and extra-community forces.

Acknowledgements

Thanks are due to the following: for help and support during fieldwork, Dr Israel Shepher; for constant advice and encouragement, Professor Norman Long; for comments on the paper, Georg Feuerstein, Dr Susan Reid, Department of Sociology and Anthropology University College of Swansea, Department of Sociology University of Stirling and the participants in the ASA conference; for finance the Anglo-Israel Association and the SSRC; and for hospitality, Kibbutz Goshen.

Notes

1. This is, and always has been the most left-wing of the kibbutz movements. It is officially atheist, whereas others are agnostic, and one is religious (see below, note 7).
2. Diamond (1957) and Bettelheim (1971) examine the attitudes held by kibbutzniks towards the *shtetl*.

3. With reference to Dr Ruel's paper in this volume, it should be noted that the terms "belief" and "unbelief" are used in the present discussion in a manner I consider appropriate to the ethnographic context.
4. See Gal (1973) for a comprehensive history and exposition of Socialist Zionism.
5. *Kashrut* = the food taboos of Judaism. See Douglas (1966) for an interesting analysis.
6. Elon (1972) gives an account of the vigour of atheism in this early period.
7. The other kibbutz movements were mainly agnostic: some tolerated religious members, and even built small synagogues for them. A tiny minority of kibbutzim were (and are) religious. See Viteles (1968) for an account.
8. Tamarin (1963) attributes this lack of effective opposition to the historical dilemma of the Jews who, suffering under intolerant regimes, had always longed for a liberal society, but had at the same time fought to preserve their ancient culture. In his view, successive Israeli governments made concessions to religious parties because they wished to preserve tradition, and were prepared to accept intolerance as the price. For many centuries. Jewish identity had been both religious and cultural: we should not be surprised that the kibbutzniks' efforts to separate these elements were strenuous, and not always consistent (cf. Deutscher, 1968; Cohen, 1980).
9. Goshen is a fictitious name for a real Hashomer Hatzair kibbutz on which I carried out fieldwork in Summer 1974 and between March 1975 and March 1976.
10. In the Jewish tradition, all festivals, including Sabbath, begin at sunset on one day and end at sunset on a later day. The kibbutz follows this convention, and always begins celebration of a festival in the evening.
11. Breakfast and lunch on the kibbutz are eaten at high speed, snatched rather than enjoyed, during breaks in the working day. On weekday evenings too, there is usually a rush, as people are anxious to be getting on with their evening activities. To eat a meal at one's leisure is considered by kibbutzniks of Goshen to be an important way of relaxing after a week's hard work.
12. Tamarin (1973) gives a detailed account of the importance which the religious authorities attach to the *mikvah*, and describes the experiences of girls who were refused a marriage ceremony unless they paid a visit to the *mikvah*. I was unable to ascertain exactly how many women of Goshen went to the *mikvah* before their marriages. It is likely that most of them did, especially those who were married in recent years.
13. It should be noted that ceremonial cycles differ somewhat from one kibbutz to another, in that they have chosen slightly different sets of ceremonies from the religious tradition.
14. This incident brought out the issue of the "generation gap" in Goshen: at that time, the younger generation was rebelling against what it called "the mafia", the ruling elite of the community, which consisted entirely of pioneers (Bowes, 1977).
15. Frankel (1980) and others have noted that synagogue services are often noisy and lacking in decorum. There is perhaps a parallel with the kibbutzniks' conduct, though this should not I feel be taken too far. Kibbutzniks were clearly acting in a contextually inappropriate manner.
16. *Citrus medica*: a fruit like a lemon, but larger, sweeter and thicker skinned.
17. There is an interesting parellel case in the London Ethical Society of the late nineteenth century (Campbell, 1971; Budd, 1977). Behaviour at ceremonies which utilized the forms but not the content of traditional religion flouted norms. The decline of the Society can be attributed (a) to the decline in institutionalised religion in the wider society and (b) to the very variable ideas of its members.

Here, the kibbutz differs, (a) because institutionalized religion is strong in Israel, and (b) because the kibbutz is selective of its members. This parallel thus provide further support for the present argument. Other possible parallels are Jewish anarchist and socialist anti-religious activities in Britain and the USA in the late nineteenth century (Gartner, 1960; Rischin, 1970; Sharot, 1976), the Socialist Sunday School movement in Britain (Reid, 1966: Simon, 1965) and anarchist activities in late nineteenth century Andalusia (Kaplan, 1977). Though there is not the space to deal with these in the present paper, I suspect a similar type of analysis to that attempted here would prove useful.

18. Criden and Gelb (1974) observe that traditionally, great importance was attached to the fact that the boy was exactly 13 years old at the *bar mitzvah*. By enrolling a whole age group of children (born over perhaps two years) at the same time, the kibbutz flouts this tradition.

19. This can be construed a Zionist sentiment, even though it is more indicative of kibbutz attitudes to Arabs than to circumcision.

20. During his fieldwork (in the early 1950s) very few kibbutzniks went through religious ceremonies. He reports one case of a couple who did so because they were going to be students in Jerusalem (the outside world). More recently (1979b) he has observed that this marriage opened the floodgates of religious marriage on Kiryat Yedidim, a development which he considers to be one aspect of the "return to normality", i.e. nature, in the kibbutz regarding the position of men and women. It will be clear from what follows (and Bowes 1978) that I disagree profoundly with this interpretation.

21. Male children could of course be circumcised, and that would serve to identify them as Jews. In fact, one of the foreign girls did have a male baby before the conversion course. It was circumcised, and therefore made a Jew.

References

Bettelheim, B., 1971: *The Children of the Dream*, London (Paladin).

Bocock, R., 1974: *Ritual in Industrial Society*. London (Allen and Unwin).

Bowes, A.M., 1977: *Ideology and Communal Society: the Israeli Kibbutz*, PhD. Thesis, University of Durham.

Bowes, A.M., 1978: Women in the Kibbutz Movement. *Sociological Review* N.S. **26(2)**, 237-262.

Bowes, A.M., 1980: Strangers in the Kibbutz: Volunteer Workers in an Israeli Community. *Man* N.S. **15(4)**, 665-681.

Budd, S., 1977: *Varieties of Unbelief: Atheists and Agnostics in English Society 1850-1960*. London (Heinemann).

Campbell, C., 1971: *Toward a Sociology of Irreligion*. London (Macmillan).

Caporale, R. and Grumelli, A. (eds) 1971: *The Culture of Unbelief*. Berkeley and Los Angeles (University of California Press).

Cohen, E., 1970: The City in Zionist Ideology, *Jerusalem Urban Studies*, No. 1. Jerusalem (Institute of Urban and Regional Studies, Eliezer Kaplan School of Economics and Social Sciences, The Hebrew University).

Cohen, P.S., 1980: *Jewish Radicals and Radical Jews*. London and New York (Academic Press).

Criden, Y. and Gelb, S., 1974: *The Kibbutz Experience: Dialogue in Kfar Blum*. New York (Herzl Press).

Davis U., 1977: *Israel: Utopia Incorporated.* London (Zed Press).

Deutscher, I., 1968: *The Non-Jewish Jew and Other Essays.* London (Oxford University Press). (Edited and with an introduction by Tamara Deutscher.)

Diamond, S., 1957: Kibbutz and Shtetl: the History of an Idea. *Social Problems,* **5(2),** 71-99.

Douglas, M., 1966: *Purity and Danger.* London (Routledge and Kegan Paul).

Drabkin, H. Darin, 1962: *The Other Society.* London (Gollancz).

Elon, A., 1972: *The Israelis: Founders and Sons.* London (Sphere).

Fishman, P. (ed), 1973: *Minor and Modern Festivals.* Jerusalem (Keter Books).

Frankel, W., 1980: *Israel Observed: An Anatomy of the State.* London (Thames and Hudson).

Gal, A., 1973: *Socialist Zionism: Theory and Issues in Contemporary Jewish Nationalism.* Cambridge, Mass. (Schenkman Publishing Co).

Gartner, L.P., 1960: *The Jewish Immigrant in England 1870-1914.* Detroit (Wayne State University Press).

Ghilan, M., 1974: *How Israel Lost its Soul.* Harmondsworth (Penguin).

Glock, C.Y., 1971: The study of unbelief: perspectives on research. In *The Culture of Unbelief* (R. Caporale and A. Grumelli, eds), Berkeley and Los Angeles (University of California Press), pp. 53-75.

Hazleton L., 1977: *Israeli Women.* New York (Simon and Schuster).

Kanovsky, E., 1966: *The Economy of the Israeli Kibbutz.* Cambridge, Mass: (Harvard University Press).

Kaplan, T., 1977: *Anarchists of Andalusia 1868-1903.* Princeton N.J. (Princeton University Press).

Leach, E.R., 1968: *Dialectic in Practical Religion.* Cambridge (University Press).

Leslie, S.C., 1971: *The Rift in Israel: Religious Authority and Secular Democracy.* London (Routledge and Kegan Paul).

Luckmann, T., 1971: Belief, unbelief and religion. In *The Culture of Unbelief* (R. Caporale and A. Grumelli, eds), pp. 21-37. Berkeley and Los Angeles (University of California Press).

Near, H. (ed), 1970: *The Seventh Day.* Harmondsworth (Penguin).

Reid, F., 1966: Socialist Sunday Schools in Britain 1892-1939, *International Review of Social History* **11(1),** 18-47.

Rein, N., 1980: *Daughters of Rachel: Women in Israel.* Harmondsworth (Penguin).

Rischin, M., 1970: *The Promised City: New York's Jews 1870-1914,* New York (Harper Torchbooks). (First edition 1962.)

Schauss, H., 1962: *The Jewish Festivals.* New York (Schocken). (First edition 1938.)

Sharot, S., 1976: *Judaism: a Sociology.* Newton Abbot (David and Charles).

Shur, S., 1972: *The Kibbutz and Israeli Society: Background and Problems.* (Hakibbutz Vehachevrat Israelit: Rekah Vebe'ayot.) Tel Aviv: (Kibbutz Artzi) (in Hebrew).

Simon, B., 1965: *Education and the Labour Movement 1870-1920.* London (Lawrence and Wishart).

Spiro, M.E., 1970: *Kibbutz: Venture in Utopia,* New York: (Schocken Books) (Second edition).

Spiro, M.E., 1979a: Symbolism and functionalism in the anthropological study of religion. *In Science of Religion: Studies in Methodology* (L. Honko, ed.), pp. 322-366. The Hague (Mouton).

Spiro, M.E., 1979b: *Gender and Culture: Kibbutz Women Revisited,* Durham, N.C. (Duke University Press).

Stern, B., 1965: *The Kibbutz That Was,* Washington D.C. (Public Affairs Press).

Tamarin, G.R., 1973: *The Israeli Dilemma: Essays on a Warfare State.* Rotterdam (University Press).

Turner, V.W., 1957: *Schism and Continuity in an African Society.* Manchester (Manchester University Press).

Turner, V.W., 1968: *The Drums of Affiction,* Oxford (Clarendon Press).

Turner, V.W., 1969: *The Ritual Process,* London (Routledge and Kegan Paul).

Vernon, G.M., 1968: The Religious "Nones": A Neglected Category, *Journal for the Scientific Study of Religion,* **7(2)**, 219-229

Viteles, H., 1968: *A History of the Co-operative Movement in Israel,* Vol 3: An Analysis of the Four Sectors of the Kibbutz Movement. London (Vallentine Mitchell).

Zborowski, M. and Herzog, E., 1962: *Life is With People,* New York (Schocken Books).

Luther and the Structure of Catholicism

Hamish F.G. Swanston

We who undergo the discipline of Theology must be content to talk not of the divine but of the stutterings of Moses, the fantasies of Apuleius, the grandiloquence of the Fourth Evangelist, the schizophrenics of the shaman, the single-minded apologetic of the doorstep conversionist. It is in this limited manner that I would speak of Luther.

I must, at my start, risk some quick characterization of the mediaeval understanding of God, world and self. It was within this tradition that Luther's experience was so unhappy, and his theological response so significant of social change.

Once upon a time, in the first world, plants grew in a Garden, animals passed quietly before Adam to learn their names, and Adam himself walked with God in the cool of the evening (Genesis 3.8). This first world of harmonies did not perdure.

Under a tree a serpent tempted Eve and Adam with the promise that they would be as gods. Harmony was brought to an end. Plants grew wild. Animals turned savage. And women and men, having for a moment had their eyes opened and indeed seen themselves as God sees them, went into exile from happiness. Though for a while the Law's demands increased their misery, there had been a Promise of renewal, (Genesis 3.15). This world, too, would not perdure.

There came a time of atonement. The earth was not put back to its Eden state but the social relations of the first world were shown to be again possible. In a desert place a man withstood the insinuations of the tempter and found a harmony with beasts and angels (Mark 1.13). He was obedient, and what Paul termed "a new creation" was inaugurated, (2 Corinthians 5.17; Galatians 6.15). Of course we are not in Eden. There are remnants of chaos clinging to us, jungles and claws and sins, but the character of the developing order is discernible. We live now in a perfecting third world.

Though the mandrake screamed, and the footpad escaped the king's justices, though sewers ran openly and convulsive devotees of St. Vitus careered through the streets, there yet remained some comfortable evidences of the divine order. At Bergen, the iron bar refused to burn the innocent at the trial by ordeal; at Ruthwell, the rood tree spoke gloriously of the young knight who mounted it on Calvary; and, at Cologne, the ermine ran from the hedgerow into Albertus Magnus' hands as a visual aid in his natural history lecture.

These happy hints of inanimate and animal participation in one order with human beings as fellow creatures of God were enlarged upon in the visions of several mediaeval mystics. In the first, for example, of the fifteen revelations made to Julian of Norwich in the space of some five hours on 8 May, 1373, the Lord "shewed a little thing, the quantity of an hazel-nut, in the palm of my hand". She asked what the hazel-nut signified, and was answered, "It is all that is made". The order of creation is adequately figured by any member of that order, for "so all thing hath the Being by the love of God" (Julian, 1927, Chapter 5). Effects were observed not only of the action of visible causes in the created order but also of the invisible. In the appropriately anonymous *Cloud of Unknowing*, written at some time between 1349 and 1395, the mystic is delighted to report that "All who engaged in this work of contemplation find that it has a good effect on the body as well as on the soul, for it makes them attractive in the eyes of all who see them" (Wolters, 1961, p. 117).

Less gifted persons might content themselves with the visibility of order on the west front of the cathedral. In the sculpted ranks of patriarchs and prophets, popes and counties palatine, there were presented images of those who were made in the image of God (cf. Bonaventure, *Comm. in Libr. Sent.*, 9 un., 4, Concl., *et ad* 4). The divine order was continued in the liturgical functions of the tonsured community. Bell-ringer, door-keeper, exorcist and lector, sub-deacon, deacon, priest and bishop, exhibited in their persons the order which persisted up to those choirs of Thrones, Dominions and Powers, who stood at the seat of God.

What was so closely seen might be imitated. Theodore of Mopsuestia delighted to discern that the deacons at the liturgy "take on the image of the invisible Powers", they are "figures of the angels" (Theodore, 1933, XV, 25). The laity might be imitators too. Pious women and men retraced the steps of the heroines and heroes of this divine order. They went on pilgrimages along the routes of the exemplars of their culture. They attempted similar wonders of abstinence, fasting, and the discipline. They went further and hoped to relive the wonder of Jesus. Some, Francis Bernardone the most notable of these, became living imitations of Jesus, bearing on their bodies the stigmata of Jesus' passion. In the easy traffic of the one creation, Caterina Benincasa, the daughter of a Sienese dyer, was held to have received the stigmata invisibly on her body after she had prayed that she might "be fastened and nailed to the tree" with Christ (Benincasa, 1721, iii, 305). Others, women most notably here, but the illegitimate, the maimed and the mad too, were deemed unable to be complete imitators of Jesus and were, for example, ineligible for holy orders. Such a spirituality has its late literary expression in the *Imitatio Christi*, a book of generous but ultimately rather depressing reliance upon the certainties of the old order.

What analogy allowed in philosophic consideration, what liturgy represented for the congregation, the mediaeval literary critic expected from the instruments of allegory. The language of the visible would articulate the invisible as they existed together. The great Grail complex, for example, presented a world which the intelligent and sensitive reader would recognize both to be and not to be his own. These stories of good knights making their pilgrimage to see the very cup Christ used at his last supper could be read on many levels, as a romantic tale for winter, as a code of chivalric conduct, as a manual of unsystematic theology, as an account of mystic revelation. And those other books to which such critics applied themselves, of Moses, of Isaias, of John, treating of so many visible and invisible realities, must necessarily employ literary forms whose meanings were also multiple (cf. de Lubac, 1959, I, pp. 110-170; Smalley, 1952, p. 196). The Scriptures were expected by the mediaeval exegetes to make sense of several levels because they were given by God as a revelation of what was going on in the several levels of the divine order, (Aquinas, 1963, Ia, 1.10). At the same time the Scriptures in the Vulgate translation of Jerome were felt to express the coherence of that order by their very linguistic unity. Hebrew and Greek became Latin.

The Latin of the Scriptures was the Latin of the schools and there, too, the language itself was a suasion of unity. The young Tommaso d'Aquino was taught logic at Naples by Martin of Denmark, natural philosophy by Peter the Irishman, and theology by Erasmus of Montecassino, (Kantorowicz, 1931, Ergensumg, pp. 266-269; Baeumker, 1920, pp. 8.33). Men from eveywhere could understand one another and praise God in a single tongue.

Though it is to the illiterate obedience of the monastic copiers that we owe most of our classical texts, the Latin of the Church, that used in the liturgy, the philosphic debate, and the law court, was derived from the rough Latin of the centurion and the regional dialects of his infantrymen, and from the summary judgements of the provincial tribundals. It was a language which most naturally expressed expectations of obedience.

Throughout the divine order the same rules applied and the same requirements of obedience. The canons of ecclesiastical law determined who could exorcise a demon, at what time of the year a young couple might marry, the way in which a soul might be released from purgatorial suffering, and how a saint might be recognized by a ceremony of "canonization". Every element of life in the universal order was regulated with pastoral care for those who might be worried whether or no they were doing the right thing. The spiritual writers were in full sympathy with this culture of obedience. "It is", says the author of the *Imitatio Christi*, "a great matter to stand in obedience; to live under a prelate: and not to be our own masters" (a Kempis, 1901, I,9). "For", says the author of that *Theologia Germanica* for which Luther had such enthusiasm, "he who in disobedience is in sin" (Winkworth, 1966, chapter 16). Only demons, or those under their influence, disobeyed. It must have been clear to others besides Bishop Cauchon and the Earl of Warwick that those spirits who appeared to Jeanne d'Arc could not have been servants of God. They advocated nationalism not the universal reign of God, transvestism not the decorum of visible order, and they spoke not in Latin but French. All quite against the rules.

Not everyone was perfectly obedient. Nor was everyone perfectly disobedient. Most women and men died in a higgledy-piggledy condition. And most of the living expected such a death themselves. They felt a kinship with their dead, they felt that the dead were still members of the one community, that the order which reached down from God through the saints to themselves included the higgledy-piggledy dead. These dead, unable now to do anything for themselves, presented a pathetic image to the living. A graduate of Wittenberg, Luther's own university, saw such a sufferer once who had been sent "unhousell'd, disappointed, unanel'd" to his purgation, and who returned to plead "remember me". As the saints aided the living, so the living must aid the dead in Purgatory. This is a faith exhibited in that episode of the *Quest of the Holy Grail* in which the coming of Galahad releases the suffering Simeon from his flaming tomb. The liberated sinner bids Galahad rejoice, "for by the goodness of your life you can save souls from earthly suffering and open to them the joys of Paraise" (Matarasso, 1969, pp. 271). Gradually that popular theology of the 1225 story was regulated by papal pronouncements: *Unigenitus Dei Filius*, 1343, which defined all human merit as "the treasury of the Church", and *Salvator Noster*, 1476, which, in raising funds for a church at Xanten, applied this treasure to the account of the dead.

Though in 1477 Sixtus IV found it necessary to elucidate the meaning of his terms in the *Salvator noster* bull, it remained papal teaching that there could be a real connection between money gifts of the living for the repair of a church building and remission of punishment due to the dead (*Romani Pontificis provida*, Denzinger and Schonmetzer, 1965, pp. 33, 1405). The gaining of an Indulgence for the dead became at once the greatest sign of participation in the communal order designed by God, and the greatest work that one human being could perform for another.

In January 1510 pope Julius II by *Liquet omnibus* enlarged the catalogue of means whereby the living might assist the dead from Purgatory and, most famously, in 1514 pope Leo X declared that contributions for the rebuilding of San Pietro in Rome would certainly qualify in the eye of God as such assistance. In his elucidation of this Petrine indulgence, the *Instructio Summaria* of 1515, Albrecht of Magdeburg and Mainz expressed the connection of grace, building stones, penance, money-box, *paternoster*, the dead relative, the five wounds of Christ, and the Kingdom of God. And he was careful for those who had no money but who should yet share in the gracious time of indulgence: these were to make their contribution by prayers and fasting, "for the Kingdom of Heaven should not be more open to the rich than to the poor", (Gerdes, 1744, s. ix; Kidd, 1911, p. 13).

Luther was a most dutiful member of the perfecting society. "I was", he said later, "the most vehement Papist, so drunk — drowned — in papal dogmas that I was quite prepared more than anyone else to kill, if I could, or at least to conspire and assist their killers, everyone who would take away a single syllable the obedience due to the Pope" (Scheel, 1929, p. 186). He worked hard at his Augustinian vocation. "I was indeed a good monk and kept the rules of my order so precisely that I can say: if ever a monk were to get to heaven by the monastic rule, I should have been that man" (Luther, 1883, 28, 143). And he expected as much as anyone from the performance of indulgenced exercises. In Rome for a law suit, significantly representing those of his order who wished to maintain the stricter observance of the Rule, he rushed from privileged church to church collecting indulgences for his dead. He even wished that his parents had been dead already so that he might have obtained a plenary indulgence for them (ibid., 31, 1.226).

He came to see that all human beings shared the condition of those souls in Purgatory. He came to see this only gradually as obedience failed him. Luther expected some encouraging sense of being on the right path. But he had no comforting assurance; contrariwise, he felt he was all wrong. He felt himself alone, unprofitable, unpleasing, an exile in the second world. He said of such a man: "When he is tormented in such a struggle it seems to him that he is alone: God is angry only with him, and irreconcilably angry against him: he alone is a sinner and all others are in the right, and they work against him in obedience to God" (ibid., 5.79.14). He is an outlaw: "He who is the enemy of God has the whole creation against him" (ibid., 16.455.15). No one understands him: "I thought, then, no one experiences this but you — and I felt like a dead man" (ibid., *Tischreden*, 2.62.403). He hated the claustral and claustrophobic life among the Augustinian canons. And at last, as he admitted years later, "I hated the righteous God who punishes sinners" (ibid., 54.179). If at the end of the day he felt that he had not done enough to please God was it not unfair that the day should be made so short and his capacity so inadequate? Was it not a mockery that

Christ should be set for our example and we be unable to follow that example? Were we not, then, in just the terrible condition of those under the old Law, knowing what to do and being able only to recognize our condemnation for not doing what was commanded us? And was not that what Paul had indeed declared to be our case when he wrote in his letter to the *Romans*, (1.17), that in the Gospel itself "the righteousness of God is revealed"?

This text became paradigmatic for Luther. It seemed, in the canonical life he was leading, to be a clear assertion that hard upon the Law, seconding its threat, comes the Gospel "threatening us with his righteousness and wrath", (ibid., 54.182). Luther's inward misery came to an end when, "by the mercy of God, meditating by day and night", he was brought to see that in its own context this condemning verse refers rather to that "passive righteousness with which the merciful God justifies us". This new reading of the text gave him a wholly new appreciation of the divine order. "I felt that I was altogether born again and had entered paradise itself through open gates" (Luther, 1883, 54.185). What he had once thought had to be won was revealed as a gift to be received. What he had once thought could only happen after a life-long, and longer, obedience was revealed as an immediate possession.

Luther thereupon employed the mediaeval methods of exegesis and argument to confirm this gracious reading of the text. "I found analogies in other terms, such as 'the work of God', that is, what God does in us, 'the power of God' with which he makes us strong, 'the wisdom of God', with which he makes us wise, 'the strength of God', 'the salvation of God', 'the glory of God'," (ibid., 54.186).

Luther had learnt from Scotus that love enjoys a primacy over reason, from Ockham that God is free to will what he will, and from Biel that bargains have more to do with the commercial than the theological enterprise. Luther has read, too, in the *Sentences* of Peter Lombard, on which he had lectured in 1509, the precise distinction for which he became so famous: "the justice of God" is that by which we are made just by his gift, and "the salvation of the Lord" is that by which he saves us, and "the faith of Jesus Christ" is that by which he makes us faithful (Lombard, 1855, P.L.192.568). And he had read the gloss of the Master of the Sentences: "this is the Justice of God, not with which he is just, but by which he makes us just". But these scholastic forerunners only made sense to him once his experience had taught him their meaning (Luther, 1883, 5.163.28; 54.186). *Experientia facit theologum,* (ibid., *Tischreden,* 16, 13 No.46).

Luther knew that in his own eyes he would never add up. He would always be tugged apart by the antitheses which confronted him at every turn, by theology and philosophy, by spirit and letter, by gospel and law, by faith and works. But God acts upon him with a singleness of love. His works are simple: the watchphrases are *sola scriptura*, (Christmas sermon, 1522), *sola fide*, (Luther, 1883, 57.19.4; 22.10; 65.1; 65.1; 69.15; 171.4), *solus Christus*, (ibid., 11.270). And God saw Luther as an integrated human being.

What God chooses to see is, at his seeing, real. His vision is creative. He sees and makes good. It had been so from the first world: "God said: Let there be. . .and there was. . .God saw. . .it was good", (Genesis 1.3-4 *et al.*) As at the old creation, so at the new creation. God looks graciously upon his creatures and they are full of grace. God's seeing renders human beings just.

There is nothing very odd in all this. I am not quite certain of the import of some sociologists' talk of roles and playing, but it is a common experience that we may take on the character that another sees. In talking with those who evidence signs of thinking me witty or intelligent or kindly, I can manage the most delightful sallies, debate the most abstruse topics, exhibit the most gracious sympathy. With those who see that I am dull or stupid or mean, I can barely bring myself to make a coherent remark about the weather without a curl of the lip. So Luther is, in a famous saying, *semper peccator, semper penitens, semper justus*, (ibid., 56.442.15-21).

It was not accidental that his attack on the old conception of divine order began with a review of Indulgences. But his contention that the living were as unable as the dead to work for their own salvation, that all were equally dependent upon the undeservable grace of God for their approach to the gates of Paradise, had reference to a larger sphere of things than may at first have appeared.

I fear that there is some real doubt whether Luther actually posted his 95 theses on the Wittenberg church door on All Saints' Eve in 1517. There is certainly some doubt whether they were understood as a challenge to the whole canonical system by the archbishop, Albrecht of Mainz, desperately hoping to recover the costs of his pallium by allowing the preaching of the papal indulgnce in his archdiocese. It is probable that Luther included the theses in his letter of remonstration to the archbishop to show that the view Luther was taking was thought quite a respectable subject for debate in the university. Only when he shewed copies to his colleagues a week later did the excitement begin. The academics understood that Luther's theses thrust against the entire structure of the old order. When the Pope recognized this, and gave Luther the customary three months in which to repent before being declared excommunicate, Luther responded, on the last day of the period of grace, by burning the books of Canon Law at the Elster Gate. Thus in the winter of 1520, Luther's inward struggle brought him to public defiance of the old regime.

Luther never wasted his considerable polemical energy to make a protest against particular ecclesiastical practices in isolation. He was always taking a stand against the general perversity of Roman theology. The totality of his revaluation is clearly discernible in the discussions among the reform party which ended in the publication of the *Confessio Augustana*, 1530. The first version of this document was chiefly the work of Melanchthon. He was pleased to say that in this "sum of our teaching" there was "nothing discordant with the Scripture, or the teaching of the Catholic Church, or the Roman Church as it is known from ancient writers", (Melanchthon, 1834, xxvi, 263ff, Art.xxii). What is sometimes thought to be a classic document of defiance was intended by Melanchthon as a summary of the likenesses of Lutheran and Roman teaching. Melanchthon had not endured Luther's experience. In his *Confession* the roughnesses of Luther's antitheses have been smoothed out or their place supplied by worrits about communion under both kinds, the abolition of fasting laws, and the permittal of clergy marriages. In June 1530, Melanchthon had come near to assuring the Emperor Charles V that the reformists were looking for nothing more than some reorganization within the obtaining ecclesiastical system. Luther became increasingly worried that the truth he had learnt in his great struggle was thought by Melanchthon to be patient of diplomatic handling within the accepted rules of debate and conference: "I am thoroughly displeased with this negotiating concerning union in doctrine, since it is utterly impossible unless the Pope wishes to surrender his authority" (de Wette, 1825, pp. iv, 146).

Luther's displeasure with the softly treading Melanchthon was, however, as nothing compared with his fury at the enthusiastic Karlstadt. And this, too, demonstrates Luther's constant effort to bring women and men to a realization of the complete opposition of his order of divine faith to the Roman order of human effort. The radical preacher had encouraged the mob of Wittenberg to think of Christian action in terms of the destruction of images, the tearing of vestments and the abolition of the Latin mass. Luther, in his attack on "the heavenly prophets", coupled Karlstadt with the Pope: "They both destroy Christian freedom, and they are both anti-Christian. But the Pope does it through commandments, Dr. Karlstadt through prohibitions" (Luther, 1883, 18.62-125, 134-214). Both entangled justification with inessentials. The prudent Melanchthon complained of the violence of Luther's language in the controversy with Karlstadt, and there is certainly something ferocious in his talk of Karlstadt's "murderous spirit", of his being "a sow rooting among pearls", and of his inciting the mob to "hew, rip, rend, smash, dash, stab, strike, run, throw, hit", (ibid.). But Luther could find no moderate words for the man who "compels us to turn from the important articles to minor ones" (ibid.). The wearing the tonsure, putting on the chasuble, pulling down the images of saints, the marryings of clergy, the exclaustration of nuns, all these were matters of indifference. In the liturgies of the more sophisticated priory, for example, Luther celebrated without chasuble and without elevating the host, but in the parish church, so as not to startle anyone, he wore the chasuble and elevated the host (ibid., 18.120).

Gradually, as other reformers interpreted the gospel differently, Luther became aware that the simplicity of the truth would not secure obedience of itself. The singleness of God's action among men had to be defended even in commerce with those who had escaped the pope. Thus at the Marburg colloquy in October 1529, in response to the eucharistic theology of Zwingli and Oecolampadius, in which the consecrated elements but signified Christ, Luther chalked in large letters on the table the decisive simplicity of the divinely-given word by which the consecrated elements were Christ *corporaliter*: "*Hoc est corpus meum*". He refused to join with the Swiss in a communion service. The divine is one, the human is divided. So Luther's theological stance again issued in social institutions. He had, however much he had meant to avoid such a thing (ibid, 5.405), to sanction specifically "Lutheran" structures of Christian community. The abolition of private masses necessitated some regulations for the provision of clerical incomes, (de Wette, 1825, ii, 379ff). The disruption of the peasants' war necessitated some regulations to supply the old episcopal discipline (de Wette, 1825, pp. iii, 136). He was asked about such things and had to make a reply. Commissioners were appointed to oversee religious matters in Saxony according to the *Instruction to Visitors* which Melanchthon put together in 1528 and for which Luther wrote a Preface, (Seckendorf, 1692, pp. II, xiii, 36; Kidd, 1911, pp. 202). Hesse adopted these ordinances in place of a native scheme which had been found properly evangelical but entirely impractical, (Richter, pp. 1.163; cf. Kidd, 1911, p. 222). Brunswick adapted Saxony's earlier regulations of 1527 (ibid. 1.106, 230). Margrave George authorized his own Church Order for Brandenburg-Nurnberg (ibid., pp. 1.176, 230). Thus, from civil obedience to civil obedience the new ecclesiastical structures were raised.

It is apparent that much, if not everything, in the ordering of the new economy, depended on the disposition of the duke. Luther was not generally unhappy about this: he liked to live in civil order. His experience had divided spheres of authority. Cauchon and Beauchamp had arranged a burning together, and Luther lit a bonfire to separate their powers. While he burnt the canon law codices, he submitted easily to that civil law which took care of drainage and brigandage. Advising Elector John in March, 1530, on the question of what a good prince might do if the Emperor moved against those of his reforming subjects who had proclaimed the gospel, even in this extremity Luther declared that it was "in no way proper for anyone who wants to be a christian to stand up against the authority of his government" Luther, 1883, 5.258). *Vim vi repellere licet* simply does not apply. So Luther generally has nothing exciting to say about a duty of civil disobedience. Rather depressingly, he encourages children to obey their parents, students their professors, and peasants their lords.

The dedication to his father of the *De Votis Monasticis Judicium* of 1521, (ibid., 8.573), reveals Luther's reformed appreciation of the duties of family life. He much repents his going against Hans Luther's will when he entered the Erfurt community. Disobedience can never be pleasing in God's sight. He much delights in guiding his own little Hans into the ways of study and prayer. The serious vocation of the parent is shown not only in the 1524 tract insisting that "Parents neither compel nor hinder the marriages of their children, and that children do not get engaged without their parents consent", (ibid., 15.163-9), and the 1530 sermon "On Keeping Children in School", (ibid., 30.2, 517-88), but also in the charming allegory of the garden, the sweet apples and the pony to ride with which he beguiles his boy (ibid., 5.377-78), and, most importantly for the young Hanschen, doubtless, in "a big fine piece of sugar" which a Nurnberger had fetched him "from the pretty garden" (ibid., 5.609). All this is pleasantly bourgeois.

There is nothing very startling in Luther's notion of academic discipline, either. Though, in the service of the gospel, he could rally the students to a bonfire protest, Luther was generally rather conservative in his conception of university authority. He had, after all, to deal with post-graduate students like Horatio who entertained notions that their philosophy could include all things of heaven and earth, and with such truant-playing, bawdy-joking, undergraduates as Rosencrantz and Guildenstern, and such an unregenerate undergraduate as Hamlet who, though he wanted to go back to school in Wittenberg, could make unseemly reformation jokes about "politic worms" and "your only emperor for diet" (*Hamlet*, IV,iii). Luther made himself unpopular among the students for a while when he preached against all tumult after a town and gown riot at Wittenberg in 1520. And he had to deal with absent professors, and with a Doctor of Divinity who had given up his proper academic title, dressed in labourer's cloth, and wanted to be called plain Andrew (ibid., 18.131). Luther much disapproved such left-wing demonstration. He made great play with the accusation that Dr Karlstadt was ministering to a congregation without being appointed by the university patrons of the living (ibid., 18.82). If the dons wanted to exercise a reforming ministry they should reorganize their teaching; "it would be well if the Canon Law should be completely abandoned", "if we bear the name and title of Doctors of Holy Scripture, the very name should make it compulsory for us to teach Holy Scripture alone", "the number of books on theology must also be reduced", and "we should not, as now, send everyone to the university for the mere sake of having many students" (ibid., 6, (381) 404-469).

When other men, using Luther's name, demanded a radical restructuring of society and a redistribution of economic resource, he was brought into a political debate for which his experience had not prepared him. He made a number of pronouncements which some of his followers found and find embarrassingly conservative. Karlstadt had, Luther declared in some fury, brought "the disorderly mob" onto the streets and let them "forget civil discipline and manners", so that they "no longer fear or respect anyone but themselves". This was "a pretty preliminary to riot and rebellion" (ibid.). When rebellion occurred, when the peasants took scythes and pitchforks in their hands and marched against the squires, Luther was quick to remove his theology of justification from their mouths, (ibid., 18.357-361). "Under the outward appearance of the gospel they honour and serve the devil, thus deserving death in body and soul ten times over". Luther told the noblemen: "Let whoever can stab, smite, slay" (ibid.). He was much criticized for this violent authoritarianism. He himself was horrified at the savagery of the retribution the victorious gentry exacted from the peasants. But he said of these aristocrats, "we must put up with them when God plagues us with them" (ibid., 18.384-401).

Luther did not say all this in the Latin of the old obedience. He made a new speech for the expression of his new life. His translation of the Scriptures has, certainly, its significance for the development of the German language. Luther's abandonment of the sentence structure, grammatical rules, and vocabulary, of Latin which had been preserved in the mediaeval translations, (Bornkamm, 1947, pp. 23-28), brought the language of the Saxon chancellery into general German use. The energy of his exposition of the psalms, the splendour of his own hymn-writing, the vulgarity of his debating technique, above all, perhaps, the brilliance of his management in a pamphlet war, ensured that Luther's folk would speak and sing in Luther's language. But it must be kept in mind that Luther's biblical translation was begun in the vernacular pericopes of those sermons and postils in which he was struggling to articulate the meaning of the gospel for himself, and that the new significances of *gerecht, beruf,* and *arbeit,* (Holl, 1926, pp. 189-219; Geist, 1931, pp. 83-113), have their origins in his understanding of his own experience. Whatever the readying of those political, ecclesiastical, or economic conditions within which he found his opportunity, the great social change of the Reformation remains a public expression of Luther's individual perception of the divine.

Parents, professors, and peasants were secular nuisances, and Luther may have a little mistaken the way of the world and the application of the gospel, but he made no mistake about the pope. Since God in his justifying regard recognizes an human being as the *gemellus* of Christ, and since good works are the appropriate response in this regard, then he who taught that by doing good works in imitation of Christ an human being might earn

62   *Hamish F.G. Swanston*

justification from God is, quite literally, Anti-Christ. He has got everything
back to front and must be plucked down. So far Luther's divine experience
shewed him. So far he was socially disruptive. If he seem strangely at ease
with other conventions of his society, it must be that he had received no
commission to proceed against anyone else.

References

A. Kempis, T., 1901: *Imitation of Christ*, (C. Bigg, trans). London (Methuen).
Aquinas, T., 1882: *Opera Omnia*, Rome (Vatican Press).
Aquinas, T., 1963: *Summa Theologica*, (translated by English Dominicans).
London (Eyre and Spottiswoode).
Baeumker, K., 1920: *Petrus von Hibernia*. Munich (Sitzungsber. d. Bayer Akad. d.
Wissenschaften).
Benincasa, C., 1721: *Opere*, iii, (B. Gigli ed.). Lucca.
Bonaventura, (Di Fidanza, G.), 1882-1902: *Opera*, (Franciscans of Quaracchi, ed.).
Quaracchi.
Bornkamm, H., 1947: *Die Vorlagen zu Luthers Übersetzung des N. Testaments,
Theol. Literaturzeit*, 72, pp. 23-28., Heidelberg.
Denzinger, H. and Schonmetzer, A. (eds), 1965: *Enchiridion Symbolorum* (33rd.
ed.). Barcelona, (Herder).
De Wette, W.M.L., 1825-8: *Luthers Briefe*, five volumes. Berlin.
Geist, H., 1931: *Arbeit. Die Entscheidung eines Wortwertes durch Luther,
Lutherjahrbuch 1931*, pp. 83-113. Munich.
Gerdes, Daniel, 1744: *Introductio in Historiam Evangelii Saeculo xvi renovati*.
Groningen.
Holl, K., 1926: '*Die Geschichte des Wortes Beruf*, Gesammelte Aufsätz zur
Kirchengeschichte*, III, pp. 189-219. Tübingen.
Julian of Norwich, 1927: *Revelations of Divine Love*, (R. Huddlestone, ed.).
London, *(Burns Oates)*.
Kantorowicz, E., 1931: *Kaiser Friedrich II*. 1957, (E.O. Lorimer, trans.). New York,
(Ungar).
Kidd, B.J., 1911: *Documents Illustrative of the Continental Reformation* (2nd. ed.)
Oxford, (Clarendon).
Lombard, P., 1855: *Sententiae, Patrologia Latina* (J.P. Migne, ed.) cxcii. Paris.
de Lubac, H., 1959: *Exégèse Médiévale, Les quatre sens de l'écriture*, four volumes.
Paris (Aubier).
Luther, M., 1883 ff.: *Weimarer Ausgabe* (W.A.) and *Briefwechsel, Weimarer
Ausgabe* (W.A. Br.), (J.C.F. Knaake *et al.*, eds). Weimar and Graz (Hermann
Böhlaus Nachfolger).
Matarasso, P.M., (trans.) 1969: *The Quest of the Holy Grail*. Harmondsworth
(Penguin Books).
Melanchthon, P. (Schwarzerd, P.), 1834-60: *Corpus Reformatorum*, i-xxviii, (K.G.
Bretschneider, and E. Bindseil, eds). Brunswick. (Reprinted 1963 Frankfurt am
Main, (Minerva.)
Richter, E.L., 1846: *Die evangelische Kirchenordnungen des sechszehuten
Jahrhunderds*. (Weimar).

Scheel, O., 1929: *Dokumente zu Luthers Entwicklung bis 1519, Sammbung ausgewählter kirchen und dogmengeschichtlicher* (2nd ed.), Quellenschriften, 2.9. Tübingen

Seckendorf, F.L. von, 1692: *Commentarius historicus et apologeticus de Lutheranismo.* (Frankfurt and Leipzig).

Smalley, B. 1952: *The Study of the Bible in the Middle Ages* (2nd ed.). Oxford (Clarendon).

Theodore of Mospsuestia, 1933: *De Sacramentis* (A. Mingana, ed. and trans.), Woodbrooke Studies Vol. VI. Cambridge (Heffer).

Winkworth, S., 1966: Translation of *Theologia Germanica* (2nd ed.). London (Stuart and Watkins).

Wolters, C., 1961: Translation of *Cloud of Unknowing.* London (Penguin Books).

Bediüzzaman Said Nursi (1873-1960):
the shaping of a vocation

Şerif Mardin

One of the most persistent bogeys of the Turkish Republic (est. 1923) and a figure which Turkish progressives still associate with obscurantism, supersitition and error, has been the Turkish religious leader "Bediüzzaman" ("nonpareil of the times") Said Nursi. Condemned by the Turkish authorities to enforced residence in a hamlet of Western Turkey following his imputed participation in the Kurdish rebellion of 1925, he was soon gathering more of a following than ever before through his koranic commentaries and sermons. He had been working on these for some years, but his exile allowed him to produce a popularized version of his theology which became an inspiration for a number of persons now gathered around him. These disciples, acquired on the spot, soon attracted him an even wider following in the surrounding villages and towns, and his influence also spread to neighboring provinces. Alarmed, the authorities arrested him in 1935, accusing him of trying to establish a secret society aimed at destroying the "laic" foundations of the Republic. Laicism was the concept which summarized the secularist ideals of the founding fathers of the Republic, and particularly, that of Mustafa Kemal Atatürk. When the issue was first debated in the Turkish Parliament in 1928, laicism had been defined as the "separation of religious and worldly concerns" (Ozek, 1962, p. 40). The principle was later to be enshrined in the Turkish Constitution by a constitutional amendment which introduced the six principles of "republican reform" into the text of the constitution; laicism was one of these (1937). After his first arrest in 1935, Bediüzzaman was condemned to a term in jail and this was followed by others in 1943 and 1948. Soon thereafter, multi-party democracy was established in fact as well as in law in Turkey. National elections took place in 1950, and the new party which emerged with a sizeable majority from this contest, the Demokrat Party, took over from the Republican People's Party, the party which for years had enforced laicism strictly and rather severely. An accusation hurled against the defeated party had been that it had interpreted secularization as a license to persecute Muslims and hound true believers. This feeling that freedom of conscience had been denied to Turks in the era when secular reform was carried through, no doubt played some role in the defeat of the RPP although opposition to it was laced with other socio-economic themes. Once in power, the Demokrat Party did, indeed soften the Jacobin secularism of its predecessor. But it is remarkable that even though the followers of Bediüzzaman supported the new government, they never could elicit its unambiguous support. In 1952 and 1953 Said Nursi was still accounting for his publications to the Public Prosecutor. Eventually, a court decision of 1956 allowed his Koranic commentaries and sermons to be published freely. Between 1950 and 1960 his following increased markedly, although this can be followed only through indirect indices such as the appearance of Nurcu activity in large cities and on university campuses. Today, the Nur movement has become a factor to reckon with in Turkish politics, for although there is no political party which was formed around the group, its support is said to be crucial in electoral contests in parts of Eastern Turkey.

Most of what we know about Said Nursi's life originates in his authorized biography first published in 1958 (Bediüzzaman, 1976). This remarkable document bears the stamp of his personality in a way that no other account of his life does. In particular, the account of his student days has a forceful, lifelike quality which is not found in other sources. It is thus a valuable document for studying the gradual emergence of his vocation, first as an aspirant Nakşibendi savant, and then as a Muslim ideologist. The picture of Said Nursi one gets from this book is that of a person embattled from the earliest days of his life. What are portrayed are Said's personal concerns, his antagonistic relations with many of his teachers, how he was persecuted and betrayed and how he overcame these obstacles. The vivid depiction of feelings, motives and emotions allow us to reconstruct the set of attitudes that regulated his behaviour at the time when he was a student of theology. A closer reading of the same source, however, reveals how motivations are incorporated into the impinging institutional framework. A third reading enables us to place the formation of Said's vocation within an even wider circle which we might name the "World System" of his time, although what I mean here by "World System" is somewhat different than the use of it which has been associated with the work of Wallerstein.

I would like to think that an overview of the operation of these three circles show the workings of something which may be termed over-determination.

Life

Said Nursi was born in a small village in the Province of Bitlis, in an area of Turkey then described in Ottoman atlases as Kurdistan. He was a native Kurdish speaker. His father was an impoverished village *molla* or prayer leader, with a small holding of land and seven children. There appears to have been considerable concern with status in his family. The rough stone which is the only mark of his father's burial place bears the title "Mirza", an attribute of noble descent. The family prided itself on the descent of Said's mother from a local notable Alişan Paşa. The conjunction of this emphasis on prestigious ancestry and of the actual poverty of the family points to a perception of status dissonance which may have been limited to Said or may have affected the entire family. Said certainly showed a marked concern for social justice he did not spare his criticism for the leading figures among the Seyhs (Sheikhs) of Bitlis whom he accused of fleecing the poor and later, in the 1920s, he stated that he understood how one could criticize the "bourgeoisie" for its egoism.

Said remained in his father's house until the age of nine. At that time he started his school education, one of the first schools he attended being that of Şeyh Mehmed Emin Efendi. Emin Efendi taught in a religious school (*medrese*) in the tradition of the Nakşibendi religious order which controlled the region. But immediately difficulties of adaptation appeared. Bediüzzaman's biography states that even at this tender age he could not bear the slightest remark made in a commanding tone, and he thus abandoned his studies and returned to his village. There he continued his studies under the tutorship of his elder brother who had preceeded him in the religious educational stream (Bediüzzaman, 1976, p. 31). Later, Said moved to the hamlets of Pirmis and Hizan where he studied with Şeyh Seyyid Nur Muhammed Efendi. Said did not get along much better with the students of this "seminary", and we are informed that they were on the lookout for an occasion to pick a fight with him. However, he was able to show his teacher that he had been set upon and that he was not at fault. Even so, after a time he left for another school where his erstwhile teacher Mehmed Emin Efendi was lecturing. Soon he was questioning the authority of the latter — stating that Mehmed Emin Efendi's powers were derived from Şeyh Abdurrahman Taği, the founder of the school. According to Said, Emin Efendi was just filling in the position and had no business voicing his own opinions. Once more, Said had to return to his village. Fortunately, the Prophet Muhammad appeared to him in a dream and this good omen encouraged him to continue his studies. But once more, during this newest attempt at school attendance, he was at loggerheads with his teacher and had to leave. There followed another series of tentative affiliations with *medreses*, ending with a three month course in the town of Doğu Bayazit with another Seyh, Mehmed Celali (Djelali).

Bediüzzaman obtained his diploma of religious studies in 1888. His own comment on the way in which his difficulties pursued him to the day of his graduation are worth quoting:

> In the past, when I was fourteen, some objections were raised to my being invested by the Master with the gown which would have been the symbol of my diploma. Due to my youth it was said that it would not be fitting for me to wear a gown which the great doctor was wearing. This was also due to the fact that the great luminaries of the time were not only in a relation of teachers to me but also in that of rivals; they perceived the ceremony as one which signified that they had surrendered [to my superior qualities]. And so no one could be found to place the gown on my shoulders and would have the self-assurance to assume the role of the Master... (Bediüzzaman, unpublished, pp. 134-135).

Shortly after having received his diploma, Said decided to visit a number of local *Ulema* (Doctors of Islamic Law) to widen his horizons. He dressed in "dervish" clothes, meaning that he took to wearing a very simple robe and carried a minimum of personal effects. He roamed in the uplands making his way towards Bitlis. One gets the impression that he was trying to prepare himself for a divine sign of his elect status but that this did not materialize. He moved back to the town of Siirt to the medrese of a new teacher, Molla Fethullah. The latter is stated to have been highly impressed by Said's abilities. This perceived brilliance led Molla Fethullah to organize a special debate to show off his star "graduate" student who had to answer questions posed to him by learned Doctors of Islamic law. His success in this interrogation is reported to have excited jealousy among other "graduate" students and among the *Ulema*, an outcome with which Bediüzzaman was already familiar. Conspiracies began to be organized against him in the community of students of religion and the *Ulema* and he was only saved from bodily harm in this confrontation by his own partisans. Apparently he had been able to elicit a number of partisans simply by being, involved in such competitive religious debates. These splits in the Muslim community seem to have alarmed the governor-delegate, the *mutasarrif* resident in town. He offered Said Nursi his assistance but this was rejected. After the fracas died down Said Nursi announced that he was ready to take on anyone who wanted to engage in a physical or intellectual contest and thereafter departed for the town of Bitlis. Possibly, the governor-delegate had decided that Siirt would be calmer without his presence.

In Bitlis, Said took upon himself to offer counsels of moderation to local families of feuding Şeyhs and to insubordinate students in the medreses. His presumption and impertinence led the religious notables to complain to

Molla Mehmed Emin Efendi, Said's earliest mentor, presumably because the latter had more influence on him than anyone else. Emin Efendi reassured the notables that the age of the troublemaker was proof that these incidents were nothing but youthful mischief. Emin Efendi, then subjected Said to a thorough going examination which must have included matters of faith as well as knowledge. Once more Said is said to have surmounted this test, and he then went on to preach in the Kureyş Mosque in Bitlis. The community of believers which attended the Kureyş Mosque again seem to have formed into a partisan group and he was thus provided with a set of followers who were aligned against his detractors. The governor of the province stepped in at this juncture and Said Nursi was asked to leave town: he went to Şirvan. Once more, the pressures of strife in this town sent Said into retreat and religious contemplation. In the hamlet of Tillo where he took refuge, Said saw in a dream the founder of the Kadiri order, Abdelkader Geylanî, who ordered him to stop the depredations of the brigand Mustafa Paşa, the leader of the Miran tribe. Mustafa Paşa had been granted the title of Paşa by Sultan Abdulhmid II who had also made him the leader of the local militia which had organized to police Eastern Anatolia and to keep under control both Kurdish autonomist tendencies and Armenian revolutionary activities (Van Bruinessen, 1978, p. 234). Said departed for Mustafa Paşa's encampment in Cizre and upon being admitted to his presence told him that he had come to make a good Muslim of him. More bemused than frightened, Mustafa Paşa organized his own contest to test the mettle of this presumptuous and impertinent young cleric. Said, according to his authorized biography, answered all questions asked of him by local sages and obtained a solemn promise from the tribal leader that he would heed his warnings He also sent him off with a number of valuable presents.

After a short and somewhat inconclusive stint with the Arab tribes of the region as a candidate for the role of conciliator in tribal disputes he moved on to the town of Mardin. Once more, he is said to have impressed the inhabitants of this town with his theological learning. According to a statement in his authorized biography, Mardin was the place where he started on his "first political life". The expression is possibly related to a widening of his intellectual horizons which resulted from meeting two students of theology who were passing through Mardin (Bediüzzaman, 1976, p. 42). One of these students was a follower of Cemaleddin (Djemaleddin) at Afganî (1839—97). Afganî, one of the most striking reformist of Islam of the nineteenth century had devoted much energy to the defence of the idea that there was nothing incompatible between Islam and the scientific attitude. His abiding interest in the reform of Islamic education derived from this stand. He was also an advocate of the strengthening of the Islamic world against the West and he encouraged the building of strong national identities in the Middle East (Fazlur Rahman, 1979, p. 216; Hourani, 1962, 103 f.). The first of these themes prefigures one of the arguments which Said Nursi was to use in his own writings.

The second traveller from which Said received information about the world of Islam outside the Ottoman Empire was a member of the Sanusi order. Since the 1840s this order had been at work forging a Muslim theocratic order in Cyrenaica by using Islam as a principle of cohesion to bring together warring Bedouin tribes (Evans-Pritchard, 1949).

The expression "first political life" probably refers to the fact that Said began to be aware that the politics of competitive learning, which he had negotiated so successfully, was only of the orbits available for the use of his background in theological studies. Said's subsequent career was to underline the extraordinary ease with which a Muslim "cleric" can shift from religious disputations to much more clearly political issues.

The reason for the ease with which the transition could be effected is clear: the Muslim community was not simply a community of believers it was by definition the group that was responsible for the political viability of Islam as embodied in a state, in this case the Ottoman state. Again, the community of believers was the fountain-head of political legitimacy and was the support of the just Caliph. It is true that the Ottoman state had established boundaries between the community and the state by repeatedly signifying that men of religion, and particularly charismatic religious leaders, had no business in politics. Nevertheless, in an area like Bitlis where the prevailing conditions were those of transition, from an old pattern of authority and leadership to a new one, the community of believers took a role which was reminiscent of that which it had assumed when the state was not around to set boundaries to its influence.

Whatever the activities Said's newly acquired knowledge generated in Mardin, they were not of a nature to please the Ottoman administration. Said was marched back to Bitlis under armed guard. One of the first supernatural interventions into his life is said to have occurred at this time: his guards halted their march to pray and soon noticed that Said Nursi had been able to get out of his handcuffs to pray with them.

In Bitlis, Said joined the staff of the Governor, Ömer Paşa, as tutor of his children. Here he extended his culture by reading a whole series of Islamic classics. He also took up the study of the secular sciences of geography, chemistry and mathematics, the newly prestigious subjects about which the graduates of secular schools boasted. Newspapers and books published in Istanbul which were received by the governor were another source of new ideas and information. His authorized biography states that it was because of the speed with which he mastered some of these Western sciences that he acquired the sobriquet of "Bediüzzaman" at the time. The Armenian question had now become a burning issue in international politics and Bitlis with its Armenian population was in the centre of the controversy. The first instance of a large scale clash had been precipitated by the refusal of the Armenians of Sason — a sub-province of Bitlis — to pay taxes both to the Ottoman Government and to their former Kurdish overlords. It is at this time that Said Nursi read a newspaper account of one of the by now routine British parliamentary denunciations of Turkish depredations on the Armenians. The speech also declared that as long as Islam had not been erased the Ottomans would never have a chance of joining the ranks of civilized nations. Said Nursi was fired by the speech to announce that he believed Islam to be inextinguishable and that he would henceforth devote his life to the defence of the miraculous nature of the Koran. Soon he was to have this mission confirmed in a dream (Şahiner, 1979, p. 73).

Said Nursi must have convinced either his audience of bureaucrats or his followers that he did, indeed, have something to contribute to the defense of Islam because shortly thereafter (1896) he was taken in tow by one of Sultan Abdulhamid's advisers, Yahya Nüzhet Paşa, who was in Iraq in an administrative capacity. The Sultan had been gathering a number of leaders of religious orders from all parts of the Islamic world in an attempt to use Islam as a political formula to instil a feeling of collective identity among his Muslim subjects. Said joined these Islamic experts in residence in Istanbul and was placed with the Imperial bird-keeper Mustafa bey in a house inside Yildiz Palace. The Sultan must not have been overly impressed by Said since he sent him back after a year. Eventually, just before the young Turk Revolution, Said was to present the Sultan with a reform project that he thereafter never entirely abandoned. This was the creation of a university on the shores of Lake Van where the local Kurdish-speaking population would be given the means to become assimilated to Ottoman culture and where the religious learning of the resident sages of the region would be stepped up by training in the positive sciences.

Personality

What emerges most clearly from Said's biography is the theme of adversity, of strife and conflict. This starkness had some relation to the cultural givens of his milieu but there is a relentlessness with which Said insists on establishing his worth which probably had roots in his personality. Said's ''marginal'' status certainly seems to have had some relation to his bitterness but this situation seems to have stamped him in a particularly traumatic fashion.

Said's determination to foil his enemies — the main theme of his authorized biography — was paralleled by clothing which projected the same hostile image. He now always wore the colourful dress of a Kurdish mountaineer of some means: baggy pants, braided waistcoat, large shawl-like belt into which were struck two daggers with silver filigree handles. This was not the way Doctors of Islamic law dressed and his colleagues did not miss an opportunity to express surprise at this strange clothing. But Said insisted on wearing these clothes even after he went to the Ottoman capital.

Another aspect of the same contentious image was Said's love of firearms: in Mustafa Paşa's encampment he engaged in shooting contests with the tribal leader and was eventually given a carbine as a parting gift. Said was also quite proud of his physical prowess and often proclaimed that no one could "lick" him. On two occasions, the Balkan Wars and the First World War, he showed extreme bravery.

The most daring performance of Said Nursi, however, was to pick as patron the saintly man who had founded the religious order of the Kadiri, who were rivals of the Nakşibendi. In a region where the Nakşibendi had established control by ousting the Kadiri this was a real act of defiance. It is difficult to believe that he had already adopted such a position before the age of nine, as one of his biographers relates (Şahiner, 1979), but there seems to exist solid evidence that he took such a stand during his student days. One of the recurring themes in his later writing (and one which shows his universalism particularly well) is that one should have no special allegiance to any of the orders since all have something to contribute to Islam.

Possibly, the most interesting feature in Said Nursi's personality is his ability to transcend the very moods of hostility which overwhelmed him in his early days. Thus he states:

> When I was ten years old I had an attitude of self-esteem and praise. I was acting as if I were engaged in extraordinarily important projects which required heroic deeds for their implementation, even though this very attitude went against my grain. I would say to myself "You are not worth five para, why then do you show this self-assurance and why are you so keen to appear courageous?..." (Bediüzzaman, 1959, p. 52).

It is this basic ambivalence which best explains Said Nursi's eventual development from a tough frontiersman to a univeralistic preacher stressing the primacy of faith, a role he was to assume in the later stages of his life and especially after 1920.

The picture that emerges from Said Nursi's biography is one of haphazard and somewhat foredoomed attacks on the structure of religious education and the religious authority which underpinned it. However, when a number of components in his background are brought together these sallies fall into a more intelligible pattern. An aspect of this background is that Said was living in a rural area which, since the beginning of the nineteenth century, had been culturally "colonized" by devishes just as another wave of dervishes had colonized Anatolia for its Turkic conquerors centuries ago. In those early centuries other dervishes had helped the establishment of nodes of settlement, and now the Nakşibendi were engaging in indoctrination in similar settlements through a stricter reinterpretation of the moral imperatives of the Koran. The Nakşibendi were working primarily from hamlets where they had established their schools. They appealed to the rural masses for clientele and because of their looser organizational network were able to spread while the Kadiri order declined. It was this Nakşibkendi complex which made up the outer boundaries of Said's universe. For him the most direct avenue of mobility consisted in rising in this complex, and though he adopted a stand antagonistic to the Nakşibendi establishment and attacked their network and their pedagogy he was still embroiled in the Nakşibendi universe. He had to accept it as a given in struggling to make a place for himself.

The strategies that he used to that end were of two kinds: the first consisted in acquiring differential status, the status of an elect, by being shown a sign of selection, i.e. a vision or a dream. Such a sign could have two consequences: at the minimum it would be a confirmation of one's vocation, maximally, it could point to the special role that one was destined to play as a religious leader. Said Nursi played on both registers but rather unsuccessfully on the second, presumably because of his age. A second strategy Said could have used was "competitive academicism" and there, indeed he had scored several successes, although he was too much of a young man in a hurry to have achieved this success without antagonizing his elders.

The reason Said did not stop at this juncture was that interpenetrating with the visionary element and with the competitive learning were two other possibilities of action for Doctors of Islamic Law where matters became more purely political. These were "Tribal conciliation" and "Mosque politics" and Said had no hesitation in embarking on both.

Culture in Bitlis

In 1891, the missionary, Mrs Isabella Bird Bishop, visited Bitlis and gave the following account of it:

> Bitlis is one of the roughest and most fanatical and turbulent of Turkish cities, but the present governor, Rauf Pasha, is a man of energy and has reduced the town and neighborhood to some degree of order (Bishop, 1891, p. 352).

The roughness of the region was the result of a number of developments some of which had taken place after the middle of the nineteenth century.

The primary structural division of the Kurdish region was that between tribal and non-tribal groups (Van Bruinessen, 1978, p. 39). Both components, however, lived according to an ethos, that of the code of honor (Barth, 1969, p. 20).

The tribal structure, the syndrome of honour, the feuding between tribes made for a society in which individuals carved their reputation by feats of courage and endurance. "Clerics" were not excluded from these obligations especially when they entered the fray as candidates for power and influence. Such a new opportunity for them arose between 1850 and 1890 when the power of the former princelings was shattered by the Ottoman Administration and no alternative system of law and order had yet emerged in its place. As a consequence,

> The emirates fell apart into many quarreling tribes led by petty chieftains who were all equally eager to fill in as much as possible of the power vacuum left by the departure of the mirs. The harsh but reliable rule of the mirs made place for lawlessness and insecurity. The entire country became haunted by feuds and tribal disputes (Van Bruinessen, 1978, pp. 289—90).

Because the Şeyhs were outside the tribal organization they were able to undertake mediatory roles in settling tribal disputes. A new field of influence was opened for them at this juncture. It is from now on that they also appear with increasing frequency as political leaders. Said Nursi himself had tried such mediation among the Arab tribes of Biro, following his departure from Mustafa Paşa's encampment, but he does not seem to have been successful. In fact, to the extent that he also had to assume the role of an impartial agent, his interference into Mustafa Paşa's affairs was also part of what we may call the "politics of mediation". But in both cases Said had arrived too late: the image that emerges from the biography in relation to his advice to Mustafa Paşa is that of a rather ineffective Don Quixote. The reasons for this are also clear: in 1891 the Ottoman state had entered into a new type of agreement with the most powerful tribal leaders who were transformed into militia chiefs and left to assume local police and gendarmerie functions. Feuds between tribes were henceforth to be settled as much as possible by this mechanism. This is the reason for which the state turned a deaf ear to Mustafa Paşa's depredations. In a way they constituted his salary equivalent.

Mosque politics

Bitlis and its surroundings cannot be conceptualized simply in terms of tribal horsemen flashing their scimitars in an area where they could only be confronted by other tribesmen in turn flourishing their lances. The province was partly populated by settled villagers, some of them working on the land of Kurdish Chiefs, and commerce was channelled through cities with well-delineated urban identities. Neither were the relations between these three components necessarily antagonistic at all times although tribesmen did often upset the system by inventing their own set of rules. What is true is that different types of relations to the central government made for different types of macro-systems and this crucially affected city politics.

The mirs, (Princes) who had ruled Bitlis from their capital city had kept the pieces of the mosaic in equilibrium most of the time. Thus neither the Kadiri order which was influential in the area before 1800 nor the tribal groups could measure themselves against the power of the mirs. The Kadiri exercized maximum influence only in a number of semi-rural centres where leading Kadiri Şeyhs had established residence such as was the case in Berzenc (nowadays in Iraq) (Van Bruinessen, 1978, p. 278). In other words, until 1849 mirs had the power to stop Şeyhs from meddling in city politics. A somewhat more flexible system of city-politics seems to have existed in other parts of the Ottoman Empire, particularly in Syria. In Syria an influential group of notables operated in the cities as intermediaries between the citizens and the Ottoman government and the majority were from established families of Doctors of Islamic law (Barbir, 1980, p. 70). Here there always existed a chance that Mosque-based contests structured around "competitive spirituality" (Ahmed, 1980) could lead to the formation of a new clique. The new group could then try to exert pressure on the existing power structure by appearing as an alternative group which would carry on the same functions as the incumbents; it could present itself as a buffer and a channel of communication between the government and the inhabitants of the city. Said Nursi's predecessor, Şeyh Halid, the man who had brought a new Nakşibendi doctrine to Kurdistan and whose lieutenants (*Halifa*) had riddled the sub-province of Hizan with their schools had attempted such a strategy at the beginning of the nineteenth century in Damascus. But his attempt had met with disaster.

A third, much more complex situation and opportunity for city and Mosque politics existed in the 1890s at the time when Said was trying to get himself a Mosque following. First of all Bitlis had become on Ottoman provincial capital. The anaemic bureaucratic structure of the mirs had been displaced by the structure of Imperial administration. A new city life had come into being with its cafés, (where, according to Cuinet, "newspapers are read"), its officer's club and secular civilian and military schools. In a sub-provincial centre dependent on Bitlis, the new structure of adminsitration would have typically consisted of an administrative council, a municipal council, a financial office, a court of first instance, a number of technical departments, a public health service, an education department and a forestry administration. That these were not simply slots that existed on paper but offices manned by relatively competent personnel was witnessed by foreign consuls. Bitlis, had, in addition a garrison of 2500 men whose effect on the town should be gauged primarily in economic terms since Bitlis became the centre for the supplies to the garrison.

In fact, as law and order were established by the administration of Sultan Abdulhamid, towards the end of the nineteenth century, prosperity in Bitlis and in some of the major towns in Kurdistan increased. The town now set an arena where a number of new processes operated: government decisions were taken there, plans for the development of the Vilayet (Province) were determined in the Vilayet Council. Government tenders were given out partly in the capital of the provinces. But this new civic structure which promised that no one would be stopped by the jealous intervention of the mirs was not what Said expected it to be. The Ottoman state was still in the wings waiting for subversive religious movements to appear. Said Nursi's attempt to carry on politics away from the rural setting into the newly active towns had failed. The reason for which Said nevertheless, thereafter, was so easily coopted into the governor's office is probably related to the reputation that he had acquired as an opponent of Nakşibendi leaders. This meant that he could be used by the state.

There was one more dimension to the growth of the city in which Said was involved and that was the Armenian renaissance. In Bitlis Province, a little less than one third of the total population of *c.* 400 000 was Armenian. Part of this population consisted of peasants — such as the rebellious peasants of Sason which I have mentioned above. But some of the Armenians were craftsmen and merchants and a smaller number occupied positions in the Ottoman administration, in key posts such as that of accountant. Since the 1850s the Armenian community of the Ottoman Empire had been experiencing a renewed prosperity. They had first been able to liberate themselves from the administration of a corrupt religious hierarchy in 1850 and by the terms of the Treaty of Paris bureaucratic posts had been opened to them. The Armenians who were well educated and who were granted the support of Protestant missionaries in Eastern Turkey used their new economic prosperity to establish good schools in various cities in eastern Anatolia. In 1880 Mikail Portugalian had established his own gymnasium on the shores of Lake Van above Bitlis. This was an important centre for the revival of Armenian culture and it was closed by the Ottoman authorities in 1885. Another gymnasium which was known to be a centre for nationalist movements operated in Erzurum. No wonder, then, that Said Nursi had proposed that an Ottoman University be established in Van. The unusual aspect of this development was that Said Nursi had been trained in a Nakşibendi network which, in a much more diffuse fashion, had been trying to create a network of Muslim revival since the seventeenth century. But this operation, carried on through the network of Nakşibendi teaching centres, was not capable of competing with the much more efficient system the Armenians were using to produce graduates in their own schools and to spread their own good work. It is at this point that Said must have harboured the gravest doubts about the success of the Nakşibendi enterprise.

The Nakşibendi order

To Muslims throughout the world the territorial decline of Islamic states and the weakness of the Ottoman Empire had caused considerable concern. Very early, however, revivalist movements had proclaimed that Islam as a whole was due for revitalization. Outstanding among these was the theory that the second millenium of Islam would not be an era of decline but an era of renaissance (Ahmad, 1964, pp. 182-190). This view was propounded by Şeyh Ahmad al Sirhindi (d. 1625) who was one of the luminaries of the Nakşibendi order in India. Somewhat later, the influence of Sirhindi spread to Syria and then to Kurdistan and its teaching became particularly well established around Hizan, the sub-province into which Said Nursi was born. The teaching of the Nakşibendi order had nothing directly "mystic" associated with it. One of its main tenets was the idea of the communion of the hearts (Hourani, 1972, p. 101) the concept that not only leader and follower were united in their hearts but that a similar communication existed between Muslims of the day and those of earlier generations. This doctrine, had an obvious strong point: it linked together both the Muslims in one place and at one time and Islam as a much wider historical phenomenon. We may call it a sort of ideology, a form of the consciousness of Islam as a historical phenomenon which liberated votaries from personal ties to any one director of conscience, which was the case in other mystic orders. It also emphasized the importance of "virtuous activity" in contrast to the antinomianism which had crept into some of the mystic orders (which did not discriminate between the various worldy manifestations of God and sometimes slid into an aesthetically satisfying pantheism). At any rate we know that for the Nakşibendi centres around Hizan what was important was no longer the transformation in which the self progresses "to its annihilation in fulfilment" (Trimingham, 1973, p. 155) but the ability to instil a new faith in the future of Islam in the hearts of Muslims. The kind of Jesuitic educational pattern that emerged from this conviction was meant to implement the new mission of the Nakşibendis. As Said Nursi explains describing his teacher Abdurrahman Taği,

He trained many students and preachers and learned men and when all of

Kurdistan began to sing his praise. I, immersed in scientific disputations of a high caliber and placed within a wide circle of science and tarikat, was convinced that these preachers were about to conquer the earth. (Bediüzzaman, 1959, p. 53).

Whether these activities had had the support of Sultan Abdhulhamid from the very beginning is not known, but what we do know is that the Sultan started to look into the prospects for an Islamic revitalization as early as 1882. As Sir William Ramsay, a British Archaeologist who had been trekking for years through Anatolia remarked:

In 1882 a change was very marked, and has been so ever since. There began a distinct revival of Mohammedan feeling. The prophecies current were no longer about the term of Turkish power, they were that the year 1300 (beginning 31st October 1882) was an epoch of Mohammedan power bringing either new life and strength or utter and complete ruin. (Ramsay, 1897, p.136)

Epilogue

Said Nursi's incorporation into Sultan Abdulhamid's Panislamic Şeyhly "advisory board" was his first step into a stance in which he collaborated with those who used Islam for the mobilization of the Islamic population of the Ottoman empire and also the population of the wider reaches of the Muslim world. The young Turks, who dethroned Sultan Abdulhamid, continued this experiment and Said Nursi also collaborated with them. Eventually, however, he was to voice his disappointment with politics and politicians and attempt to work for the revitalization of Islam, through a reinstilling of faith in the heart of the average Muslim. The political frame which he had to adopt at first, however, shows the close conjunction between religion and politics in an Islamic setting and the way in which these two forces, in turn, were incorporated at the time into the accelerated change taking place in the world of the 1890s. Here, a basic transformation was occurring in the pattern of "clusters of settlement, modes of transport, centres of cultures, areas and centres of language, divisions of caste and class, barriers between markets, sharp regional differences in wealth and interdependence" (Deutsch, 1966, p. 187), and the Kurdish areas of the Ottoman Empire were increasingly drawn into "the uneven impact of critical historical events" (Deutsch, 1966).

References

Akbar S. Ahmed 1980: *Millenium and Charisma among Pathans.* London Routledge and Kegan Paul.

Aziz Ahmad, 1964: *Studies in Islamic Culture in the Indian Environment.* Oxford (Clarendon Press).

Barbir, Karl K., 1980: *Ottoman Rule in Damascus 1708-1758.* Princeton (Princeton University Press).

Barth, F., 1969: *Ethnic Group and Boundaries: The Social Organization of Cultural Difference.* Boston (Little, Brown & Co.)

Bediüzzaman Said Nursi, n.d.: *Sikke-i Tasdik-i Gaybi,* (Istanbul)

Bediüzzaman Said Nursi, n.d., *Emirdag Lahikasi.* Istanbul (Sinan).

Bediüzzaman Said Nursi, n.d., *Tarihçe i Hayati* Istanbul (Sözler Yayinevi).

Bishop, Isabella L. Bird, 1891: *Journeys in Persia and Kurdistan,* Vol II. London (John Murray).

Deutsch, Karl W., 1953, 1966 (2nd ed.): *Nationalism and Social Communication.* London (John Wiley).

Evans-Pritchard, E.E., 1949: *The Sanusi of Cyrenaica.* (Oxford).

Fazlur Rahman, 1979: *Islam* (2nd ed.). Chicago and London (University of Chicago Press).

Hourani, Albert, 1962: *Arabic Thought in the Liberal Age 1789-1939.* London (Oxford University Press).

Hourani, Albert, 1972: Shaikh Khalid and the Nagshbandi order. In *Islamic Philosophy and the Classical Tradition* S.H. Stern, A. Hourani and V. Brown, eds. Cassrer.

Özek, Çetin, 1962: *Türkiyede Lâiklik.* Istanbul (Baha).

Ramsay, William M., 1897: *Impressions of Turkey*

Şahiner, Necmeddin, 1979: *Bilinmeyen Tazaflasiyle Bediuzzaman Said Nursi.* Istanbul, (Yeni Asya).

Trimingham, J. Spencer, 1973: *The Sufi Orders in Islam.* London (Oxford University Press).

Van Bruinessen, M.M., 1978: *Agha, Shaikh and State: On the Social and Political Organization of Kurdistan.* Rijswijk (Europrint).

The Dinka and Catholicism

Godfrey Lienhardt

When Daniel Comboni, one of the Veronese priests who pioneered the mission of the Verona Fathers in the Southern Sudan, was sailing up the Nile in 1858, their boat ran onto a sandbank. Comboni describes their situation:

> Our position was very critical; we were in the middle of the White Nile; on the one side were the Dinka who only last year had massacred the crew of a boat, on the other, the Shilluk, one of the most powerful and savage tribes of central Africa, living by robbery and rapine. We could not move... If those savages had wanted, they could have destroyed us in a matter of minutes... When we had discussed every side of the difficulty we said that if the Shilluk should come to attack us, with crucifixes on our breasts we would surrender everything to them, boat and all. Without doubt they would take us as slaves before their king, perhaps to be killed, but by the grace of God and by charity we would win the affection of these savage people, and so, without seeking any further in the vineyard of Christ wherein to work, we would plant our Cross and found our mission station there. (Quoted in Dempsey, 1955, p. 100).[1]

Naturally the Dinka and Shilluk were suspicious and hostile, since foreigners travelling through their territory had often been raiders and slavers. But 30 years ago, when slave-raiding lived on only in the memory of old people, and after almost a century of missionary presence among the pastoral Nilotes of the Southern Sudan, mission stations there were still very few and far between, and their evangelical influence weakly diffused through the vast territory. In the villages and cattle-camps of the great bulk of the population, one might come across individuals here and there who had been through mission schools, and some of them baptized, but the presence of Catholic missions was not obvious outside the few towns and townships. That the first two Southern Sudanese priests in the Bahr-al-

81

Ghazal were ordained[2] only in 1944 and 1946, while Dr Francis Deng's book on traditional and modern values among the Dinka (Deng, 1971) indexes only eight page-references to "Christianity and Dinka culture" in 388 pages, suggests that the growth of the Church among the Nilotes had been slow.

This is no reflection on the dedication, energy or personalities of the missionaries. For many years non-Christians had been on good terms with them and made use of their medical and educational services. They were concerned for the people, learnt their languages and customs, and travelled widely among them visiting their few scattered outlying schools and catechists. Since the missionaries were for the most part Italians, and the civil administration on the whole very British, and Presbyterian or Anglican by upbringing, the Catholic Church was not the Church of the rulers as in the colonies of Catholic states, and the missionaries were not distanced from the people by social conventions. Their influence was local and limited.

So to describe the Southern Sudan as Christian (as journalists, political commentators and religious sympathizers have often done) misrepresents the situation. Most educated Southern Sudanese were indeed the products of a Christian form of education, as are today the many more western-educated southerners who provide the political leadership and administration of the South; but in the 1940s proselytizing Southern Sudanese Christians, except for those few in the service of the Church itself, were not conspicuous. It was not primarily as Christians that southerners fought against the northern Government until almost ten years ago, but as non-Arabs and non-Muslims against Arab and Muslim domination. In that world, what kind of translation, as it were, of experience was required for a Dinka to become a nominal or believing Christian?

The Church is the bearer of a theoretically unified body of theological and social doctrine. The two are already represented in the reported reaction of the early missionaries mentioned in the quotation with which I began — the wearing of the crucifix and the intention to demonstrate their charity. They bear the symbols of their faith, and hope to recommend them by their works. The doctrinal symbol of the crucifix caused immediate difficulties, for Fr. Dempsey says that the Shilluk "ran away from men so cruel as to wear on their breasts a cross with a man fixed to it" (1955, p. 103) and expresses his view, as a missionary priest, that for the Shilluk (and for the Dinka this is equally true) educational and medical and other practical services of the Church necessarily must precede any hope of evangelization (1955, 124ff.). He recognizes also that the freedom of movement taken for granted by the Shilluk population (and the pastoral Nilotes are much more mobile) creates a difficulty for missions, for the Church's forms of organization elsewhere presuppose a settled population, a Catholic community with priestly guidance and leadership. Thirty years ago certainly the practice of Catholicism was associated with towns and mission stations, providing a very different form of social life from that of the villages and the cattle-camps. For traditional Dinka, towns have always been places of ill-repute, attracting social riff-raff, and Dinka of good family did not wish their children to be corrupted by such company as they might find near established mission-stations. Hence there were scarcely any Christian chiefs. Catholicism had not grafted itself on to the local leadership.

The Dinka indigenous leaders combined religious with political status; but although some of the priest-chiefs, "masters", of the fishing spear, had a higher reputation for their religious power than others, there was no hierarchy of authority. Each priestly family provided spiritual and political guidance for the people of the area in which it was dominant. Its position was validated by elaborate myths, basically common to all Dinka, which set the priestly clan in a religious tradition closely bound up with the ecological conditions and basic experiences of life and death of the Dinka in their own places in Dinkaland. The myth itself represents the first priests as descended from the union of a spirit with a woman who could not have a child by human agency, and the first priest gives a teaching, performs various miracles and shares his power among his followers. The Dinka thus already had a story of the founding of their religious belief and practice which corresponded at some points to the Christian story of the birth and earlier career of Christ, and to the authority inherited through the Apostles at his death. Although such correspondences might appear advantageous for those wishing to persuade the Dinka to accept the Christian version, they could also appear simply as alternative and foreign versions of religious truths already familiar on their own terms to the Dinka, and unlike the Christian version, intimately connected with their own way of life. Ideas of a high God, of sin, of sacrifice, of redemption by blood and God's forgiveness (to mention only a few of the components of Christian doctrine) were also central to Dinka religion. Dramatic religious conversion, ideas of turning away from idolatry, being freed from spiritual bondage and excited by new cultural expressions of religious fervour, characteristic of the effects of fundamentalist missions in particular among peoples defeated by foreigners, could scarcely be expected on any large scale among the Dinka. The pastoral Nilotes have a very non-material — indeed anti-material — conception of the nature of religious forces, and at one level of thought could easily accept the commandment that "thou shalt have no other God before me", or the Moslem "there is no god but God', and they make no "graven images", the effectiveness of which could be questioned by an appeal to a more spiritual or scientific interpretation of religious forces.

The Dinka knew also that in different parts of the country there were many differing versions of the validating myth of their own priesthood, each giving its own account of the original characters and action in relation to local clans and communities. As there was no hierarchy of religious control, so there was no idea of a hierarchy of doctrinal authority. I took down many different versions of this myth among people who knew that I had been told stories different from their own. I never heard of any concern to establish one true version, for myth is "what people heard from the people of long ago", and different peoples heard different things. Only within each community was it accepted that some versions were more correct and fuller than others, and here the more authoritative version, the "true doctrine", as it were, was that of on the whole older men, recognized to have taken a special interest in tradition, and to have had it handed on in more complete form from fathers and grandfathers who had themselves been similarly specially instructed. But the very idea of missionary activity, of teaching and propagating a more comprehensive religious truth, was absent, except in the case of the few "charismatic leaders", called "prophets" in the anthropological literature, whose teaching did not deny the basic tenets of traditional Dinka religion, but revived them with their own personal revelations and divine guidance. They claimed revelation from God, so another theme in Catholic doctrine represented, for example, by the statement of Cardinal Fumasoni-Biondi, "the Catholic Church comes from above and not from outside", was also familar to the Dinka themselves.

Thus there were enough parallels between Catholic theological and social doctrine for the Christian message not to appear entirely new, but (and this must be a particular problem for evangelists in such circumstances) Christian arguments against Dinka religious and spiritual conceptions could involve calling into question also the Christian ones to which they were analogous. Why (to take just two examples) if Dinka accepted the Christian miracles, should they reject similar miracles attributed to great religious leaders in their own indigenous tradition? Why leave their own established religious leaders who called upon their people to become reconciled with God and each other, who made blood sacrifices to cleanse them from sin, who often called for peace, in order to follow others with a similar message?

The higher philosophy of missions, as it was represented in the 1950s, was intended to take account of such questioning, but, it seems to me, assumed native populations more readily convinced than the Dinka that the Christian message incorporated all that was good and true in their own religious experience, and hence somewhat misunderstood the way in which Christianity was in practice propagated, as though it were a matter of confronting "lower" with "higher" spiritual ideals. I quote a few passages from the papal encyclical on the missions, *Evangelii Praecones*, promulgated by Pope Pius XII in 1951, as representing the official Catholic approach at the time of which I am writing:

> ...The Church, from the beginning down to our own time, has always followed this practice: Let not the Gospel, on being introduced into a new land, destroy or extinguish whatever its people possess that is naturally good, just or beautiful. For the Church, when she calls her people to a higher culture and better way of life, under the inspiration of the Christian religion, does not act like one who recklessly cuts down and uproots a thriving forest. No, she grafts a good scion upon a wild stock, that it may bear a crop of more delicious fruit.

The "wild stock" of Dinka religion involved a fundamental identification of each clan with its own tutelary divinities, addressed as "you of my father" in all Dinka prayers. That conception of religious communion by descent, and symbolized by animals and other creatures and objects which the Dinka therefore held in reverence, was difficult to use as a stock upon which to graft Christianity, for it went so deep into Dinka personal and social life that to reject it would be to reject the very idea of an abiding spiritual truth, transmitted from generation to generation *per omnia saecula saeculorum*, upon which the Church based its own claim to religious authority. The encyclical continues, referring to Tertullian:

> Human nature, owing to Adam's fault, is tainted with original sin, but has in itself something that is naturally Christian; and this, if illumined by divine light and nourished by God's grace, can eventually be changed into true and supernatural virtue.

Here again the Dinka myth of the origin of mankind is one of many such telling of the anger and withdrawal of God-in-the-sky from men, as the result of a human act of disobedience, of an original sin. The myth of the spiritual leaders of the Dinka represents them as in a way remaking the relationship of man with God by restoring to man a "true and supernatural virtue", though not perhaps of the ethical kind suggested by the encyclical. It continues:

> This is the reason why the Catholic Church has neither scorned nor rejected the pagan philosophies. Instead, after freeing them from all error and contamination, she has perfected and completed them by Christian revelation. So likewise has the Church graciously made her own the native art and culture which in some countries is so highly developed. She has carefully encouraged them, and has brought them to a point of aesthetic perfection that of themselves they would probably never have attained. By no means has she repressed native customs and traditions, but she has given them a certain religious significance; she has even transformed their feast-days and made them serve to commemorate the martyrs and to celebrate the mysteries of the faith.

This programme is in a liberal tradition of Catholic thought which must recommend itself to those who find no authority in Christian teaching for the condemnation of indigenous dancing and drinking, for example, which seems to figure so largely in the message of some Protestant sects. But it presupposes a comprehension of "pagan philosophies" as formulated by systematic thinkers like the Greeks, Chinese or Romans, and thus doctrinally comparable with Christian teaching. The earlier missionaries among the Dinka could not possibly have any such comprehension of a Dinka philosophy. The Dinka themselves did not think doctrinally, and the missionaries, partly by the very nature of their convictions and vocation, could not suspend their own belief to reach the comparative level of thought required to reinterpret the encyclical in local terms. Thus despite the Catholic view that the Church comes from above and not from outside, and the Church's claim to be teaching *quod ubique, quod semper, quod ab omnibus*, in the eyes of the Dinka the Catholic Church could not but appear to come from outside, in the form of "red foreigners" (their term for Europeans) often bearded, and dressed in special garments unlike those of European officials. They provided in the schools and missions a way of life and teaching foreign to the Dinka, and turned those they could influence into a different kind of person from the herdsman, warrior, and husband of many wives and father of many children, who represented the Dinka ideal.[3] The introduction of Christianity involved in some ways a more, and in some ways a less, radical reformation of Dinka ways of thought than the encyclical, and other Christian aspirations on the same lines, assumed. The familiar Malinowskian, functionalist view of all social institutions as intricately interconnected would have suggested that eradicating "bad" beliefs and customs, and retaining and adding to "good" ones, was a more complex task than this liberal tradition of Christian thought allowed for.

The Nilotes regarded the missionaries like all foreigners as inferior to themselves in all but technological and medical skills, and were as secure in their own standards as the missionaries in theirs. So the missionary presence was valued above all for one contribution to Dinka well-being which reflective and influential Dinka slowly came to see as necessary for their cultural and political survival — education. The Dinka were made increasingly aware that much though they might have preferred to live without external interference in their traditional mode of life, that interference had already begun to endanger their independence. They saw that they needed enough of their own people capable of thinking in foreign ways, of meeting foreigners on their own ground while remaining Dinka in their loyalties, to understand and circumvent encroachments on their own autonomy.

Education, and therefore evangelization where it took effect, started in the Dinka language, moving on to elementary English and now Arabic. Dr

Deng has described the situation of the earlier Dinka schoolboys (and I imagine it has not changed very much, except through the considerable increase in the numbers of school-educated Dinka) as follows. He is introducing the section of school songs in his volume of Dinka poetry (Deng, 1973, p. 250).

> The position of schoolboys somewhat resembles that of age-sets, as their songs reveal, though the songs emphasize the boys' newly-acquired skills rather than fighting potential. They often express the dilemma of a person asserting the value of his new wisdom and abilities as the means of progress in a yet largely traditional system. In consequence he still has to appeal to leaders who, while recognized as leaders, are also regarded as lacking the new virtues... They [the songs] are of course very recent and relevant only to a small minority of all Dinka.

In the 1950s, outside mission stations and among people speaking wholly in Dinka, one rarely heard any word which could be understood as a version of the word "Christian"[4] as if referring to religious commitment only. Schoolboys and people around missions whether Christians or not, were *mith abun*, "the children of the mission," *abun* presumably being a loan word from the Ethiopian *abuna*, a father and Bishop. Baptism was *doc piu nhialic*, "blessed with God's water", an idea quite familiar to Dinka in their own religious practice, though here become a specialized term for the Christian rite. Thus missionized Dinka were seen as belonging to another kind of family, different from their natal family, and when away from it, forming a community with customs, and linguistic usages, of their own. Then "the children of the missionaries" were fed and brought up by the missionaries instead of their own parents. A redefinition of vernacular terms makes possible the construction of a framework of reference coming from Dinka family life, now applied to the Church, seen as a kind of family, but not a Dinka family.

A few extracts from one of the songs recorded by Dr Deng give a lively impression of the amalgamation of Dinka and Catholic ideas, through which some Dinka came to classify themselves as Christians. Dr Deng entitles the poem "The tribe has remained behind":

Who was the first to put the flank in order?
The man who governs the land
It was Can, the Crested Crane, our chief,
Akol, Hair on the Head, our chief
Do not let the tribe of your father stray
. . . . .
The feast of Aweil has begun
The feast of the Tribe of Lang has begun
And the feast of the Tribe of Giir has begun.

. . . . .
Kwajok Mission is our summer cattle-camp
Kwajok is our home
It has become our home
The home of the Great Priest.
We kissed the Master

. . . . .
The Governor of Wau asked,
"People of Akol Mayuok,
Why has your tribe remained behind?
Your tribe has remained far behind
You have been surpassed in learning
Apuk of Jok have gone ahead,
And Kwac of Yot have heard the word."
Eee-ee-ee. . .
Deng Makuei, our master, will teach us to write
Our master will teach us to write papers and books
In the Great Awan of Can e Nyal.
Let us go sharpen the horns of Great Can at Kwajok.

(1973, pp. 254-5)

Here the proper names, except for that of Deng Makuei who is a school-teacher, are those of well-known Dinka chiefs, and the imagery is of fighting (by booklearning in the mission) for superiority between the young men of different tribes, in their case fighting for ("sharpening the horns of") their own tribal leader. Though the priest at the mission is included among their leaders whom the song is intended to praise, neither this song nor any of the others quoted by Dr Deng resembles conventional Christian hymns, with their emphasis on individual moral and spiritual self-development. The basic aspiration indeed is not towards the worship of God but towards "going ahead", towards "progress".

To traditional Dinka, that idea of progress was quite foreign. There was little evidence that life had ever been different from what it was today, nor, until the coming of the Europeans, that it was ever going to change in the future. But by the 1940s, it had become apparent to many thoughful Dinka that in lacking education their people were lacking some of the essential skills for political survival in the modern Sudan, and they came to accept the idea that they were in some ways which put them at a disadvantage in the modern world, backward. This idea was suggested to them, with no disrespect for their own culture, by missionaries and government officials alike, since both were anxious that the Dinka should be able to speak for themselves in councils of state outside their own homeland when the Sudan became independent.

I do not doubt that some Dinka were converted by a love of God and drawn into the Church by the attraction of some Christian principle, by prayer, by individual, introspective activity of the conscience, or by the example of such priests and other Christians as they had among them. But in general, the road to Christianity, or at least to a Christianized way of thought, and the incorporation of some Dinka into the wider civil and ecclesiastical organizations of the modern world, came with the acceptance of the idea of progress through education. And "getting ahead", as is shown in this and other songs, was interpreted in terms of familiar Dinka intertribal rivalries and encouraged by them. So the acceptance of the Church came through foreign secular ideas of progress and development, for the most part material, which had little to do with the main evangelical purposes or teaching of the missions.

The usage of the expression for "to go ahead, to go first" — in Dinka *lo tweng* — for "to progress" or "to get on in the world" is a small but telling example of the way in which at many such small points a foreign system of thought was introduced, not simply as a replacement of the traditional system but as an alternative to it, through a kind of linguistic parallax. The SOED definition of "parallax" (*Astron.*) is "Apparent displacement of an object, caused by the change (or difference) of the point of observation". Far from thinking themselves "backward" among their non-Dinka neighbours in the Sudan, the Dinka thought themselves superior to them, as indeed did their Nuer neighbours to the Dinka. *Tweng*, "ahead", meant either further on in a journey, or senior. Age-sets were divided internally according to seniority into three generation groups, according roughly to the relative ages of the young men who had been initiated at about the same time, and the period at which it seemed appropriate to give an up-and-coming generation its own name as a separate set. The senior in each generation were *nhom tweng*, literally "head forward" and thus both "ahead" "higher" and "in front" (as with quadrupeds, especially cattle); the middle were *ciel*, "in the middle"; and the junior *cok cien*, "foot behind" and thus "in the rear". These groups were in periodic competition, self-assertive juniors trying to wrest the leadership from their seniors when the time came for establishing their own superior prowess and vitality, in order to be recognized as the seniors of one generation of sets instead of the juniors of another. This followed roughly the biological cycle of adolescence, aggressive unmarried manhood, settling into middle-age and then retiring from much dancing, courting and fighting into the wisdom of elderhood.

When the idea of acquiring more foreign knowledge and competence — a continuous process over the generations — has been placed in the context of trials of strength between Dinka age-sets, a sporadic activity repeated in each generation, the "point of observation" has modified the understanding. The Dinka view of age-sets, based upon a cyclical notion of local history, begins to be displaced by a dynamic view of history, accompanied by a philosophy of progress, and with teleological overtones.

Through the associaton of generational competition for local status with ideas of cumulative development and advance, "getting ahead" begins to be directed towards some distant, more universal end, defined in foreign terms. A social process is metaphorically translated into social progress. Here social philosophy is affected by the linguistic parallax I have mentioned, and the possibility of thinking that mankind should strive towards some *civitas dei*, some superior form of society conceived of by the Catholic Church as, differently, by rationalist evolutionists, but never before by the Dinka, begins to be introduced.

A similar process of translation from indigenous to foreign concepts involving a reformulation of experience and thought may be seen in relation to theological doctrine. The Dinka concept of *wei*, meaning breath, life, what animates, is discussed in another paper (Lienhardt, 1980) and I shall mention it only briefly. This word for breath and life may be the nearest approximation to anything that could be meant by "soul" in the Dinka language. But the Christian "soul" goes with a whole set of eschatological doctrines, conceptions, and ideas of human personality, which have no relation to the meanings of the Dinka word *wei* as breath/life. Added to this is the use of *wei*, as in *wei santo* (using the Italian adjective) for the Holy Spirit. There can be no doubt that Dinka with a Christian education use their own words in this parallactic way. I wrote in the earlier paper:

> Missionaries, using *wei*, breath and life, as the best approximation to translate "soul", have presumably successfully reshaped the Dinka word for their converts into a unitary term for a moralized and spiritualized self-consciousness of each separate individual in relation to a personalized God. (Lienhardt, 1980, p. 75)

But though Christian doctrine would require a Dinka Christian to assert that an ox had no "soul", I doubt if even the most scrupulous Christian Dinka would ever be able to assert that an ox had no *wei*, since this is what the strong animal has in superabundance, far more than human beings, and what is released to give them the power and vitality they ask for when the beast is sacrificed.

The "greatest commandment" includes the injunction to love God "with all thy soul". In this context again, the Dinka *wei* would have to be modified in meaning to make sense, but so would the Dinka word for "to love", *nhiar*. I doubt if "I love God" or "God loves me", using *nhiar* for "love" and *nhialic* for God (as the missionaries do) would ever be said in traditional Dinka. In the memoirs of the first Dinka to come to England, sometime in the 1880s, he tells how when he was a boy his father was killed while trying to save him from slavers, though his father might have saved himself. Many years later, when he had been adopted by Christians and was on the way to becoming an evangelist in Nottingham, he records how:

I reached the stage when I could sincerely pray for myself, that light might be vouchsafed me.

It came at last...when I read the Gospel of St. John iii, 16-18 [God so loved the world that he gave his only begotten Son] I read and re-read and presently I was able to see God's way of salvation clearly. I was able to draw a comparison from my own stormy life. My dear father had died for me. He could have saved himself but he chose to die rather than desert his son... in just the same way had Christ chosen to die for me and the whole world of sinners, that we might be saved from eternal destruction. My father had died to save me from the bondage of my body [slavery] — Christ had died to save me from the bondage of sin. (Wilson (Kathish), n.d., pp. 223-9)[5]

The Dinka "God" is often addressed as a father; but in the indigenous usage it is the relationship of respect (*thek*) for the father that the Dinka "God" *nhialic* brings to mind, rather than the affection of a father for his children.

So a transmission of Christian doctrine, and all the organization, both of society and of experience which go with it, first through the Dinka language, and then through English, involve a complex reorganization of meanings and their relationships. The associations of particular religious terms, either in Dinka or in Catholic teaching, are mutually defining, and in order to convey a new set of meanings in the same language as the old, an alternative pattern of associations is introduced.[6] This is much more than the rejection of some ideas and the retention of others envisaged in the papal encyclical I earlier quoted.

The process by which I suggest this occurs is indicated in the earliest conversation reported between Dinka and the missionary Beltrame and supposed to have taken place in the 1850s (Beltrame, 1880, pp. 98-9). There already, among many statements, questions and answers in Italian and Dinka which *do* represent Dinka usage even to the present day, a reformulation of Dinka meanings has already started to take place. The missonary asks where a bad man goes after death. The Dinka are reported to have replied — I translate from the Italian translation of the Dinka text — that when a bad man dies, the Demon (*Demonio*, with a capital D) will come from the wilds and take his soul (in Italian *l'anima*) to the house of fire. The missionary then asks what happens when a good man dies, and is told that his souls will go with Great Deng (the name of a very important Dinka divinity, sometimes identified with God-in-the-above, *nhialic*) into the sky. The divinity Deng is here translated as *Dio*. The Dinka are then asked if these souls will stay in the home of fire, or in the above, for ever and the Dinka reply (for once in that particular exchange sounding authentic) "We don't know". Now as I have said, the Dinka word *wei*, here translated as "soul", *anima*, does not mean the kind of entity which could be consigned to hell or heaven. It becomes so in this conversation, and once the Dinka word for breath-life begins to be used in this way it is supported

Godfrey Lienhardt

by significant shifts of meaning, which in relation to each other place Dinka words in a foreign universe of discourse. The Dinka expression *pan e mac*, the home of fire, used here to suggest hell and all that goes with it, would be meaningless in traditional Dinka. *Pan alo mac* might indicate some homestead from which fire could be obtained when one's own fire had gone out. *Wei* as breath-life has no such association with burning and punishment.

Similar in implication is the introduction of the *Demonio*, the Devil, into the conversation as a translation for the Dinka *jok*. I once translated *jok* as a "power", in order to indicate some sorts of abstract and spiritual force invoked, in the main, to account for various diseases. Where we should say "it is malaria" or "it is a fever", the Dinka would say that it is *jok*, a *jok* has seized him. And as when serious symptoms of illness appear, we ask a medical doctor to diagnose the disease and prescribe treatment, so the Dinka consult diviners who identify which spirit (*jok*) is causing trouble, and recommend action, for the Dinka usually animal sacrifice. *Jok* thus is both the illness and its unknown spiritual cause; and since illness is bad for men, and some illnesses are worse than others, so *jok* (the plural *jak* is rarely used), are on the whole "bad", and must, if the patient is to survive, be removed and kept away and kept satisfied. For it is often divined that they have a just complaint against the sufferer, who is thus in his own way "bad" to attract their attentions.

Beltrame records a conversation in which the missionary asks Dinka what they say to a very sick man who is about to die. They reply that they do not say anything, but they bring in a doctor (in Dinka here *beny wal* "master of grass, herbs, magical potions"), who will tell them to kill a bull and anoint the body of the sick man with its dung, so that *il Demonio* (with a capital D) will go away from him, and will not carry him off to its home.

In Christian thought of course the absolute goodness of God has its counterpart (perhaps less emphasized nowadays than it has been in the past) in the absolute evil of the Devil, Satan. The arts of Christendom have the profuse imagery of a loving Father in Heaven above, with the good spirits and blessed souls, and the hateful Devil below, with the demons and damned souls. Such cosmic moral dualism was foreign to Dinka thought, nor on the whole were God and "spirits" imagined in visual terms. If, to take the example of a well-known Dinka "spirit" *garang*, often divined as the source of a feverish overheated condition, a diviner says that *garang* has seized a sufferer, the Dinka no more consider what *garang* would appear like in itself than we should consider what malaria would appear like in itself. What concerns them is each particular manifestation. Only certain harmful powers regarded as coming from outside Dinkaland (the best-known is called *matthiang guk*, and there is a good deal of doubt about the derivation and definition of that name) could be thought of as being bad in themselves, as distinct from in their manifestations in human suffering. But these are man-manipulated sources of suffering, and show human malevolence. Though their use may be thought of as displeasing to God they are not the opposite of God, *nhialic*, "the in the above" for God has no spiritual opposite in Dinka.[7]

Traditional Dinka priests certainly pray and make sacrifice so that sufferings (for the most part physical) which afflict their people and their beasts should leave them and go elsewhere. Since they do not think of the causes of illness and so forth as material and physical, they can only be described as spiritual, and hence as "spirits", and in this we are not far away from Dinka conceptions. But when in schoolboys' songs recorded by Dr Francis Deng the missionaries and the Virgin Mary are honoured for protecting their flock from "evil spirits", the "badness" of Dinka suffering for which the moral fault of the sufferer, not the malevolence of the spirit may be the explanation, begins to be assimilated to the Christian conception of supernatural moral evil, spiritually hypostatized in Satan.

Theologically, of course, the term "hypostasis" belongs to metaphysical speculations and definitions which are central to the exegesis of the mystery of the Trinity, and of the relationship between the humanity and the divinity of Christ. These doctrines are concerned with realities, substances, which underlie appearances, and attributes — metaphysically speaking the "accidents". Some reflection of the meaning may be found in the question "What is the substance of this complaint?" So the hypostasis of the three Persons of the Godhead — the Father, the Son and the Holy Ghost — is the Trinity: "Lord God, king of heaven, omnipotent Father, eternal God, who with your only begotten Son and the Holy Spirit is one God and one Lord, *not in a singularity of one person, but in a Trinity of one substance*" as the preface to the Tridentine Mass expresses it. The person of Christ himself is the hypostatic union of his two natures, the divine and the human. The Christianization of the various Dinka usages of the word for breath, animation, life, vitality as meaning "soul", the spiritual substance of each individual human identity, is thus characteristic of a metaphysic which is central to the formulation of very important Christian doctrines, as is the translation of a Dinka word for illnesses and their spiritual causes as "evil spirits", and hence, hypostatically, the Evil One, Satan.[8] I do not doubt that the Dinka schoolboys' understanding of the Dinka word *wei*, and of the Dinka word *jok*, lay or alternated between that of the missionaries and those of non-Christian Dinka, meaning to them both "breath-life" and "spiritual essence of the person, soul", and "bad illness" and "evil spirit", respectively. But in subsequent generations, and in families which have inherited the Christian faith and live in nominally Christian communities, the ambiguities of the ideas of this generation may be resolved in favour of the foreign interpretations with their doctrinal concomitants similarly redefined. So a systematic set of doctrines may slowly be introduced, through the mutual redefinitions of Dinka words and meanings, and a doctrinal orthodoxy carrying with it the acknowledgement of the authority of selected persons to define and maintain it. If developments in Dinkaland resemble those in many other parts of the world, there may in turn be those who, while coming to deny that doctrinal and personal authority, propose to replace it not by the *laisser-faire* principles of traditional Dinka belief, but by other religious, or more likely political, doctrine. Amusingly, I think, a Dinka quoted by Dr Francis Deng in another work of his, (Deng, 1978, p. 71)[9] had already summed up the processes of change and linguistic and intellectual modification I have tried to indicate in this paper, by the one word "What". "What", as it were, appears here as the Dinka hypostasis of all modern technological and intellectual developments:

> God asked man, "Which one shall I give you black man; there is the cow and the thing called 'What', which of the two would you like?"
> The man said "I do not want 'What'."
> Then God said "But 'What' is better than the cow!"
> The man said "No".
> God said "If you like the cow, you had better taste its milk before you choose it finally".
> The man squeezed some milk into his hand, tasted it, and said, "Let us have the milk and never see 'What'."

But once the "what is..?" questions have been asked, formulated definitions and doctrines, previously made unnecessary by consensus in linguistic usage, begin to supply answers.

Notes

1. In fact they paid the Shilluk to help them, but they made off without doing so.
2. One is now Archbishop of Juba. Neither was from a pastoral Nilotic background.
3. But another concern of the Encyclical, represented by the statements that "Charity indeed can remedy to a certain extent many unjust social conditions, but that is not enough. For in the first place there must be justice, which should prevail and be put into practice", is much in line with Dinka attitudes.
4. "Christian" is difficult to pronounce for untaught Dinka. "Jesus Christ" is transliterated in a Dinka New Testament as "*Yecu Kritho*".
5. He dates this experience to 1882, and says he was born in 1859. "Kathish" and "Masha" are poor transliterations of Dinka personal names.
6. I should not be surprised if in future some Dinka came to assert that *wei* meaning "breath-life", and *wei* meaning "soul", were "two different words". The word *atyep* or *atiep* has also been used for "soul", but since this means basically a shadow, a reflection, and hence "ghost", has no moral qualities and is not immanent, that usage has implications similar to those discussed for *wei*.

7. Most "supernatural" manifestations may be referred to as *nhialic*, "divinity", including those to which sickness is attributed (i.e. the Catholic "demons").
8. A very interesting paper on the linguistic and semantic implications of the anthropologists' hypostatization of the vernaculars of those they have studied is G.B. Milner's essay "Hypostatization". He refers to Professor Sir Raymond Firth's examination of the way in which *mana* was hypostatized from a term which had no single consistent meaning throughout Polynesia, and became an anthropological "concept".
9. It is interesting that when Dr Deng recorded Dinka lore in the 1970s for this book, some Dinka had started to claim that they had traditionally possessed the missionary stories, but had not been able to preserve them by writing them down. For comparative material from a very different culture, see Riviere (1981).

References

Beltrame, Giovanni D., 1888: *Grammatica e Vocabolario della Lingua Denka*, Vol. III. Rome (Memorie della Societa Geographica Italiana).

Dempsey, James, 1955: *Mission on the Nile*. London.

Deng, F.M., 1971: *Tradition and Modernization: a Challenge for Law among the Dinka of the Sudan*. New Haven and London (Yale University Press).

Deng, F.M., 1973: *The Dinka and their Songs*. Oxford (Clarendon Press).

Deng, F.M., 1978: *Africans of Two Worlds: the Dinka in Afro-Arab Sudan*. New Haven and London (Yale University Press).

Lienhardt, Godfrey, 1961: *Divinity and Experience: the Religion of the Dinka*. Oxford (Clarendon Press).

Lienhardt, Godfrey, 1980: Self: public, private. Some African representations. *Journal of the Anthropological Society of Oxford*.

Milner, G.B., 1966: Hypostatization. In *In Memory of J.R. Firth* (Bazell, Catford, Halliday and Robins, eds). London.

Rivière, P.G., 1981: 'The wages of sin is death'. Some aspects of evangelisation among the Trio redrawn. *Journal of the Anthropological Society of Oxford*.

Wilson, Salim C., n.d.: (Hatashil Masha Kathish). *I was a Slave*. London (Stanley Paul and Co. Ltd). (Probably published in the mid-1930s.)

Provoked Religious Weeping in Early Modern Spain

William A. Christian Jr.

The relative frequency and intensity of emotions and their public expression varies from culture to culture, and within cultures over time. This variation has a certain logic that we ought to be able to study and understand. Johannes Huizinga pointed to the ease with which people of the Netherlands and France wept in the late Middle Ages as evidence for a special emotional intensity. While his explanation of such a special intensity is not convincing (he attributed it to life's violent contrasts and impressive forms; "all experience had yet... the directness and absoluteness of the pleasure and pain of child-life"), his examples of weeping, especially public religious weeping, should be addressed. They included the mother of St. Colette weeping and lamenting the Passion, preachers like Vincent Ferrer and Bernardino of Siena making congregations weep, and the people of Paris weeping during processions in 1412 (Huizinga, 1963, pp. 1-3, 173-175, 182). People in sixteenth century Spain wept in similar circumstances, and their diaries, autobiographies, letters, inquisition testimony, and devotional literature point to compelling, systematic reasons why.

Weeping is not necessarily a spontaneous manifestation of emotion; it may be a formal, ritual act, as with the Andaman Islanders (Radcliffe-Brown, 1922, pp. 116-117, 238-243), the Tapirapa Indians of Central Brazil (Wagley, 1978), and ritual mourners of southern Italy (De Martino, 1958). In these societies, some weeping has been described as voluntary, something people can decide to do, which in the very act provokes emotion in those weeping and those watching.

Similarly in early modern Spain, weeping was considered something that people could learn how to do, in the course of exciting their emotions. People went to certain places and did certain things in order to weep. For the pain, pious tenderness, or sorrow that accompanied weeping were part

97

of an economy of sentiment that could influence God. Conversely God, angels, and devils could cause emotions. The principles for discerning the supernatural meaning of strong, unexpected sensations were known to literate and illiterate alike, women and men, clergy and laity. The various potential religious significances of emotions meant that attentiveness to feelings, the engendering of certain feelings, and the public display of certain feelings were all encouraged. Tears were considered significant visible evidence for some feelings. Because they were visible and their presence was recorded, they permit us in retrospect to observe some of the occasions on which private and public sentiment was provoked for religious purposes.

Public weeping in early modern Iberia

Huizinga gave an example of one kind of collective, provoked weeping — the processions of Paris in 1412, centering on relics, for the royal campaign against the Armagnacs. According to the journal of a bourgeois of Paris, people wept piteously while they watched or followed "the most touching processions in the memory of man" (Huizinga, 1963, p. 3). Such processions in times of crisis were intended to obtain a specific end. In 1507 in Barcelona during a great plague, a procession was held to lay the cornerstone of a chapel to St. Sebastian, the plague saint. Periodically the procession would pause, and a group of children who were flagellating themselves would fall on their knees and cry out for mercy to a man dressed as Sebastian, complete with arrows. "And those who said this wept with tears and lamentations so piercing that it almost broke the hearts of those who cried and those who heard them" (Dietari, 1894, p. 201).

In these processions the public was a knowing, willing participant. Other tear-provoking scenarios were sprung on the public by surprise, and some of them, at least, no less effectively. On the week before the feasts of Saint James and Saint Anne in 1552 the people of Gandía could receive a jubilee indulgence if they received communion; and almost all of them did. The Jesuits, however, were upset that on the feasts of Saint James and Saint Anne, as was usual, a bullfight and jousting were to be held, in indecorous contrast, they thought, to the climate of piety. Four priests and four brothers decided to disrupt the festivities by provoking penitential tears. One father carried a crucifix, and others went with a skull, barefoot and bareheaded, and with ropes around their necks; with them went two flagellants whipping themselves. When they reached the plaza where people were gathered for the festivities, the people began to cry out "Misericordia," as in a crisis procession. One of the Jesuits went to the town gibbet and preached to the crowd, and the others continued through the streets. When they returned to the plaza, "everyone began to weep once more and cry out for mercy," and the Jesuits went to the opposite side where the Duke, Duchess, gentlemen, ladies, and clergy were seated, and one of the Jesuits preached there. "From time to time great cries of misericordia spread through the plaza, the Duchess weeping along with everyone else, the people coming down from the stands and following after the Jesuits with copious tears and cries for mercy." There was no bullfighting or jousting, "although it had been prepared at great expense" (Litterae Quadrimestres, 1894, I, pp. 742-744, VIII-31-1552).

Barefoot and hatless, with ropes around their necks and whipping themselves, the Jesuits were acting out the humiliation of the Christ they carried on the crucifix, were living images like the Barcelona St. Sebastian with arrows. In the same year of 1552 the rector of the Jesuits of Coimbra did a self-imposed public penance, whipping himself and weeping copiously.

> I think I went to twelve different places and knelt down asking for pardon and saying in a loud voice, 'nobles and commoners of Coimbra, for the wounds, death and passion of Christ our redeemer I ask that you forgive me all the scandals and disedifications that you have received from the Jesuit school, for before God I confess that it was my fault and that my sins were the cause of it all,' and almost every time I said this Our Lord gave me so many tears that I could not finish (LQ II, p. 58, XI-14-1552).

Part of the power of this Jesuit's act came from the fact that it was unusual for priests to whip themselves in public. However, lay flagellants and other public imitators of Christ, mass participants in this same kind of emotional public drama, periodically paraded in the streets and highways of sixteenth century Iberia (Christian, 1981a, pp. 182-190; Llompart, 1969, 1972). The Jesuit's tears were as important an element of his public penance as the whipping, and were a feature of the most serious public processions. The town of Ajofrín (Toledo) made one annual procession (and others in times of drought) 50 km to the shrine of Mary in the town of San Pablo de los Montes. An elderly priest of Ajofrín wrote in 1596, "In the last forty years I have taken part in many processions worthy of memory, which truly can be called processions, for they were made with much devotion and shedding of tears and even blood and many bare feet". He remembered in particular a procession in the drought of 1567: "they walked as true penitents without saying a word to each other, carrying rosaries in their hands, their feet bare, and tears on their cheeks". In the region it was considered that the procession of Ajofrín was particularly efficacious for rain. Some villages fed the pilgrims "and received them very well with many tears and much self-flagellation". So that at times both the people in the procession and delegations from towns they passed were weeping.[1]

There was also the calendrical collective weeping of Holy Week. In a brief aside in his widely read devotional guide, *Audi Filia* (1556), Juan de Avila referred to the dressing of images, probably in Holy Week, to provoke tears. "When they want to take out an image, *to make people weep*, they dress it in mourning and arrange it so it provokes sadness" (1963, p. 2642 my italics). In the following decades newly carved specialized Holy Week images began to be used in which mourning (of Mary) or scenes from the Passion (of Christ) were incorporated as part of the imagery. In 1580 the Brotherhood of the Sepulcher of Jaén had a flexible image of Christ that, on the appropriate day, they took down from the cross, wrapped with a shroud, and placed in a tomb, "provoking many people to shed tears". As in several Holy Week processions today, in seventeenth century Jaén an image of Mary was carried to meet an image of Christ in the streets. The Marian image was articulated so that on meeting Christ her head nodded and her arms stretched out to embrace her son, "which deeply moved those who, in dramatic silence, observed it" (Ortega Sagrista, 1956, pp. 32, 39). The weeping images of Mary were a way of incorporating the profound Marian devotion of Iberia, evident in the vast majority of powerful shrines, in the heightened attention to the Passion of Christ.[3] Mary weeping was thus as much as a model to imitate as Christ being whipped.[4]

This kind of Holy Week weeping survives today, the only collective religious weeping that I know of in present-day Spain. A Sevillano (with tears in his eyes) describes the weeping at the departure of La Macarena (a weeping Madonna) from her shrine on the night of Holy Thursday as "aesthetic tears". He does not consider himself a Catholic, and so refers to his attitude as "idolatry", but says it stems from an identification with La Macarena on a human level as a suffering person who is intensely loved. He says it probably also has to do with staying up all night, the end of winter, the scent of orange blossoms on the air, the full moon on Holy Thursday night, and the effect of a very realistic and artistic image. This kind of public weeping, then, like that of the crisis processions, was provoked by a religious dramaturgy in which relics, images, or people representing saints played an important part.

The weeping that stopped the bullfight at Gandía was provoked by a combination of penitential drama and preaching — symbolically from the *picota*, the place of punishment and symbol of secular justice. The Jesuits were effective practitioners of a long tradition of medieval preachers and celebrants who provoked tears, including, as Huizinga mentions, Vincent Ferrer and Bernardino. The quarterly letters of Jesuit houses to Loyola in Rome commonly refer to priests whose effectiveness is measured by their ability to make their audiences weep. The rector at Gandía, Juan Bautista la Barma, regularly made people weep who heard him say mass ("they cannot keep from weeping'' LQ II, p. 212, IV-6-1553). The sermons in Seville, wrote Gonsalvo González in January, 1556,

> continue with much concourse of people and emotion and especial devotion, which the Lord gives them, of compunction and tears that they cannot stop; especially after some sermons about death and the judgment they went weeping and moaning in the streets, straightening out their lives and preparing to do penance (LQ IV, p. 84).

Like the weeping in penitential processions and that provoked by dramaturgy involving saints, weeping provoked by preachers also has its modern survivals, particularly in the sermons of missionaries, in Lent or at other times of the year. It was especially characteristic of famous charismatic preachers like Diego de Cádiz and Antonio María Claret, who, like Vincent Ferrer and Francisco Borja, were itinerant revivalists. In Lent, 1919, the first time people saw the eyes of the famous Christ of Limpias (Santander) move and shed tears was immediately after the climactic mass, in which most people wept, of a week-long mission given by two Capuchin friars (Diario Montañés IV-8-1919). Spanish newspaper accounts show that weeping was common in the final days of missions conducted by Jesuits, Claretians, Redemptorists, Passionists, and Capuchins during the religious revival of 1947–54, particularly those associated with traveling statues of the Virgin of Fatima. The more modern weeping, however, seems more limited to the services, more isolated in rural areas, and less vehement and spontaneous than that described in the Jesuit letters. In some American evangelical churches, especially in Appalachia, weeping is still a common feature in ordinary Sunday services as well as revivals.[5]

Other incidents described in the Jesuit letters indicate that there was a general easiness of tears, not only in ritual settings. When on Palm Sunday, 1553, Juan Bautista la Barma went from Gandía to another village to preach, he was accompanied by many people he met along the way, in the manner of Christ's entry into Jerusalem. As they proceeded together, he invited them to tell how they had been blessed in their lives, and many of them wept. I will cite this incident at length, because it provides a good example of the ambiance of devotion in which so much of the public weeping took place.

> They went with him slowly, reciting a litany and invoking the angels and saints of the town they were going to. And then the Father said that since on that day Jerusalem had received the Lord with praises, they too should praise the Lord, each inviting the others to praise the Lord because of a personal blessing. The Father began, saying they should praise the Lord because He had made him a priest. Another said because he had been a great sinner, had realized it, and now he wanted to serve God. Another, because he had been a *Moro*, but had

been brought to his true understanding. Another, because he had been a great swearer and blasphemer and never tired in sinning, and then became very sick, at which time he realized what he was, and now he was well and wanted to serve God. In this way they walked on, each saying in turn so many things, and with so many tears, that it was heartbreaking (LQ II, pp. 212-213, IV-6-1553).[6]

The tears were shed in public by single persons as well as persons in groups. After Lent in 1553 six brothers from the Jesuit house in Medina del Campo received permission to *peregrinar*. Their chief purpose seems to have been to edify. At one town they came across people dancing and enjoying themselves. One of the brothers began to preach to them about heaven and the life of Christ, and those who were dancing fell on their knees "to hear the word of God with great attention and reverence". The village parish priest was there and "went up to the pilgrims, prostrated himself, and weeping with great sorrow, with his white hair worthy of respect, said he was a great sinner, and that for the love of God that they commend him to Our Lord..." Another day they came to a village where they heard there was a woman who had not spoken to her relatives for seven years. "Then our brothers in their poor garments went to the woman, and Our Lord gave them such words that not only did they soften the woman's hard heart, they even broke it, and with tears and ardent love she went to embrace her enemies". (LQ II, pp. 269-270, V-4-1553).[7]

While the creativity and fervor of the early Jesuits (like that of Loyola himself) may have been especially strong stimulants to religious sensibilities, evidence from other sources (including extensive testimony in investigations of divine signs) supports the notion that at least in public, people in early modern Spain wept more easily than they do now.

Self-observation: emotions as signs

In early modern Spain, some emotions were considered a form of obscure communication; like dreams they were messages to be deciphered. For this purpose "emotion" must be considered equivalent to "feeling." People did not make such an arbitrary distinction as now between emotion and sensory perception, physical pain and sorrow, happiness and healthiness. People's emotions were a kind of test for their spiritual condition. One of the tasks of the spiritual directors of persons actively seeking holiness was to discern the meaning of their confessants' feelings. Because there was an important religious significance to unexplained emotional shifts and movements of the heart, lay people as well as religious were attentive to them.

In 1523 Francisca la Brava, the wife of a wool carder in the agricultural town of La Mota del Cuervo (Toledo), described to town authorities the emotional events leading up to her first vision of Mary. She was very attentive to her feelings. "... she could not sleep the whole night because a sorrow [or pain] came to her heart, although in her face and body she did not feel bad, but rather healthy [or happy]." Sleepless, "she prayed to Our Lady the Virgin Mary to guide her in what was best for the salvation of her soul to a completely sound mind, and shortly after this she fell asleep". The next night the same thing happened. "She asked Our Lady, since she was so sad without knowing why, to guide her and tell her what was the cause of the great sorrow [or pain] she felt in her heart..." (cited in Christian, 1981b, pp. 164-165, 315-317).

Note how in describing the pain and sorrow, Francisca located it in the heart, checking to make sure it was not in her face or body; and the important fact that it was a sadness she could not account for. This kind of attention to the heart's feelings as possible spiritual signs, I submit, has by and large disappeared. A modern equivalent might be the notion of a bad or guilty conscience, but one generally knows the cause of that, and in Francisca la Brava's case the cause is unknown (and could even be unrelated to her actions).

Two years earlier, in 1521, a soldier named Ignatius Loyola was reading the lives of saints and the life of Christ while convalescing in the Basque country. He was struck by a correspondence between the emotions he felt and the thoughts he had been thinking. Later in life he described how he came to this perception:

> When he thought about the profane world he had great pleasure, but when he was tired of it he found himself dry and discontented; and when he thought about going to Jerusalem barefoot, and eating only herbs, and doing all the other privations that he saw the saints had done, he was not only consoled while he was having these thoughts, but he remained contented and happy afterward. At first he did not notice this, or stop to think about the difference, until one time when his eyes were opened a little, and he began to marvel at this contrast and reflect upon it, learning by experience that from some thoughts he remained sad and others, happy; and little by little he came to know the difference in the spirits that were at work — one of the devil, and the other of God (Loyola, 1947, pp. 133-134).

This perception, at the root of Loyola's conversion, was made an integral part of his *Spiritual Exercises*. The tens of thousands of persons who followed the exercises in early modern Europe were instructed to notice how they felt as they said each word of their prayers, "noting and pausing at those points in which I have felt more consolation or desolation or more spiritual feeling". The range of possible feelings were described in detail in the commentary accompanying the exercises, and rules were given "to feel and know the various motions caused in the soul: the good ones so they will be received, and the bad ones so they will be ejected". In this way those taking the exercises were sensitized to the "reality" of the divine and the demonic at work within them (Loyola, 1969, pp. 198, 374-394).

In 1527 when Loyola was a student at Alcalá, he was already giving rudimentary exercises to a group of young women and having them pay attention to their emotional states. María de la Flor, a young weaver who characterized herself as someone who had been "a bad woman, who went with many students," told inquisitors investigating Loyola that after following him in prayer for some weeks:

> four times there came to this witness very great sadness, and nothing seemed good to her, and she could not raise her eyes to look at Ynigo; and that when she was sad and spoke with Ynigo or Calixto, the sadness left her. And the wife of Benavente and her daughter said they too experienced the same sadness, or even stronger. And [María] asked Ynigo what that sadness was and where it came from. And he said that when one enters the service of God the devil introduces it; and that she should remain strong in the service of God, and that they were undergoing this for the love of God (Loyola, 1904, p. 612-613).[8]

Like Francisca la Brava, María de la Flor identified her sadness as spiritual. Both sought guidance from religious sources — Francisca from the Virgin Mary, and María from her spiritual guide. Even before consulting Loyola, however, María had noted when it came, how many times it came, and when it went away.

Loyola was hardly the inventor of the discernment of spirits by emotions, although his use of it as a tool of spiritual pedagogy was innovative. This kind of discernment dated from pre-Christian times, was approved by Church Fathers, and was commonly practised by religious to know if they were being inspired by God or misled by the devil. In fifteenth century Spain it was a criterion commonly used to test lay visionaries (Christian, 1981b, p. 193, 199-201). The printing of spiritual handbooks in romance in the first decades of the sixteenth century by Catherine of Siena, Angela of Foligno, Vincent Ferrer, and Francisco de Osuna gave to all who could read instructions for the evaluation of emotions. But when the Protestant heresies arose, auto-evaluation of religious sentiment and inspiration was seen as a dangerous business.

For in practice it was very difficult to distinguish "true" from "false" happiness or consolation. Visionaries like Francisca la Brava and Jeanne d'Arc would insist that their visions made them happy, and thereby acquire in their own minds a kind of immunity from the arguments put forth by their spiritual superiors. The Franciscan preacher, Francisco Ortiz, was sure, in the jail of the Inquisition of Toledo in 1529, that his friend the *beata* Francisca Hernández was doctrinally correct, he said, "because of the continued increase of holy joy and happiness that every day God gives in my soul for preaching against the culpable malfeasance of the representatives of the Inquisition". (Ortiz had been hauled out of the pulpit for denouncing the Inquisition after the *beata's* arrest.) The inquisitor asked him how he knew his feelings were not illusions of the devil. Ortiz replied, "For the devil never places truth in the heart nor a true despising of the world and of life in favor of God". Ortiz said he knew, "as the saints have said," that the devil can give "some sweetness and false happiness, but all the saints say that very soon the old serpent shows his tail and leaves the heart unquiet and sad: that this is the condition of miserable sin".

The inquisitor, however, had some counter-examples. "Sometimes there has been someone who despised the things of this world and received death willingly, affirming that he or she serves God and has the spirit of God, and the Church has held that person to be a heretic and in error." Fray Francisco allowed that the inquisitor had a point, but said that in those cases appearances were deceiving. "Many appear to despise the world who really do not, for they were really seeking their own glory, which they loved more than God. In that way many Romans died for honor, and many true heretics received death with outward signs of joy... [but inwardly] with proud and rebellious hearts, full of true sadness, confusion, and protest from the soul." His own feeling, however, he well knew. It was far from pride, and consisted only in love of God and humble subjection to the Church.

The inquisitor moved on to another matter; he was not convinced, and the formal charges eventually read that Ortiz had been tricked by the devil, but there was no way the inquisitor could prove how Ortiz felt. That only Ortiz could know. Ortiz eventually gave in when he learned that his friend Francisca, though still a virgin, was not as chaste as he had thought (Selke, 1968, pp. 131-133, 204, 209). But his interrogation shows the problematic nature of the use of emotions to determine truth for a Church that considered itself beleaguered (cf. Huerga, 1978, pp. 407-411, 430-431).

One strategy to counter this situation was to limit information on the evaluation of spirits available to the lay public, and to encourage individuals with spiritual questions to consult ordained directors. In 1559 much devotional literature in the vernacular was banned and burned. In one section left out of Juan de Avila's *Audi Filia* when it was reissued in 1574 were some signs for distinguishing true from false revelations; people were instead instructed to consult their spiritual directors (1963, pp. 48-49).[9]

This in fact controlled the problem only in part. For in practice the spiritual-minded who trusted their own reading of their emotions could look around until they found a spiritual director who agreed with them.[10] Teresa of Avila through much of her life was in doubt whether the consolations and graces she received were of God or the devil. Different confessors had different opinions; at one point six theologians were consulted — they agreed that it was the devil and instructed her to give it *higas.* Only gradually did a consensus emerge that her spirits and feelings were good ones, and even after her death there were efforts to ban her books. A chapter in her autobiography on the evaluation of the causes of emotions is as nuanced and subtle as that of Catherine of Siena. Reading emotions for their spiritual meaning, perhaps in part because it was so difficult, was a highly developed art.[11]

Tears as evidence for changes of heart

The special arena of spiritual emotions was thought to be the heart.[12] That is where Francisca la Brava located her sorrow and what Francisco Ortiz referred to as the locus of emotional truth and demonic inquietude; it was the heart of the obdurate woman that was softened by the Jesuit brothers until it broke and she wept, and the hearts of onlookers and listeners that were broken by the Barcelona processional drama and the life histories that people told to each other on the way out of Gandia on Palm Sunday. *Hard-hearted, a change of heart, tender-hearted, heart-rending,* and *broken-hearted*, are terms that we still use in a secular sense. In sixteenth century Spain they also had rather precise religious meanings derived from the Bible, referring to a person's relative openness to the love of God.

The eyes were thought to have a special connection to the heart, to express it to the outside. "I want you to know," said Catherine of Siena, "that every tear comes from the heart, for there is no part of the body that wants to satisfy the heart as much as the eye" (1969, p. 235).[13] The Lord could hear hearts, but people could not. Because it was difficult for people to know the nature of the motions of their own hearts, much less anyone else's, outward signs like tears were especially important.

Weeping was one of the ways one could know one's own heart. According to Teresa of Avila, writing in 1562, seeing oneself weep was itself a consolation given by the Lord in return for devotion. "If [in contemplating the Passion] there is some love, the soul is rewarded, the heart is softened, and tears come; sometimes it seems we draw them out by force, other times the Lord seems to make it so we cannot resist them. It appears that His Majesty repays our small attention with a very great gift, which is the consolation that he gives a soul when *it sees itself weep* for such a great lord" (Libro de la vida, 10:2, my italics).[14] Perhaps some inkling of this kind of consolation is the kind of peace and calm one experiences after sympathetic weeping in films or at funerals.[15] Most devotional weeping (like Huizinga's example of St. Colette's mother, who wept daily for the Passion) was solitary, and could only be a visible sign of a softened heart for the weeper.

Spiritual treatises in use in sixteenth century Spain refer to a number of kinds of devotional tears, generally ranked in order of preferability. On the first level or levels were tears that purged sins, and this was the kind most emphasized in most handbooks for lay people.

Though not obligatory, tears were considered a favorable sign of contrition (Tentler, 1977, pp. 237-248). "Our tears have great force before God," wrote El Tostado. He instructed sinners, "to have sorrow for their sins, moving themselves to sorrow and tears the most that they can, for because of this sorrow their sins will be forgiven" (Tostado 1517, a ii v°, a v r°; also Hernández García, 1960, p. 322).[16] "Tears wash sins away..." begins a chapter on tears of a fifteenth century book of exempla (*Especulo*, 1951, p. 246). Juan de Avila recounted the story of Hezekiah from Isaiah (38:4) to show the power of tears. "Hezekiah turned his head to the wall and wept with many tears, asking the Lord for mercy.... he asked the judge himself to be his lawyer, appealing from the just to the merciful. His defense is self-accusation; his rhetoric is sobs and tears." The Lord answered, "I heard your heart and I saw your tears," and granted him 15 more years of life. Avila apostrophized on this sudden suspension of the Lord's punishment as a result, "of a few tears, shed not in the temple, but in a corner of a bed, and not by eyes looking to the sky, but rather at a wall, and not by a just man, but by a sinner". He told the sinner to take heart, "and humble yourself weeping to him whom you ignored while sinning, and receive forgiveness from he who wants so much to give it to you" (1963, pp. 217-219).

Like tears of contrition, tears wept externally in the contemplation of the Passion were thought to have a purgative effect on sins, and in Spain this remained the great spiritual exercise of the sixteenth century (Bataillon, 1966; Corrientes, 1963). The *Vita Christi* of Ludolphus of Saxony, first published in Catalan 1495-1500 and Castilian in 1502-1503, was one of the books Ignatius Loyola was reading when he reached his understanding of spiritual emotions. "El Cartujano", as the author was known, invited the reader to "understand, contemplate, weep over, and feel the course of this most holy death". In reading the Passion, one was encouraged to experience an ordered series of emotions, one of which, compassion, would call forth tears (Ludolphus, 1502-1503 IV: Ch. 58, 48rv. 55r).

Wept under these circumstances, tears would have great value.

> The extent of the efficacy of tears shed in prayer, and particularly in memory of the passion of Christ is very clear from a certain person's revelation. The Lord appeared to the person in spirit and said: 'If anyone in memory of my passion weeps tears with devotion, I wish to take them into my kingdom as if they had suffered for me.' So that when a man remembers this *paso* [Christ sweating blood in Gethsemane] he should fall to the ground on his face, praying with the heart... and try as hard as he can to have tears, having compassion and sorrow for Jesus Christ. And if the eyes, tired from love, will not shed them, shed them at least with the will (Ludolphus, IV: Ch. 59, 65v).[17]

Similarly, Loyola instructed the participants in the first week of his spiritual exercises to try to weep: "and here begin with much effort to force [yourself] to sorrow, mourn, and weep, and continue doing so while considering the following points" (Loyola, 1969, pp. 282, 214, 374).

In her *Life*, Teresa of Avila recounts episodes of purgative weeping. "I felt so bad for not having thanked [Christ] for those wounds that my heart was rending, and I threw myself next to Him [a crucifix] with copious weeping, asking Him to fortify me once and for all so I would not offend Him". Earlier, her failure to weep when reading the Passion at age 16 (in 1531) she attributed to a hardness of heart: "And if I saw a [nun] have tears when she prayed, or other graces, I was very envious of her, for my heart was so tough (*recio*) that if I read the entire Passion I would not shed a single tear; this caused me sorrow".

For Teresa the contemplation of the Passion was the beginning stage in a spiritual progress. "In thinking about and dwelling on what the Lord underwent for us we are moved to compassion, and this pain and the tears that result from it are savory." (Libro de la vida, 9:1, 12:1, 3:1). Similarly, Tomás of Villanueva, the Augustinian saint who was Archbishop of Valencia, wrote in his *Brief Way of Serving Our Lord*, "Our soul considers our Redeemer bound to the column or nailed on the cross and understands that the innocent Lamb suffers for our sins. From this consideration one becomes sad, moans, and weeps for having offended God and caused his death. This way is called purgative, for by it one purges one's sins". Following earlier treatises, he presented the purgative as the first step in a spiritual progression (Tomás de Villanueva, 1952, p. 511).

Spiritual writers agreed there were other, "higher" kinds of weeping. Frequent tears were a feature of early Cistercian spirituality. The *Liber Miraculorum* of Caesarius of Heisterbach has many cases of copiously weeping monks and nuns. Tears were some monks' greatest desire; the source of vainglory for others ("How I wish there was someone here to see this grace of mine!"); and their absence was considered a spiritual trial (1929, BkI: Ch. 35; II:19-22; IV:30; VIII:11-13). For Catherine of Siena the highest form of tears, higher than those of contrition, are those wept when one is not concerned with self at all, but only in the love of others and of God (1969, pp. 233-261).

Spiritual weeping was an important element in recollection (*recogimiento*), a form of Franciscan spirituality popularized by Francisco de Osuna and considered by him an alternative to contemplation of the Passion (Francisco de Osuna, 1972, pp. 334-353).[18] Its practitioners tried to clear their minds for God's grace and consolations, and tears were both a technique and a result of the method. For beginners they were wept with effort and were weapons to use in obtaining grace, like those of contrition. For the more advanced they were like a fountain ("issuing without moan or sigh hot from the heart and flowing easily from the eyes without interior or exterior noise, for these people are not thinking of things to provoke their crying, but only attempting to recollect their hearts''). And for the perfect they were a fountain that was ever-running, effortless tears of joy. Osuna was proud to say that "weeping comes more easily to the followers of recollection than to other people" (1972, pp. 338, 342, 337).

Teresa of Avila, who learned the method from Osuna's book, experienced this "gift of tears", as did Ignatius Loyola, whose spiritual diary (1544-5) is in large part a record of the occasions on which tears came to him in prayer, the diary itself being a prime example of the observation of one's own emotions. For Loyola also the most preferable tears were those "in consideration of or love for Divine Persons". Laínez, who later succeeded Loyola as the head of the order, observed Loyola in prayer on a terrace in Rome. First Loyola took off his hat and looked at the sky, then he knelt and made a reverence to God, then he sat on a small bench, too old and weak to kneel for long. "There he remained, his head uncovered, weeping two trails of tears with such softness and silence that one heard no sob or moan, nor any movement of the body" (Loyola, 1947, pp. 644-645).[19]

I doubt that this kind of mystical weeping was widespread in early modern Spain; but saints weeping this way were painted in pictures and described in books, and it would have been clear to the faithful that in addition to purgative weeping there were other kinds performed by the spiritually advanced.

Public tears as evidence of collective contrition

In most of the instances given at the beginning of this paper, the collective public weeping was purgative in nature. In the crisis processions it would be an acknowledgement of collective sin in the hope of receiving the kind of forgiveness Hezekiah received for his tears on a collective basis, a collective appeal to the merciful God from the just God to avert plague, drought, locusts, military defeat, and other collective afflictions. The Holy Week processions and the Lenten and revival sermons provoked on a collective level the kind of purgative weeping encouraged in the private contemplation of the Passion. Processions in Holy Week, in which the home town became Jerusalem, were efficient ways to provoke compassion and tears that served the purgation not only of the individuals in question, but also of towns as collectivities. They thereby averted, hopefully, future collective punishments from God. There was thus a collective, as well as individual, economy of sentiment.

Such weeping had to be public. In these collective situations it was as important to see your neighbor's tears as your own, for only if tears were shed generally could it be known that the hearts of the entire community had been moved. Hence drama that provoked collective weeping not merely served an individual's spiritual promotion; it was also a way to know by tears, the outward signs of the heart, that collective repentence was in progress.

Small wonder, then, given theological notions of the times, that people were easily moved to tears. A certain kind of tender heartedness and consequent weeping was of vital practical importance to communities, as well as of spiritual importance to individuals. Without it God would not be moved. Weeping was not, as Huizinga would have it, the expression of a child-like sensibility that we have largely outgrown. Emotions were serious business; provoked, collective, weeping could be effective. One is tempted to say it was rational to weep. A science for provoking public tears and compassion existed, with specialized artists, sculptors, choreographers, and actors.

Note that this was a tenderness of heart in relation to Christ above all, not necessarily to other people. The ruthlessness of the Spanish reaction to the iconoclasts of the Netherlands was doubtless due at least in part to the particular nature of this tenderness, which was above all cultivated through the contemplation of images of the Passion and the imitation of the Passion in penitential behavior. From a Spanish Catholic's perspective, the destroyers of images were willfully repeating the Passion that the Spaniard had been taught to contemplate and weep over. Teresa of Avila could not understand those who did away with images, for she could not do without them.

> I had so little ability to represent things in my mind, except for what I could see. I could profit nothing from my imagination, [unlike] other persons who can see things in their minds wherever they pray. . . . for this reason I was such a friend of images. Unhappy those who by their fault lose this good! It surely seems that they do not love the Lord, for if they loved him, they would delight in seeing his portrait, just as here one is still happy to see someone one loves dearly (Libro de la vida, 9:6).

Afterthoughts

Obvious factors in the relative incidence and intensity of emotions in a given society will be external conditions like nutrition, climate, and the level of security. Less obvious but perhaps equally important are the societal solutions to the universal problem of maintaining a relative psychological balance or homeostasis in individuals (Rosenthal, 1941). People in society produce their own stimuli — entertainment in the form of theater, games, celebrations, religious rituals — that provoke necessary emotions, whether laughter and fun, tension and release, weeping and sorrow.

Weeping appears to be involved in the reduction of stress, the relief of suffering, and the release of tension (Darwin, 1872; Frey, 1980). Surely these must be some of the psychological byproducts of (or equivalents for) grace, atonement, and consolation. In early modern Spain they were obtained on an individual and communal basis by the cultivation at a high pitch of sympathetic sorrow. So that while people might consciously manipulate their emotions for religious purposes, the strictly emotional consequences were real and no doubt effective in and of themselves. In some churches in the mountains of West Virginia, according to K. Stewart, (unpublished data) a similar process appears to serve people as well now as it did in Spain four hundred years ago.

In *The Civilizing Process*, Norbert Elias has addressed some of the ways in which body functions have been privatized over the intervening centuries through the spread of notions of decorum from centers of power. The privatization of weeping also corresponds to a de-emphasis in theology on punishment and contrition and the virtual disappearance of the notion of collective community responsibility to God. I am unsure whether the tension, stress and suffering that public weeping addressed has been reduced, or merely transferred to issues that are considered personal and not soluble by collective ritual.

Acknowledgements

Many people contributed to this paper with suggestions and references. I am particularly grateful to F. Márquez Villanueva, K. Stewart, T. Tentler, R. Trexler, T. Yager, and L. W. Bonbrake. I wrote this essay while on a fellowship from the American Council of Learned Societies with funds provided by the National Endowment for the Humanities.

Notes

1. Biblioteca de la Real Academia de Historia, Madrid, Collección Salazar N-7, folios 294-301, an untitled manuscript memoir dated June 10, 1596 by Pedro Gómez Molino about the devotion of the town of Ajofrín to the shrine of Mary in San Pablo de los Montes. 295v: "yo de xl años a esta p^{te} me e hallado en muchas digas de memoria y q verdaderamente se pueden dezir proçesiones por ser hechas con mucha deuocion y derramami° de lagrimas y avn de sangre y muchos pies descalços... 297r: yban como verdaderos penitentes sin hablarse vna palabra uno a otro sino los rosarios en sus manos los pies descalços las lagrimas por sus mexillas... 297v: y en el camino los regalaron mucho y fueron muy bien

recebidos con muschas lagrimas y disciplinas..." See also Trexler (1980).

2. "Cuando quieren sacar una imagen, para hacer llorar, vistenla de luto y pónenle todo lo que incita a tristeza."
3. See table of shrines to Mary compared with those to other saints and Christ in Christian, (1981a, p. 74).
4. Shiite Moslem weeping of a more violent nature, accompanied by flagellation, occurs in a commemoration similar to Holy Week, the ten days of mourning for Husayn, the prophet Muhammed's martyred grandson (Fischer, 1980).
5. Kathleen Stewart, unpublished field notes on the region of Beckley, West Virginia, 1981.
6. "que era para quebrantar los coraçones"
7. "no solamente ablandaron el corazon duro de la mujer, mas aún lo quebrantaron"
8. Maria de la Flor, testifying on May 10, 1527 in the third Alcalá investigation of Loyola by the Inquisition of Toledo.
9. See introduction by Luis Sala Balust. Juan de Avila, following Gerson, had played down the use of emotions of joy or sorrow for discernment, instead emphasizing the seers' pride or humility and the veracity and orthodoxy of the vision messages (pp. 203-207).
10. This was commonly the case with urban *beatas* investigated by the Inquisition of Toledo in the late sixteenth and early seventeenth centuries.
11. Teresa de Jesús, *Libro de la vida*, (Ch. 25); Caterina da Siena (1969, pp. 284-287); also Tomás de Villanueva (1488-1555), *Sermón sobre la Anunciación de la Virgen María*, (1952, pp. 236-239).
12. On the symbolism of the heart see bibliography in Bauer (1973).
13. "Io voglio che tu sappi che ogni lagrima procede dal cuore, perché neuno membro e nel corpo che voglia tanto satisfare al cuore quanto l'occhio."
14. "Parece nos paga Su Magestad aquel cuidadito con un don tan grande, como es el consuelo que da a un alma ver que llora por tan gran Señor."
15. It has been suggested that such weeping may be a way of eliminating toxic substances from the body and redressing a chemically-based emotional imbalance (Frey, 1980).
16. This publication is evidence that the discernment of spirits and the cultivation of private devotional tears continue in modern Spain.
17. "Pues quando el hombre se acordare deste paso: derribese en tierra sobre su cara orando con el coraçon...r esfuerçe quanto pudiere por tener lagrimas aviendo conpasion r dolor de jesu christo. E fatigados por amor/ r si por los ojos no las pudiere derramar: derramelas a lo menos con la voluntad."
18. On the practice of the method see the introduction by Melquiades Andrés (Francisco de Osuna, 1972), Andrés (1976), and Selke (1968, pp. 239-243).
19. Ignatius Loyola, letter to Francisco Borja, IX-20-1548, and Pedro de Ribadeneira, *Vida de San Ignacio* I 325; both cited by V. Larrañaga in his introduction to the *Diario Espiritual* (Loyola, 1947, pp. 644-645).

References

Andrés, M., 1976: *Los recogidos*. Madrid (Fundación Universitaria Española).

Bataillon, M., 1966: *Erasmo y España*. Mexico City (Fondo de Culture).

Bauer, G., 1973: *Claustrum Animae* I. Munich (Wilhelm Fink Verlag).

Caesarius of Heisterbach, 1929: *Dialogue on Miracles* I-II. London (Routledge).

Caterina da Siena, 1969: *Il Libro* [*The Dialogues*]. n. p. (Edizione Paoline).

Christian, W.A. Jr., 1981a: *Local Religion in Sixteenth Century Spain*. Princeton (Princeton University Press).

Christian, W.A. Jr., 1981b: *Apparitions in Late Medieval and Renaissance Spain*. Princeton (Princeton University Press).

Corrientes Espirituales en la España del siglo XVI, 1963: Barcelona (Flors).

Darwin, C., 1872: *The Expression of the Emotions in Man and Animals*. London (John Murray).

De Martino, E. 1958: *Morte e pianto rituale nel mondo antico dal lamento pagano al pianto di Maria*. Torino (Edizioni Scientifiche Einaudi).

Dietari of Barcelona (*Manual de Novells Ardits*), 1894: Volume III. Barcelona (Henrich).

El Especulo de los legos, 1951: Madrid (Consejo Superior de Investigaciones Cientificas).

Fischer, M.M.J., 1980: *Iran, from Religious Dispute to Revolution*. Cambridge, Mass. (Harvard University Press).

Francisco de Osuna, 1972: *Tercer abecedario espirtual* (1527). Madrid (Biblioteca de Autores Cristianos).

Frey, W.H.II., 1980: Not-so-idle tears. *Psychology Today*, January.

Hernández García, E., 1960: *Guiones para un cursillo práctico de dirección espiritual*. Comillas, Santander (Pont. Univ. Comillensis).

Huerga, A., 1978: *Historia de los alumbrados* I. Madrid (Fundación Universitaria Española).

Huizinga, J., 1963: *The Waning of the Middle Ages*. London (Edwin Arnold).

Juan de Avila, 1963: *Avisos y reglas cristianas sobre aquel verso de David: Audi, Filia* (1556). Barcelona (Flors).

Litterae Quadrimestres (LQ) I-VII., 1894-1897: Madrid (Augustinus Avrial). 1920, 1925: Madrid (Editorial Ibérica). 1932: Rome (A Macioce and Pisani). (Monumenta Historica Societatis Iesu).

Llompart, G., 1969: Desfile iconográfico de penitentes españoles (siglos xvi al xx). *Revista de Dialectología y Tradiciones Populares* XXV, 31-51.

Llompart, 1972: Penitencias y penitentes en la pintura y en la piedad catalanas bajomedievales. *Revista de Dialectogía y Tradiciones Populares* **XXVIII**, 229-249.

Loyola, I., 1904: *Scripta* I. Madrid (López del Horno) (MHSI 25).

Loyola, I., 1947: *Obras completas* I. Madrid (Biblioteca de Autores Cristianos).

Loyola, I., 1969: *Exercitia Spiritualia*. Rome (Institutum Historicum Societatis Iesu) (MHSI 100).

Ludolphus de Saxonia, 1502-1503: *Vita cristi romãçado por fray ambrosio* I-IV. Alcalá.

Ortega Sagrista, R. 1956: Historia de las cofradías de la Pasión de Semana Santa. *Boletín del Instituto de Estudios Giennensis* **III**, 10, 9-71.

Radcliffe-Brown, A. 1922: *The Andaman Islanders*. Cambridge (Cambridge University Press).

Rosenthal, H. M., 1941: On the function of religion in culture. *Review of Religion* **V**, **2, 3** (January, March).

Selke, A., 1968: *El Santo Oficio de la Inquisición; proceso de Fr. Francisco Ortiz (1529-1532)*. Madrid (Ediciones Guadarrama).

Tentler, T. N., 1977: *Sin and Confession on the Eve of the Reformation*. Princeton (Princeton University Press).

Teresa de Jesús, 1967: *Obras completas*. Madrid (Biblioteca de Autores Cristianos).

Tomás de Villanueva, 1952: *Obras*. Madrid (Biblioteca de Autores Cristianos).

Tostado, A., 1517: *Tratado de confession llamado tostado*. Alcala de Henares (Arnao guillen de brocar).

Trexler, R., 1980: *Public Life in Renaissance Florence*. New York and London (Academic Press).

Wagley, C., 1978: *Welcome of Tears: The Tapirapa Indians of Central Brazil*. Oxford (Oxford University Press).

From the Mouths of Babes:
christianization by children in 16th century New Spain

Richard C. Trexler

> The Spanish [soldiers] could have...attained heaven if...they had killed the
> old men and women so that those of the new generation lost all knowledge of
> the old [religion] (Duran, 1967, I, 79).

Anthropologists and historians usually consider Indian tribes of 16th
century Mexico as social and cultural units and, almost uniformly, they play
down those units' internal conflicts. Economic historians at times employ
the topos of the imperial power seducing certain classes among the
colonized, but intratribal group tensions are rarely taken seriously. The
fashion in which imperial Spain appealed to the boys of the Mexican
peninsula has gone largely unstudied, for the Spanish Conquest has been
viewed as pitting only two social and cultural units against each other, Spain
and some particular tribe. In his learned, if Christo- and occidentophilic,
work on *The Spiritual Conquest of Mexico*, Robert Ricard (1933, p. 320)
casually deplored the "disagreeable fact" that Indian children commonly
denounced their fathers to the Spanish authorities, apparently an
aberration in the otherwise adult struggle between two paternal societies.
The problem of the relation between the old and young in early colonial
society has, alternatively, been avoided by simply casting the Indian nations
as children and the conquerors as adults.

The role of the Indian young in the evangelization of Mexico was,
however, a central rather than an incidental phenomenon, one only
obscured by the hegemonic ploy of casting nations as generations. The
strategy of the Christian clergy involved pitting the young people of New
Spain against their fathers and elders; in the early Spanish Conquest the
liminal group of the Indian young crossed or were carried over tribal
borders and found new fathers among the priests. That had a significant

impact on colonial social structures and on the differential experience of Christianity by young and old. The purpose of this paper is to study the strategy of conversion, its execution, and the religious experience produced by an organization of celibate fathers and their native sons, pitted against Indian elders.

European backgrounds

> How this Conversion of the Indians was Carried Out by Means of Children, in Keeping with the Talent God gave Them (Mendieta, 1971, p. 211; Torquemada, 1969, III, p. 33).

How odd initially, and yet on reflection how reasonable, that such a paean to lay child genius should have been sounded by early missionary historians of the spiritual conquest, and should have been so edifying for European fathers who brooked no disobedience from their own sons. The explanation for the missionaries' magnanimity lies in contemporary European views of children. The attitudes toward the young which the first evangelists brought to the New World were a potent mixture of traditional clerical views and new pedagogic ideas which, applied to the *tabula rasa* of the Indian nations by fully empowered clergy, had an impact in New Spain which was impossible in old Europe. For centuries hagiographers had vaunted the oblate-saint shielded from the *saeculum* when still a child and the youthful clerical convert like St. Francis who disobeyed a blind though not evil father; the model of a clergy ever-invigorated by youthful disobedience toward carnal fathers was ancient. A celibate group isolated by *rites de passage*, the clergy itself was indeed that segment of the European population whose membership was partially exempt from the biopsychological classifications applied to secular society's age groups. Clerks were types of eternal children. When Franciscan friars in the New World delighted in having become "as little children" to learn Indian languages (Mendieta, 1971, p. 219), they but rejoiced in the clergy's ancient traditions. The Franciscan Juan Torquemada (*c.* 1610) appealed to that same ancient view of the child when he wrote that if god was author and master, "a little age is a lot, for through the power of god you have no age, but only will" (1969, III, p. 84).

Such traditional clerical self-images fuelled the general re-evaluation of the lay young which was underway in fifteenth-century Europe, and the first evangelists of New Spain grew up at the time of that most radical juvenile experiment, the Savonarolan boys' movement in Florence from 1496—8 (Trexler, 1980, pp. 474-90). That recent event, its significance, and certainly the writings of the Dominican leader (Torquemada, 1965, III, p.

594) were known to those who then evangelized the Indies: organized into age-specific confraternities, innocent sons could convert worldly fathers; real children rallying to God's children could assure the salvation of corrupt adults. In the Savonarolan years, some said that the inspired children aimed at establishing a republic of children if their fathers did not mend their ways. A Mediterranean model of saintly child evangelists was clamorously in the air as the first clerks left for New Spain in 1523 and 1524. Here force of arms would insure that no law or tradition stood in the way of its full practical realization.

The internment of the children

It is the law among these people... that the brood follows the mother (Pérez de Ribas, 1944, II, p. 226).

When the Twelve Apostles of the Indies arrived in Mexico City in mid-1524, the Spanish strategy for winning over the young Indians was already visible. The lay brother Peter of Ghent had arrived in the Valley the previous year and started his mission, and in early 1524 Cortés himself had decreed a far-ranging program to intern the boys (Cortés, 1871, p. 32-4; Trueba, 1959). how, however, an elite corps of Franciscan friars assumed full control. Greeting the friars on their arrival in the city, a magnificently attired Cortés dismounted and, on his knees, kissed the rags of the Mendicants in welcome. A calculated inversion of expected behavior, Cortés's action toward these children of Europe became legally binding for all Indians on meeting friars: a friar was a father and was to be addressed and treated as such (*padreme*: Sahagún, 1949, p. 107; Torquemada, 1969, III, p. 21). The Indian boys clearly benefitted from this new order, able now to leave their villages and return in the friars' retinue. They would be "disciples" even as their masters were "apostles" (Mendieta, 1971, p. 258). The social and cultural boundaries set for the pre-Christian youth would be broken by the crossing-over of boys from their fathers to the Fathers.

Ghent's and Cortés's determination to intern the boys was adopted by the Apostles: the chiefs were to turn over their young men (*hijos pequeños*) for education in Christian doctrine, good manners, reading, writing, and singing; in Ghent's school, the boys were additionally taught Spanish crafts unknown in Mexico. The caciques themselves were to build the monasteries which would house the friars and the sons of the principals, who would spend day and night with their mentors (Mendieta, 1971, p. 214; Torquemada, 1969, III, p. 25). How long would the boys be kept? The friars said only that they would stay until they were indoctrinated, and I could find only one term of residence specified: in Michoacán in the early years, the sons of a lord were told that they would be kept in Mexico City for a year (Chronicles, 1970, p. 86). In fact, however, the boys would not be released after indoctrination, for they then began to instruct their lower-class compatriots in the church patios. Furthermore, a primary understanding of the friars was nowhere stated but everywhere implicit: the boys would be domiciled in the friaries at least until their fathers converted or until the boys married (Focher, 1960, pp. 74-5). Thus the boys' evangelism was more central to the plan than their mere indoctrination and, except when their fathers had unquestionably converted, the boys stayed attached to the friaries from their arrival—the youngest were about four years old, the age above which children could not be baptized against their will (Focher, 1960, p. 68; Motolinía, 1970, p. 316; Pérez de Ribas, 1944, II, p. 165)—until marriage at about 20 years of age. The niños y mozos of the friaries (Torquemada, 1969, III, p. 48) were from the start hostages for their unbelieving fathers, and an elite cadre for subsequent evangelization.

At the strategic level, such hostaging served military purposes more pressing than either indoctrination or evangelization: taking a tribe's young warriors away to school removed that tribe's ability to resist the Spaniards or to engage in inter-tribal rivalries. As a frontier Jesuit of the early seventeenth century would say, schools for boys brought peace (Pérez de Ribas, 1944, II, pp. 215, 252). At the level of the individual missionary entering hostile territory, furthermore, hostaging preserved his life, and in mid-sixteenth century a Dominican superior warned his missionaries that "it is customary to take hostages from the sons or relatives of the caciques and the principals" on entering new areas (Othón de Mendizábal, 1976, p. 92). Evidently, coercion was the rule (Gibson, 1952, p. 33). Mendieta (c. 1590) told how the Indians of Oztoticpac, 600 strong, came out to meet the missionary:

> without the children they had reared. They did not dare bring the bigger children [mayorcillos], to avoid their being taken from them. For they knew that the religious collected them and placed them in schools (1971, p. 750).

If the boys were surrendered, said Motolinía (c. 1540), it was because fathers feared for themselves (1970, p. 270).

Religious considerations conspired with military ones to distance the boys from their tribal ambience. In the earliest days, Peter of Ghent was ready to send his boys out evangelizing to distant parts, but forbade them to socialize with their nearby unconverted parents (Cuevas, 1921, II p. 200). Moral rather than physical distance was, therefore, the primary goal. Thus the friars baulked at a royal request that some boys be sent to Madrid for education so as to reassure fathers that their boys would not be enslaved (Mendieta, 1971, p. 482). And when an ecclesiastical network of schools had been established in New Spain, boys went to the friary school nearest to them. But until that network was developed, boys obeyed rudimentary colonial geography rather than tribal lines. On March 20, 1524, even before the Apostles arrived, Cortés decreed that all Spaniards having Indian pueblos under them send the male children of the local Indian principals to the nearest city for instruction, accompanied by individual servants[1] who would be sent out of the monasteries to procure the necessities for those young masters far removed from their parents (Cortés, 1871, p. 32). Ghent tells us that boys came to his school from distances of 20 to 40 leagues (Cuevas, 1921, II, p. 200), and Mendieta says simply that these boys came from the whole land (1971: 608, 258).

Severed from their parents and interned in these friaries, the boys might then be punished with the stocks if they tried to escape or whipped if they became inebriated (Espediente, 1883, p. 40, 501, 509). Here was no mere continuation of indigenous pedagogy under enlightened management, as Mendieta and some modern scholars suggest. Forced internment at great distances from home was as revolutionary in Mexico as elsewhere (Duviols, 1971, pp. 236-70; Soriano, 1963, p. 71). So was the goal of the pedagogy: to weaken and attack sons' attachments to fathers and not, as was one goal of indigenous schooling, to inculcate the latters' authority. The friars effected a structural scission in the fabric of upper-class Indian society which would have a profound impact on the experience of Christianity.

Throughout this article, the children of the Indian elite will be the center of our attention. The masses of non-noble boys are another story. Dependents of this juvenile elite, they lived at home, merely visiting the patios each morning to be indoctrinated by these superiors before returning to their fathers with the good news of the gospel (Motolinía, 1970, p. 270). Instruction did not include reading and writing, and the friars tried to keep it that way.[2] In this chapter these boys remain in the background, and we shall soon move inside the friary to watch the elite boys learn Christianity. Before doing so, however, we must note a decisive legal difference among these interns which was created by the imposition of Christian marriage upon their fathers. The successful enforcement of monogamous Christian marriage, we shall argue, produced a large number of displaced bastards who would long remain wards of the monasteries.

Simply put, the friars refused to baptize any polygamous Indian, and the sedentary Indian elites were everywhere polygamous (Soustelle, 1961, p. 179). When the friars broke the resistance to monogamy, around 1530, innumerable chiefs drove all but one of their wives from the house and sent the children with their mothers, creating an army of "widows" and bastards (Motolinía, 1970, pp. 66-7, 263-5; Mendieta, 1971, pp. 301, 306). The caciques' standing was measured by the size of their households and the wives' by the standing of their husbands (Pérez de Ribas, 1944, II, 226;

Zorita, 1963, p. 90; Soustelle, 1961, p. 179), so the impact on both status and welfare was devastating. Compare Pérez de Ribas' assurances that some pretty women did find new husbands with the same author's vivid accounts of desperate women crying out that Christianity had made them widows (1944, I, p. 344; II, pp. 101, 226). It is unlikely that the one-time "satisfaction" such husbands paid their wives on departure actually sufficed "to feed and maintain the children who left them", as Motolinía suggested (1970 p. 264).

That the majority of upper-class Indian children were reduced to bastardy and thus to legal disadvantage seems to follow from these institutional innovations; contemporaries studiously avoided the issue, and modern scholarship has not studied the matter (Gibson, 1964, p. 151-2; Höltker, 1930).[3] My reading of the evidence does, however, provide an explanation for the hoards of oblates and juvenile hangers-on who were such a feature of the missions (Mendieta, 1971, p. 220, 245, 444, 744; Pérez de Ribas 1944, I, p. 311-2; II, pp. 30, 159, 220-1). Directly to the point, this reading allows us to better assess the legal and moral condition of our interns: shamed by their spurned mothers, the majority were bastards whose hopes of a paternal inheritance had been decisively compromised.

Teaching paternity in the friaries

> If one can stop a father from killing his child, one can certainly stop him from killing that child's soul (Focher, 1960, p. 68).

Within the friary, a new day dawned. Rising from their eternally lit dormitories (like those of nuns, Mendieta (1971, p. 415) said), these now docile crew-cut Samsons (Pérez de Ribas, 1944, II, p. 227) donned their altar boys' dress which distinguished them here and on mission (Mendieta, 1971, pp. 226, 415, 431; *cf.* 444, 744), and began their mixed duties of domestic work and learning. They cooked, swept, portered, dug graves and in certain circumstances begged for the friars, freeing the latter for "more important" tasks while humbling these noble sons who held such an exalted position as residents of the House of Mary (*NCDHM*, II, p. 64; Mendieta, 1971, p. 380; Torquemada, 1969, III, 223). That humility was all to the good, since in their schooling the boys learned a particularly flattering sociology of eternity.

All their ancestors had gone to hell, the boys were taught, for they had worshipped "idols" (Sahagún, 1950: I, 27 *et seq.*; Mendieta, 1971, p. 318; Torquemada, 1969, II, p. 119 and III, p. 23; Pérez de Ribas, 1944, III, p. 26); the innocent children of the Christian era would be the first to attain heaven, and from those heights they would intercede for their living elders' and tribes' accession. Children and not adults were the "first fruits" gathered by the Christian grim reaper, and everyone should be happy to die on mission, from plague, or from any other illness. "Rejoice," the Jesuit Pérez de Ribas told grieving parents on the pandemic deaths of their children; "convert," he warned them, it they wanted to join those scions in heaven (1944, II, p. 157, III, pp. 49, 83, 225, 269-70; Mendieta, 1971, p. 244; Torquemada, 1969, I, p. 763 and III, pp. 100-2). The religious experience of early colonial Mexico structured the parental and tribal futures around children. The past was "simple" and "silly," the boys learned, their elders so "infantile" as to worship female divinities (Sahagún, 1950, I, pp. 27-30), and the present was dangerous, given "the errors, rites, and idolatries of their [living] fathers" (Mendieta, 1971, p. 224). The pedagogy turned aggressively against the living. "There was but one god and not many, like those their fathers adored," the children heard (Mendieta, 1971, p. 218). Filial piety was not a required course in these schools; ridicule of blind ancestors and dislike of recalcitrant living fathers was no mere elective.

A rich lore about their "evil fathers" (Torquemada, 1969, III, p. 94) soon developed. There were those objects of contempt who concealed sons at home instead of surrendering them, and stories about such men taught the boys that if they knew such cases they were required to confess the matter to the padres. Carnal fathers' daily activities, such as their "pagan" religious practices and their drinking, became the object of *exempla*. Finally, these boys who would themselves become illegitimate through their fathers' subsequent monogamy were taught to detest polygamy. We may still hear friar Motolinía thundering the lesson to his charges: "each house of the lords of these indigenous people," he wrote, "was nothing more than a forest of abominable sins" (1970, p. 66).

The boys were led to conclude that the clerks and not their recalcitrant fathers were the ones who really loved them, the ones to whom they had the greater debt (Pérez de Ribas, 1944, II, 225). The same friars who commended the Aztec fathers' care for their children to their Spanish compatriots (Olmos, in Zorita, 1963, pp. 140-52; Mendieta, 1971, pp. 503-4; Acosta, 1954, pp. 205-6) now typecast those who resisted their sons' conversion as acting "not so much [from] a parent's love as from the rabidity of the demon" (Torquemada, 1969, II, 761). They were "demons in the figure of fathers," fathers who had "lost the natural sentiment of love for sons" (Pérez de Ribas, 1944, II, p. 160; Mendieta, 1971, pp. 238, 658). The powerful theme developed that the friars filled this gap, having "more tender love for the converted Indian boys than any father had for his sons" and certainly more than did their own carnal fathers (Pérez de Ribas, 1944, III, p. 276; Mendieta, 1971, p. 631). The leader of the Twelve, Martin of Valencia, was typical: he treated the boys as though they were his own sons and mourned them as his own when they died (Motolinía, 1970, pp. 318-20; Mendieta, 1971, pp. 241-3).

Part of the purpose of this competition was to insure that the boys would end by loving the friars more than their fathers, and missionary historians like Mendieta insisted that was what happened. It was a miracle of the Holy Ghost:

> Though these friars were so new and so foreign to [the boys], [the latter] denied the natural affection toward their fathers and mothers and heartily gave it all to their masters, as if they were the ones who had engendered and reared them (1971, pp. 222, 638).

Every allowance being made for the self-deception of clerical celibates fantasizing about fathering, and with full cognizance of the few alternatives,[4] it seems success often crowned the clergy's efforts. Here is not the place to inquire why the indigenous fathers lost so many battles, though it must be said that child sacrifice and harsh native pedagogy seem less probable as explanations than the fact that it was often only their spiritual fathers who could provide them with wife and goods. For after the initial shock of capture and internment, the boys generally did stay in the friaries. Pérez de Ribas for all his self-satisfaction seems to have spoken the truth: "the *niños* were so well off because of their good treatment that when some of their fathers tried to extract them from the seminary, they hid themselves and resisted the return to their homes" (1944, III, p. 276).

What can have been the religion of these sons as, now trained in doctrine, they began their evangelical tasks "masters of their fathers and of all other [fathers] in matters of faith" (Moles and Daza, in Ricard, 1933, p. 121)? The friars had done everything possible to turn them against their living and past culture, to make them outsiders to the world they had now to convert. The boys were still Indians, however, and the friars even while telling them to forget the past encouraged them to atone for the pre-Conquest sins of their fathers and ancestors. Marked for life by their natives names which derived from the "filthy gods" (Sahagún, 1950, I, p. 27), the boys with their fathers were required to restitute all the usury which they had taken, "that from the time of their infidelity as well as that since then" (Motolinía, 1970, p. 238; Mendieta, 1971, p. 289). The guilt of errors past, that of a "pagan" race, weighed on the boys, in a perverse sense preserving their cultural identity even while assuring the friars of material support.[5] "For although already Christians," Motolinía noted, "the sons unburden themselves and leave their patrimony...." (1970, p. 238). The same author best describes the boys' sense of a cultural guilt more sacred than baptism:

> [The boys] asked their [carnal] fathers if, when they were *niños*, they were reared in the House of the Demons, and how many times their ear blood was

sacrificed, if it was, and if they had been given human flesh to eat and other foods dedicated to the demon of idolatries. There were many who accused themselves and said: "I sinned from the belly of my mother.... When I was in the womb of my mother, she offered and promised me to the demon." And others said...: "When my mother had me in her womb she became inebriated and ate human flesh, so that for my part I ate human flesh and sinned. Thus I sinned in that also." (Motolinía, 1970, p. 105).

Into evil homes

The father being old and the son a child, the child manages the elder. Illuminated by god, our child... admonished the blind and unenlightened elder, his kin (Torquemada, 1969, III, p. 84).
For the masters of the evangelists were *niños*. The *niños* were also preachers, and the *niños* [were] ministers of the destruction of idolatry (Mendieta, 1971, p. 221).

A first at, Peter of Ghent sent his boys on mission to distant areas even while keeping them away from their own relatives (Cuevas, 1921, II, p. 200); the Twelve Apostles soon encouraged their boys to work on relatives. This fleeting distinction allows us to isolate the revolutionary nature of the early clergy's strategy, which was to outflank the fathers by appealing to the caciques' dependents. From the boys' first appearances as instructors in the monastery patios, they appealed to subjected cohorts not to tolerate their parents' "idolatry", and these cohorts' subjection to the interns was of the essence: the *criados y vasillos* of the noble fathers were more the targets of the patio instructors, Torquemada said, than the nobles themselves (1969, III, p. 83). Thus when these interns went into the countryside to preach, class and status were not ignored. The first boys the Twelve Apostles sent out were, in fact, two young relatives of the fallen Montezuma (Mendieta, 1971, p. 259), and in general, rich boys were sent to rich dependencies and poorer boys to less well-endowed villages (Motolinía, 1970, p. 70). The motivation was evident: in this way, the boys could undermine the authority of their own noble fathers among outlying dependents.

Ghent leaves no doubt as to the spectacular nature of the boys' intervention in this world of dependents, writing to admiring colleagues in Europe that whenever he heard of a native feast, he expedited the toughest of the toughs, *los más habiles*, "to disrupt the feasts" (Cuevas, 1921, II, p. 200). Thus street attacks were common from the start, and we shall return to their analysis. For the present, however, let us turn to their more domestic tasks, which were to preach, to gather information, and to search out Indian images. We know nothing about their sermons but, as critics of their being sent out unaccompanied by friars would say, "the boys get into other things than preaching" (Espediente, 1883, pp. 475, 496; Motolinía, 1970, p. 264). That was nothing more than was expected of them.

The information-gathering of the boys was constantly praised by the friars, who pictured the younger generation as that group within native society able and desiring to reveal its secrets (Motolinía, 1970, p. 207). In 1525 the Indian tribes around Tenochtitlan conspired against the Spaniards but, the friars rejoiced, "through the Indians whom the friars taught, the [latter] learned everything", and a revolt was avoided (Mendieta, 1971, p. 231). The mission annals are filled with "priests' boys" who saved padres' lives through revealing some demonic plot, but only occasionally do they record juvenile reports of the Spanish laity's injustice toward the Indians (Chronicles, 1970, p. 96). The boys "revealed everything", Mendieta said, and that more than anything else was the proof of how much they loved the friars (1971, pp. 222; 233; Motolinía, 1970, p. 316; Torquemada, 1969, III, p. 34).

In addition to such political intelligence, the boys provided information about the location of Indian images, secrets commonly gleaned from their age-cohorts in the villages. Sometimes the big boys, the *más grandecillos* (Mendieta, 1971, p. 235) themselves took matters in hand, "turning everything in the houses upside down" to find the images and other diabolical property, to then either smash or burn the images in the streets (Espediente, 1883, p. 475; Procesos, 1912, p. 11; Mendieta, 1971, p. 657; Motolinía, 1970, pp. 318-20). Such breaking and entering followed by destruction of property was the case in the famous "martyrdom" of the Indian boy Antonio and his servant Juan who, as Motolinía approvingly narrates, left the friary to missionize, insisting "with the maximum arrogance" that they too had the right to die for Christ (1856, p. 20). Killed by occupants after they had broken into a house and smashed some "devilries" in front of horrified elders, they (like "many other little Indian boys" violating native norms) became part of the martyric lore taught subsequent interns (Mendieta, 1971, pp. 245, 751; Motolinía, 1970, pp. 318-20).

At other times, however, these young "persecutors" (Camargo, 1892, p. 247) "steal [the images] and faithfully bring them to the religious", in the bishop Zumárraga's commending words (Mendieta, 1971, p. 638). In Savonarolan Florence the boys were limited to words in correcting corrupt fathers; in New Spain they searched out or destroyed all evidence of the devil, and that, as Motolinía said, was to be found in all the homes of the elite (1970, p. 66). With the full encouragement of the friars, the boys violated property and personal rights as even Spanish society in Iberia would have defined those rights.

Out in the hustings on mission the boys did perpetrate things which no friar would have approved; that much needs be said. Well-founded evidence that certain boys had hanged Indians "because they were not good Christians" combines with independently corroborated claims that in 1529 other boys had raped girls after insisting on preaching to women separately (Espediente, 1883, pp. 475, 510, 533). Yet only Motolinía even alluded to the problem, disputing the claim that another boy had ever used bad judgment (1856, p. 17); the friars neither reported such unedifying (Boxer, 1978, pp. 94-5) events in their histories, nor did they seem ready to act on accusations. Quite the opposite. In the rape case, for example, a travelling Spanish civil official, himself risking excommunication, had the boys whipped in his presence because the Indian accusers dared not report the matter to the friars (Espediente, 1883, p. 533). The reason for such clerical reticence is not far to seek. The very basis of the children's martyric heroism was their breaking, entering, and theft of cultural properties, which received the approbation of the friars. The friars' denunciation of rape would have weakened their boys' legitimacy, as much as the friars might regret such activity. Ricard's characterization of such theft as the work of "precocious Tartufes and *canailles*" who "abused" their place (1933, pp. 122, 320-2) is contradicted by Zumárraga himself. The archbishop understood that if the boys' attacks on their very parents were to be considered laudable, those on strangers could not be less so.

Inebriation, domestic religious rites and, improbable as it might seem, the fathers' polygamy were the bread and butter of the battles against the fathers; the "disruption" of the parental life-style was the aim of the Apostles from their arrival. It began with a boy outflanking his father through the latter's dependents, including the intern's mother, and continued in personal combat between the two (Torquemada, 1969, III p. 393). The domestic conflicts between the generations in such father–son encounters make some of the most revealing reading of the spiritual conquest. In what follows, we shall first examine what the boys said to their fathers, and then the range of paternal responses. Let it be said at the start: we are dealing here with a brash saint who might pity his father's ignorance, but was determined to save father from himself through aggression.

With equal credibility, the contemporary Motolinía and the mestizo historian of Tlaxcala, Camargo, told the most famous story of all, the conflict between the 13-year-old Cristóbal and his noble father Acxotécatl. It began with the boy coming to his father's house from the monastery and abruptly warning Acxotécatl that he, Cristóbal, would reveal his father's sins to the friars; Camargo, himself a child at the time, added that the boy warned his father "grown old and evil in sin" (Motolinía, 1970, p. 316) that if he did not reform he would "forfeit the obedience and respect that he had for him as a father" (1892, pp. 245-6). All this pleading "went in one and out the other" paternal ear, Motolinía continued (1856, p. 7), which moved the boy to say that he would "lose all sense of decorum" and himself burn his father's images, break his pulque vats, and generally defame his father before the Christian community of Tlaxcala if something were not done (Camargo, 1892, pp. 245-6). Camargo has the boy make one last desperate appeal to his father, telling him that he lived "reproached and shamed" in the monastery because of Acxotécatl's life-style, indeed was so shamed that he "did not dare appear before his masters the religious" (1892, pp. 245-6). There can be little doubt that a pattern of competition in the monastery granted cloistral love in the measure that the boys succeeded in reforming their fathers.

When Cristóbal carried out his threat and began rupturing pulque vats, first Acxotécatl's vassals and then one of Cristóbal's stepmothers, with her obvious interest in having her son and not Cristóbal inherit the father's wealth, confronted the father. The wife asked why her husband tolerated the impudence of the boy, who threw everyone and thing into confusion. "Flay and kill him", she is said to have demanded, "for why do you want a son who spits in your beard and puts himself above everyone else?" (Mendieta, 1971, p. 237). How well the friar historians recognized both the tenor and implications of such confrontations! Cristóbal had in fact been involved in the most flagrant public defamation of his father. For when the boy's own mother defended him before her husband, she (and the friars) had to justify defamatory drawings which Cristóbal had done in public. According to Motolinía, the mother asked her husband if he too had not "thoughtlessly committed some misdemeanor with the pen, dirt, or picture? Didn't you do the same misdemeanors when you were young" (1856, pp. 10-11)? Unremitting. Acxotécatl murdered his son, a decorously lengthy affair as the friars spun it out, near the end of which the boy cried out with all the spite he had imbibed:

> Oh father, don't think that you've made me angry with you for the things you've done to me. I'm not anything but happy. Know that you've done me a great favor, and that you've given me more honor than if I had inherited your lordship! (Motolinía, 1970, p. 318).

The friars thus paint for us a justified, truly Franciscan "divine ire" of the sons against the fathers. They show us as well fathers who write off their sons, and just want to be left alone.

The heresy trial of Carlos of Texcoco in 1539 provides us with our best document of the attitudes of upper-class Indian adults toward the young evangelists. During the proceedings, one Francisco told the court how his uncle Carlos had publicly criticized him while he was teaching doctrine — less because Francisco's doctrine was wrong, it seems, than because the youngster had stepped out of the role which the natives believed a noble wise man should assume:

Why do you travel about to say what you have to say? For it is not our custom to do what you are doing. For our ancestors say and teach thus: that it is not good to know the active life. Rather, [the wise man] should stay [in one place] as did [our ancestors], withdrawn and grave, and not associate with the lower class (Cuevas, 1921, I, p. 372).

Francisco had obviously outflanked the authority of the chiefs by appealing to the lower-class *macehuales*, and Carlos resented alike the evangelical type of truth-saying special to the Mendicant friars and its retailing by boys on mission. The appeal to the *macehuales* was as important a strategy to the European clergy (Mendieta, 1971, p. 662) as it was threatening to the Indian elite, and for Carlos, the message was clear: the Indians and their class structures should be left alone. "Each person," Carlos told Francisco, "should follow the law, customs, and ceremonies that he wants to" (Cuevas, 1921, I, p. 372). Carlos of Texcoco displayed an upper-class resentment against young, mobile truth-squads. The experience of Christianity through the friary boys' social organization had generational, class, and spacial-dynamic aspects.

The Indian father's desire to be spared youthful evangelism is, finally, directly documented in the 1539 trial of Xpobal. Testifying against his father and his uncle Martin, Xpobal's intern son Gabriel gave a routine description of what he found when he visited his home: the elders's drunkenness, which gave bad example to the *macehuales*, paternal rites and chants to sun and moon, the determination that his elders did not know their Christian prayers. But Gabriel admitted that he had not seen all his father's and uncle's drunken misdeeds, because, he said, "they had fought to keep him away [from the house] so that they would have more room for their rites, [and] so that the son would not reveal them" (Procesos, 1912, pp. 163-6). This decision to exclude intern sons must have been common enough for fathers like Xpobal, who not only wanted to be spared their son's zeal, but also the humiliation, documented in this case, of having their sons sent home by the civil authorities to stop their fathers' customary religious chanting.

The mestizo Camargo plausibly imputed these final anguished words to Acxotécatl before that worthy set about killing Cristóbal:

How can it be, my son! Did I beget you so that you would persecute me and go against my will? What difference does it make to you that I live according to the law I like and that which suits me? Is this the payment you make me for my having reared you? (1892, p. 246)

Why, the father who wants to be left alone seems to ask, did the son want to change his father into his son? Acxotécatl mourned the passing of an order which Carlos of Texcoco could still conceive as a *ius gentium*, but which the father of Cristóbal clung to only as a defense against filial ridicule. Xpobal simply hid from his son.

Into the streets

> [I and my students] travel roundabouts destroying idols and temples, and raising churches to the true god. In such a fashion we pass our time..., so that this faithless people will come to know the faith of Jesus Christ (Ghent, in Trueba, 1959, p. 22).

In the very year that the Apostles arrived in Mexico, the boys of the Tlaxcalan friary attacked a native priest during the public celebration of the feast of Omacatl, the god of sociability. In the marketplace, that priest criticized them for "leaving [Omacatl's] house and going to that of St. Mary," so the big boys in the group, undaunted by the priest's fierce mask and unusual public presence, assasinated him. Shocked at first by the news, the friars soon praised the boys as heroes, for they could believe that the victim was a demon and not a mere priest; Indian priests, they said, almost never left the temple as had this apparition (Motolinía, 1970, p. 314-6; Mendieta, 1971, p. 234-5). This incident was archetypal. It was the first of the disruptions of festivals which initiated the struggle for the control of ritual space. Performed in the presence of *macehuales* whose hearts and minds were at stake, the spectacle left the natives "frightened out of their wits at seeing such great daring among boys" (Motolinía, 1970, p. 316; Torquemada, 1969, III, p. 63).

On January 1, 1525, the boys began to destroy the temples. In a series of lightning attacks, they desecrated first the great cue of Texcoco and then those of Tenochtitlan, Tlaxcala, and Huejotzingo, assisted, our sources indicate, by some converted *macehuales* determined to prove they were really Christians, and watched by the friars (Mendieta, 1971, p. 227; Nuttall, 1933, p. 293). Who led these "children and youth"? Mendieta tells us that the friars had specifically selected "the sons of the very Indian lords and principals" of each town. Because the boys attacked the heritage of their own fathers, he said, "God gave them the strength of giants"[6]. The scene was alive with emotion, the boys "lifting their voices in praise..., ecstatically happy", while "those [spectators] who were not happy were terrorized and stupefied, it breaking the auricles of the heart, as they say, to see their temples and gods in the dirt" (Mendieta, 1971, p. 227; Torquemada, 1969, III, p. 63; Motolinía, 1970, p. 209). As in the previous murder of Omacatl, the natives viewed this new world-historical event in relation to the power of their boys:

> For the most part the Indians showed themselves vanquished. They did not try to resist the lesser [actions which followed], when the friars went, or sent their

disciples to search out the idols [the Indians] kept [outside the temples] and take them from them, [nor when] they destroyed the lesser temples which remained. Such was the cowardice and fear provoked by this [burning of the main temples], in fact, that [afterwards] the friars only had to send some of the boys with the rosary or some other sign. Finding [adults] in some idolatry or wizardry or inebriation, [the boys simply] told them to stop it, [and that] the padre wanted to see them. This incredible subjection was necessary to the conversion (Torquemada, 1969, III, p. 51; Mendieta, 1971, p. 230).

Thus in Torquemada's view, the subjection of the adults to their own young was a key to their subjection to the friars. The stage was set for the last aspect of clerical strategy for re-orienting ritual space, the Christian procession.

The boys' early participation in the processional remodeling of formal spaces is first evident during the Christmas season 1526–7. Ghent tells us that he had had little success in luring the *macehuales* to his mission church until he discovered the importance of singing and dancing to the Indians' own religious rites: the Christmas celebrations at this time were a success, he said, because Indians sang and danced to the new god (Cuevas, 1921, II, 202). Motolinía (1970, p. 252) tells us that these performers were children, while Pérez de Ribas (1944, pp. 3, 318) leaves no doubt why *macehuales* boys were taught to sing and dance: "so they could serve in ecclesiastical festivals."

The boys' entry into Christian crisis as distinct from celebratory processions can only be seen in vague outline, a regrettable fact considering the important role which "*niños* doing a procession of blood" came to play in classical Mexican propitiation (Pérez de Ribas, 1944, II, pp. 116, 124, 184; Ricard, 1933, p. 228). Yet the process had begun by 1527, when a march to induce rain in Tlaxcala involved a statue carried by a sacristan who was doubtless an intern (Gibson, 1952, p. 36; Mendieta, 1971, p. 431). This image of Mary had an important history. Cortés had given it to Acxotécatl in the earliest days of the Conquest, and this later filicide had installed it in his home with all the paraphernalia of sacrality. Fascination for Cortés being what it was, the Virgin quickly became a pilgrimage goal for the Tlaxcalans, and it was carried from Acxotécatl's home and back in public ceremony long before the friars arrived there in 1524, and removed the image to their monastery (Gibson, 1952, pp. 35–6). All the more crucial, therefore, that an Indian boy carried this first symbol of Tlaxcalan Christian history in a crisis procession which brought rain. As the movement of the image from the home of Acxotécatl to the monastery symbolized the shift of proto-Christian Tlaxcalan Christianity from a ritual geography which had the home of Acxotécatl as its hub to one where the friary was at center, so entrusting that image to an Indian adolescent reinserted saving grace back into the Indian community in the person of the children. Did other Indian boys follow the example of Fray Martin of Valencia in this procession and flagellate themselves for rain as they had been taught to do in the friary (Mendieta, 1971, p. 599)? We do not know. But we are sure that they did come to play a central role in public penitential activities to save the new, Christian, nations, Adults would offer them a banquet on the feast of the Holy Innocents, a symbolic final meal before their sacrifice for their elders.

The marriage of the innocents

> It pleased not only the spiritual fathers, but [the boys'] carnal ones. . . , [this office of] the *niño fiscal*. To increase this cult of children, which is the principal harvest of these new Christianities, the padres initiated a feast held just for them, which was celebrated the day of the Holy Innocents. . . . [The priests] served the little barbarians their meals. . . , there being a trumpet blare at each course, [the boys] being [thus] saluted as if they were adults. . . . The carnal fathers stood there astounded, and the boys learned the doctrine of Christ well (Pérez de Ribas, 1944, III, pp. 261, also 320).

From such Feasts of the Innocents to the boys' marriage feasts of Cana was only a small step in the early history of Mexican Christianity; in each region, the Spanish clerics soon after interning the boys were faced with the task of marrying them. The *Wunderkinder* of the conversion had to become respectable young husbands of a new Christian society which would educate its own children at home. The status of the missionaries was on the line: the *macehuales* watched to see if the friars could end their masters' polygamy and thus free wives for them;[7] the bastardized interns also depended on the friars' success for their future.

The Christian clergy had three perceptible goals in marrying their interns. First, they aimed to monopolize the ceremony of bestowing wives. Thus in the years 1524–30, when almost the only Christian marriages performed in New Spain were those of interned boys, the friars adopted a highly ceremonial marriage procedure to emphasize the honor they could grant an alumnus. Motolinía describes the 1526 marriage fanfare for Don Hernando Pimentel of Texcoco and seven of his fellow graduates in just such solemn terms, calling the first marriage in New Spain what Mendieta said was only the first celebrated with great pomp (Motolinía, 1970, pp. 66-7, 262-3; Mendieta, 1971, p. 296). Matrimony was in short a public reward bestowed on good students, as Mendieta explained in describing his "first marriage", that of Don Calixto. Even though he was already a big boy, Calixto had entered the friary as an intern along with the *niños*, so when the time came for him to marry, the friars, said our historian, "wanted to send him off from the church with that honor of marrying him" (1971, p. 296).

In addition to bestowing wives, the friars wanted to show they could guarantee goods and status: such were the other, more difficult, goals of the clergy. The Spanish laity's and clergy's expropriation of native property created massive uncertainty as to title, property, and rank. From the beginning the clergy intended to prepare their minions "for the regiment of [the boys' own] pueblos" (*NCDHM*, II, p. 62; Pérez de Ribas, 1944, III, 42-3). But which pueblos, with what honor, and with what property? The only thing certain was that success in placing the boys was crucial to the Christian clergy. "In dividing the land," the Franciscans and Dominicans agreed as early as 1526:

> One should pay great attention to the *niños* and *señoritos* who are in the monasteries. Where possible, the division should sooner fall to them than to others. For these boys are central to the conversion of all the other [Indians] (*CDHM*, II, p. 551).

The missionaries' success was never in doubt. The friars themselves noted that some Indian lands passed to their rightful upper-class heirs in the friaries, the Christian god sometimes killing the caciques so as to expedite the transfer (Motolinía, 1970, p. 208). The same sources stated with gratitude that the lower-class boys whom elite fathers sent to the monasteries as their sons, though they were not, sometimes ended by inheriting those chiefs' properties, god thus mocking the Indian fathers' duplicity (Mendieta, 1971, p. 217). These subversions of the fathers' last wills, rightful inheritances, and the enormous properties which the friars disposed of through usury restitution, enabled them to place their charges. In 1554 some 13 principals from the northern half of Mexico City (Tlaltelolco), from Cuautitlán, Atzcapotzalco, and Huitzilopochco were restrained, almost impassive when they were queried by the Spaniards on the treatment their people had received from the Europeans. But they came alive when asked who were now being made caciques in their towns and villages. "Persons of low birth, or boys reared in the churches or monasteries", they spat out, and not the lawful heirs (Zorita, 1963, p. 286). That assessment adds up to something more than a minor social upheaval as Benjamin Keen astutely recognized. The Indian elders were convinced that Christian religious institutions, associated as they were with the confounding of property and status rights, benefitted Indian interns once they married.

If the friar Motolinía writing in 1540 could already vaunt the number of his interns who had settled into marriage life and were rearing Christian children (1970, p. 262), he did not mention the destruction of tribal structures which those innocents had wrought, nor did he view them as victims of that destruction. When the friars arrived in New Spain in the

1520s, they were quick to praise the authoritarian paternalism of the cultures of central Mexico and, in the generations to come, the Christian clergy would imagine no greater glory for the Christian god than a utopian Christian republic led by them and peopled with native families (Phelan, 1956). Yet this paper has shown a peculiar association in these early decades of the evangelization between the paternal authoritarianism of the clergy — those children of Europe — and a celebration of juvenile genius. The imperial padres and their indigenous boys mediated between the European *and* indigenous paternalism of pre-Conquest days, and the new paternalism of colonial Mexico.

Summary

They will give birth though they are very old (Aiton, 1927, p. 140).

During the early Conquest of Mexico, a specific ecclesiastical organization consisting of a handful of Christian clergy and large numbers of young Indian interns attacked several native structures. The ritual and property structures need no further comment, but the impact upon exchange structures bears review. First, monogamy radically modified exchange through wives and children. Second, the cohort solidarity of the Indian young people against adults rather than against foreign enemy youth was important. Third and of equal import was that age group's association with the class of the *macehuales*: elders' fear of cross-liminal conspiracies between "the young and the plebs" is too well documented in the Old World (Trexler, 1980, pp. 29-30) for us to mistake its relevance to the New.

Finally, native normative structures suffered heavily at the hands of the new religious organization through its legitimation of breaking, entering, and theft by Indian boys who had themselves been taken by force. Then as now, European and Amerindian law abhorred the violation of sacred objects more than of profane ones, yet in New Spain, such actions were good not bad, saved rather than damned their perpetrators. If the early historians were right that Indians vices were greater after the Conquest (Motolinía, 1970, p. 136; Mendieta, 1971, pp. 503-4), the legitimation of the theft of *sacra* must be part of any explanation (Duviols, 1971, pp. 48-50).

Caution is called for as we move from structure to religious experience. As this article makes clear, it is difficult to document the Indians' reaction to the Christian religious organization in their own, even if Spanish-mediated words. And since we have avoided the natives' pre-Christian religious organization and experience, we can only haltingly compare the old and the new. What we shall summarize is the religious experience the friars and their interned boys made available to the natives, that which the friars themselves largely recorded.

The friars and their boys offered the Indian adults what can be described as a new dynamics of moral space which worked horizontally and vertically. At one pole was the charismatic or spiritual center of the friars in their monastery, which performed miracles. At the opposite end was adult Indian society, the receptors of the benefits of that charisma. The young Indian interns mediated the two. Their power was peculiar, for within the monastery they wer servile to the friars, and were not said to exercise any religious force upon the outside from the inside, as did the friars. Yet on entering tribal adult society they exercised an effective *plenitudo potestatis*, carrying with them the sacred objects (rosaries, images, and the like), coercive symbols for that adult world just as, within the monastery, the friars coerced their god for them.

Thus a specific sense of space was a fundamental characteristic of early colonial religious experience, as it is of any such experience. A second ground of religious experience is a specific valuation of objects, and the world we have studied was told to value youthful ones, if in a limited fashion. Youth's cohort solidarity in action was shown by pairs rather than large groups of boys: adults only felt rather than saw the force of the corporation of the young. Nor were these boys like their peers in other missionary cultures who worked miracles and had visions (Vasconcellos, 1865, p. 71). No *fascinans tremendum* in New Spain. The Indians adults were stunned by the boys' daring, not by their sacredness, by their very human spite rather than by the "divine ire" of which the friars spoke. In the early 17th century there was apparently a clerical move afoot to have the "martyr" Cristóbal canonized (Torquemada 1969, III, p. 93; Gibson, 1952, pp. 246-7), but it never happened. From the earliest days, Aztecs were forced to celebrate their defeat by the Spaniards on the feast of St. Hippolytus; no Indians, it seems, have ever celebrated their children's victory.

Acknowledgements

I should like to thank William Christian for reading an earlier version of this work, and John Davis for helping shorten it for publication.

Notes

1. These servant-master teams continued together, reappearing as companions in the missionary effort. See for example Antonio and Juan below.
2. In less dense missionary areas lower-class and elite children sometimes were

interned together, leading to the emergence of the former in leadership positions, as complained of below.

3. One way of studying this problem would be a scientific rather than edifying examination of early charitable institutions, to determine who were their beneficiaries.

4. The theme of rapacious Spanish laymen attacking Indian rights which were defended by the clergy was, of course, propagated by an interested clergy. But there is no doubt that it was often true. Thus the boys often stayed in the monastery to avoid impressment by the Iberian laity, sometimes encouraged by their fathers. See most strikingly Espediente, (1883, pp. 472, 495).

5. As in Europe, so here in Mexico the friars were "fathers of the poor," and thus took in much of the restitution, which they were then held to re-distribute to the needy.

6. "Llevando los frailes en su compañia los niños y mozuelos que criaban y enseñaban, hijos de los mismos indios señores y principales, que para aquello les daba Dios fuerzas de gigantes, ayudándoles tambien de la gente popular los que ya estaban y se querian mostrar confirmados en la fe", Mendieta (1971, p. 227).

7. Motolinia (1970, pp. 66-7, 262) describes a dramatic demographic situation where the *macehuales* males had no one to marry because the principals monopolized all the marriageable women.

References

Acosta, Jose de, S.J., 1954: *Obras*, Madrid (Ediciones Atlas).

Aiton, A., 1927: *Antonio de Mendoza. First Viceroy of New Spain*. Durham (Duke University Press).

Boxer, C., 1978: *The Church Militant and Iberian Expansion, 1440-1770*. Baltimore (Johns Hopkins University Press).

Camargo, Diego Muñoz, 1892: *Historia de Tlaxcala*. Mexico (Oficina Tip. de la Secretaria de Fomento).

CDHM, 1858-66: *Colección de documentos para la historia de México* (Joaquín García Icazbalceta, ed.) 2 vols., Mixico.

Chronicles of Michocán, The, 1970: (Eugene R. Craine and Reginald C. Reindorp trans. and eds). Norman (University of Oklahoma Press).

Cortés, Hernan, 1871: *Escritos Sueltos*. Mexico (I. Escalante y Ca).

Cuevas, Mariano, 1921: *Historia de la Iglesia en México*, 2 vols. Tlalpam, D.F. (Impr. del asilo "Patricio Sanz.").

Duran, Diego, O.P., 1967: *Historia de las Indias de Nueva España e Islas de la Tierra Firme*, 2 vols. Mexico (Editorial Porrua).

Duviols, Pierre, 1971: *La lutte contre les religions autochtones dans le Pérou colonial. 'L'Extirpation de l'Idolâtrie' entre 1532 et 1660*. Paris (Institut Français d'Etudes Andines).

Espediente promovido por Nuño de Guzman. . . contra Fray Xoan de Zumárraga (1529), 1883: In *Colección de documentos inéditos, relativos al descubrimiento, conquista y organización de las antiguas posesiones españolas de América y Oceanía*. vol. 40. Madrid (Manuel G. Hernandez).

Focher, Juan, O.F.M., 1960: *Itinerario del misionero en America*. Madrid (V. Suarez).

Gibson, Charles, 1952: *Tlaxcala in the Sixteenth Century.* Stanford (University Press).

Gibson, Charles, 1964: *The Aztecs Under Spanish Rule.* Stanford (University Press).

Greenleaf, Richard, 1961: *Zumárraga and the Mexican Inquisition.* Washington (Academy of American Franciscan History).

Höltker, Georg, 1930: Die Familie bei den Azteken in Altmexico. *Anthropos* **25**, 465-526.

Mendieta, Geronimo, O.F.M., 1971: *Historia Eclesiastica Indiana.* Mexico (Editorial Porrua).

Motolinía, Toribio, O.F.M., 1856: *Traduccion de las vidas y martirios que padecieron Tres Niños Principales de la Ciudad de Tlaxcala.* In *Documentos para la historia de Méjico.* ser. 3, vol. I, 1-27.

Motolinía, Toribio, O.F.M., 1970: *Memoriales e Historia de los Indios de la Nueva España* . Madrid (Ediciones Atlas).

NCDHM: Nueva colección de documentos para la historia de México, 1886-92: (Joaquín Garcia Icazbalceta ed.), 5 vols. Mexico.

Nuttall, Zelia, 1933: *Documentos referentes a la destrucción de Templos e Idolos; Violación de Sepulcros y las remociones de Indios e idolos en Nueva España durante el siglo XVI.* Mexico (Editorial Cultura).

Othón de Mendizábal, Miguel, 1976: In *Rebeliones indígenas de la época colonial* (Ma. Teresa Huerta and Patricia Palacios eds.). Mexico (Sep. Inah).

Pérez de Ribas, Andrés, S.J., 1944: *Paginas para la Historia de Sinaloa y Sonora. Triunfos de nuestra santa Fe entre gentes las más bárbaras y fieras del Nuevo Orbe,* 3 vols. Mexico (Editorial "Layac").

Phelan, John, 1956: *The Millenial Kingdom of the Franciscans in the New World.* Berkeley (University of California Press).

Procesos de Indios idolatras y hechiceros, 1912: (L. Gonzalez Obregon ed.). Mexico (Archivo General de la Nacion).

Ricard, Robert, 1933: *La 'conquête spirituelle' du Mexique.* Paris (Institut d'Ethnologie).

Sahagún, Bernardino, O.F.M., 1949: *Colloquios y doctrina.* In *Sterbende Götter und Christliche Heilsbotschaft* (G. Kutscher ed.). Stuttgart (W. Kohlhammer).

Sahagún, Bernardino, 1950: *Florentine Codex. General History of the Things of New Spain,* vol. I, Santa Fe (School of American Research).

Soriano, W. Espinoza, 1963: La Guaranga y la reducción de Huancayo. Tres documentos ineditos de 1571 para la etnohistoria del Peru. *Revista del Museo Nacional* (Lima) **32**, 8-75.

Soustelle, Jacques, 1961: *Daily Life of the Aztecs on the Eve of the Spanish Conquest.* Stanford (University Press).

Thoonen, Francis, 1930: Conversion of Parents through the Children. In *Les Conversions. Compte-Rendu de la Huitième Semaine de Missiologie de Louvain.* Louvain (Editions du Museum Lessianum).

Torquemada, Juan de, O.F.M., 1969: *Monarquia Indiana,* 3 vols. Mexico (Editorial Porrua).

Trexler, Richard, 1980: *Public Life in Renaissance Florence.* New York and London (Academic Press).

Trueba, Alfonso, 1959: *Fray Pedro de Gante.* Mexico (Editorial Jus).

Vasconcellos, Simão de, S.J., 1865: *Chronica da Companhia de Jesu do estado do Brasil.* Lisbon (A.J. Fenandes Lopes).

Zorita, Alonso de, 1963: *The Lords of New Spain. The Brief and Summary Relation.* (Benjamin Keen, trans. and ed.). London (Phoenix House).

True Buddhism and Village Buddhism in Sri Lanka

Martin Southwold

The terms *gamē Buddhagama* and its literal English translation "village Buddhism" are regularly used by Sinhalese themselves. They signify the kind of Buddhism supposed to be characteristic of villagers (*gamē minissu*) — or, as we might say, in Redfield's[1] sense, "peasants". Village — or "peasant" — Buddhism is assumed to be homogeneous and distinctive. This is part of a folk model apparently shared by all Sinhalese; reality is rather less tidy.

Some people go further than this: they state plainly and emphatically that village Buddhism is not true Buddhism, it is a corruption of Buddhism, even that it is not Buddhism at all. Several people actually told me that I was making a grave mistake in studying village Buddhism, and if I meant to persist I ought at least to find out what true Buddhism is. When I asked how I might do this, I was referred to works issued by the Buddhist Publication Society — with which, as it happened, I already had familiarity. Others told me that the true Buddhism exists only in books — I failed to ask them which books. Still others indicated that true Buddhism is manifested in practices which I knew, and they knew, are more typically supported by non-villagers than by villagers. In the ordinary sense this is also a folk model, though not of the common folk. Those who express it either are, or seem to be seeking to be, non-villagers — which is to say members of an élite. I shall resist the temptation to term it a *herrenvolk* model. It is more compelling than it might be because it is endorsed by a quantity of literature, much of it erudite.

Gombrich must have had a similar experience, for he writes of "the frequency with which I had been told, by books and by people, that Sinhalese village Buddhism was corrupt" (Gombrich, 1971, p. 45). He goes on to explain why he thinks that judgment is mistaken. In particular he

137

takes up for vehement dissent some remarks from one of the books —
remarks that he considers worth a digression because they "are typical of a
view of traditional Buddhism by no means confined to scholars and
Europeans, but common also to English-educated Sinhalese" (ibid., p. 51).
The book is *Exorcism and the Art of Healing in Ceylon* (1954) by Paul
Wirz, an amateur though accomplished ethnographer. The remarks,
referring to Sri Lanka, are: "In reality, it is the same here as in other
Buddhist countries; only very few comprehend the true Buddhist dogma in
its real profoundness; the rest are Buddhists in name only, among them also
a great part of those who wear the yellow gown [i.e. the Buddhist
clergy]..." (Wirz, 1954, p. 236; Gombrich, 1971, p. 50).

Gombrich asks sardonically what might be "the true Buddhist dogma"
which Wirz comprehends so much better than many Buddhist monks. He
suggests that Wirz probably picked it up from English-educated Sinhalese
and their European mentors, among whom he mentions two German
monks. One of these was the founder of the Buddhist Publication Society,
which publishes booklets and a journal, mainly in English and largely by
European authors. These people in turn got their views largely from the
work of nineteenth-century European scholars who studied the Buddhist
scriptures. Among these Gombrich mentions Neumann, Rhys Davids, and
Max Müller: quoting from the last a passage in which he writes of seeking
Buddhism's "earliest, simplest, and purest form as taught by the Buddha
and his immediate disciples".

The gentle irony of Gombrich's style makes his scepticism evident. He
goes on to state that the modern Buddhism that has been formed in this way
is something new, rather than a Buddhist revival; and to wonder whether its
bearers "are not heading towards the first genuine syncretism in Ceylonese
Buddhist history". (In this paragraph and the last I have summarized
Gombrich, 1971, pp. 54-6.) By the end of his book he is not merely challenging
the conventional wisdom but, behind a heavy academic smokescreen,
standing it on its head: for he concludes with the sentence: "If this is
popular Buddhism, could it be that *Vox populi vox Buddhae?*" (1971, p.
327).

This account, severely compressed as it is, may give some idea of how
complex and confusing the situation is, and indicate the various questions
we have to sort out if we are to get beyond a vague but cosy consensus that
villagers are vulgar.

(1) Whose allegations, that village Buddhism is not true Buddhism, are
we considering: those of English-educated Sinhalese, or those of the
authors, mainly non-Sinhalese, of books? If both, are we sure we can
disentangle the one from the other?

(2) On what grounds, in terms of differences between the two
Buddhisms, are these allegations based? Are the differences based in facts,

and facts properly interpreted? How do such grounds relate to motivations for making the allegations?

(3) What is the ontological character of the true Buddhism with which village Buddhism is compared? Has it reality only, as some say, or mainly, in books, i.e. pious compositions? If so, are the allegations merely a truistic, but tendentious, comparison of myths and professions with practice? What is the actual place of such books in a religion, and Buddhism in particular?

(4) If this true Buddhism is largely a product of Europeans and their pupils, does the contrast between it and village Buddhism have any bearing on the relationship between high theology and popular religion in a purely Buddhist civilization? Before Europeans muddied the waters, was there actually such a relationship, and if so what was it?

Constraints of space prevent me from offering adequate answers to all these questions; which is as well since, partly from not having clearly perceived the matter in this way when I was in the field, I do not have adequate answers to all of them. But the list may serve at least to articulate the answers I shall offer.

I must point out that my account is over-simple and somewhat idealized. I have tried to distinguish two varieties of Buddhism and to associate them with two distinct classes of Sinhalese; but in reality the distinctions are not sharp and the association far from perfect. What Gombrich called "modern Buddhism", and I call "true Buddhism", has in fact considerably influenced the Buddhism of villagers, as Malalgoda pointed out in his review of Gombrich's book (Malalgoda, 1972, pp. 160-4); hence my account of village Buddhism abstracts those of its features where such influence is least apparent. Again, my data do not fully warrant the generalizations I offer. My account of village Buddhism is based mainly on my observations in a few villages in one small area of Sri Lanka (in Kurunegala District); while much of what I report is clearly common, I have little doubt that there are villages in which the pattern of Buddhism differs in important respects. My knowledge of the Buddhism of the non-villager élite is unsystematic, since this is not what I set out to study, and my observations derive largely from conversations with people I happened to meet both in the rural area where I was doing fieldwork and elsewhere. My pupil, Mr Mark Hodge, who has since made an admirable study of the varieties of religion and their association with social class in a southern Sinhalese town, tells me that my account of the Buddhism of the non-villager élite is too simple, though broadly correct: in reality their Buddhism commonly has more of the features of "village Buddhism" than I (or my informants) acknowledge. But these points, had I space to develop them, would only strengthen my criticism of the widespread assumption that village Buddhism is not true Buddhism.

It may have been noted that the self-styled "true Buddhism" is firmly rooted in books, all of which are dependent, more or less directly, on some very special books, those of the Pali canon, the Theravada Buddhist scriptures. This is — or rather, has usually seemed to be — an inescapable consequence of any attempt to discriminate a true from a less true Buddhism. Buddhism has never had a Pope empowered to declare the true doctrine; indeed the lack of any decisive structure of authority in the Sangha, the community of clergy allegedly founded by the Buddha to continue his teaching, has been a major factor throughout Buddhist history (cf. Tambiah, 1976; Dutt, 1962, p. 28; etc.) From time to time, though not recently, councils of senior clergy have been called to decide questions in dispute or in doubt; but these have always lacked autonomous authority. The decisive source of legitimate authority has always been taken to be the word of the Buddha; and since that word is unknowable if not from the scriptures (or the oral compositions which preceded their reduction to writing), authority has been located in the scriptures. Declarations of the true Buddhism have therefore always been either tendentious or derived from the scriptures. That the latter implies the former we shall have to expose. My immediate purpose is to remark that contentions that village Buddhism is not true Buddhism cannot be assessed, though they are sometimes presented, without reference to the scriptures.

"By books and by people"... Gombrich characterizes the people who disparage village Buddhism as "the English-educated Sinhalese". I would describe my own observations in slightly different, though consistent, terms. Those who most regularly and predictably told me that village Buddhism is not true Buddhism were Sinhalese who speak English and who are, *ipso facto*, members of the "national élite"[2] (Roberts, 1974), the self-styled "middle class". Others who did so had occupations which might be called "lower middle class" and were socially ambitious; though not members of the middle class they may be surmised to have it as a reference group. But I must not exaggerate the social determination of such views. I knew people objectively similar to those in this second category whom I never heard disparage village Buddhism; and my surmise that those who did are those who have the middle class as a reference group is not independent of my recognition of the kind of Buddhism they professed. This kind of Buddhism, marked by disparagement of village Buddhism and by certain other characteristic features to be noted, I shall, for the sake of brevity, refer to as "élite" or "middle class Buddhism". Descriptively, these terms are not quite exact, and they may well be considered prejudicial; but in both respects they balance the counterposed term, "village Buddhism".

The books in question are expositions of Buddhism, both scholarly and popular, and descriptive accounts, both scholarly and popular, of people in Buddhist countries; most of them are written by Europeans (or Americans).

It is relevant to consider this wide range of literature, since it is the virtual consensus in all that one reads that leads one to assume, as I did when I was in the field, that the inferiority of village Buddhism is a matter not of opinion but of simple fact. I shall, however, concentrate my critical attention on modern ethnographic studies. That books of all these kinds, like books generally, are mainly written by members of élites for members of élites may not be considered irrelevant.

A common charge against village Buddhists, levelled both by books and by people, is that, contrary to Buddhism, they are heavily involved in traffic with gods and other spiritual beings. Gombrich effectively refutes this charge (1971, pp. 46-9). Remarking that, on the evidence of scripture, "supernatural beings were as much a part of the Buddha's universe as they are of a Buddhist villager's universe today" (ibid., 48), he concludes "Belief in gods like this is not logically (or otherwise) incompatible with Buddhist doctrine" (ibid., 49). I might add that in practice, if not in profession, élite Buddhists are hardly less, and sometimes more, concerned with gods than villagers are.

Another charge I heard from élite Buddhists, and discern in some of the literature, was that the Buddhism of villagers is largely a matter of rituals, whereas true Buddhism is in the mind. I found that neither in practice nor in profession did village Buddhists generally attach greater value to ritual than élite Buddhists did, and they too readily acknowledged that Buddhism is essentially in the mind — and, no less, in ethical conduct. Their involvement with ritual, such as it is, is consistent with scripture which, taken as a whole, cannot be said either to prescribe or to proscribe ritual performances.

Both these charges seem to be ill-founded, and to be useful only as evidence of the tendency or bias of those who make them. The second, however, at least hints at a difference between the two Buddhisms which I find to be real and significant — though I did not hear it explicitly elaborated as a charge against village Buddhism.

Élite Buddhists attach great value to the practice of meditation, for laymen (including women) as well as clergy. It is very common for élite Buddhist lay persons to take trouble to learn the techniques of meditation, and to claim to devote regular time to putting them into practice. Though I have no real evidence, I do not doubt their claims. Typical village Buddhist lay persons have very different attitudes. Mostly, they show not the least inclination to practise meditation; and their attitude towards its alleged practice by other lay persons, and often even by clergy, smacks of ribaldry. Time and again, when I referred to the practice of meditation, they indicated that they did not distinguish it from snoozing. I said "mostly" to accommodate a minor exception. There is a practice known as taking the Eight Precepts (*ata sil*) which involves attending all day (usually once or twice a month) at a temple, and there devoting most of one's time ostensibly, if not very evidently, to meditation. In my experience, only a few people attempt this practice, and these are mainly, and notoriously, old women. Many village Buddhists, especially men, and including some clergy, regard the practice with derision.

Everyone agrees that all clergy ought to meditate, and it is therefore not surprising that every cleric whom I asked whether he meditated told me that he did. But some neither carry, nor make much effort to carry, conviction; and Gombrich reports much the same (1971, pp. 280-1). It is in fact a matter of common knowledge, or belief, among villagers that certain clerics in the locality never meditate. Lay village Buddhists regard this as a defect, but a fairly minor one: they may go on to list his other virtues, and conclude that on balance he is a good cleric. The clerics themselves, whose claims to meditate were perfunctory, similarly drew my attention to their other good works, with no hint of self-deprecation. An élite Buddhist is quite different: if he tells you that a certain cleric does not meditate, he presents it as a horrifying indictment. He does not allow that other accomplishments may compensate; he is more likely to cite them as further evidence to depravity. Similarly, the sweeping indictments of almost all clergy that one sometimes hears from élite Buddhists refer not only to their alleged moral depravity, but also to their involvement in ritual and, of all things, social service.

There is a minority of Sinhalese clergy — amounting, according to Michael Carrithers, to nearly 800 (out of some 20 000) — who devote their whole time, so far as possible, to meditation, withdrawing for this purpose to isolated monasteries or yet more remote hermitages (Carrithers, 1980, p. 196). Adapting one of the indigenous terms for them, they may be called "the forest-dwelling monks." Gombrich remarks that they are part of the modern Buddhism which we saw to have been of largely European inspiration; and that their practice, though intended as a revival of ancient practices, may to some extent be a "pseudo-revival" (1971, pp. 283-4). It is not surprising, therefore, that élite Buddhists tend to venerate these monks, often saying that they are the only worthy clerics, even that they are the only really good Buddhists. Those whose account of "true Buddhism" does not state or imply that it exists only in books refer primarily to the practice of these monks, and the practice of laymen who support them and engage in meditation themselves.

Again village Buddhists seem strikingly different. Through failure to see clearly enough the diagnostic value of these monks, I did not ask villagers systematically how they regarded them. Some people did speak of them with respect, and I cannot say that all of these were clearly adherents of élite Buddhism. I have been told that respect for forest-dwelling monks is common in other villages. But simply from the fact that in most of my interviews and conversations they were never mentioned, I infer that at best most villagers were indifferent to, if not unaware of, them. On the other hand, often without my raising the subject, a substantial minority of my village informants, both laymen and clergy, did speak of these monks not with veneration but with withering contempt. The mildest comment, which I heard from several people was: "They say they spend their time in meditation, but how do we know what they get up to at night?" The most usual charge against them is that they are selfish; when one considers that Buddhism is directed to the eradication of all sense of self, this is indeed a damning indictment. They are also said to be futile in that, for all their austerities, they no more attain nirvana than anyone else does; and useless in that, if Buddhism had been left to them it would have died out long ago.

Though I recorded these opinions from only a minority of villagers, it was a significant minority in that its members predominantly held positions of leadership. This suggests to me that other villagers, less accustomed to be outspoken, may tend towards the same view — which is impressive both for its logic and for its orthodoxy. But the tendency, if any, is probably latent: forest-dwelling monks, like most other aspects of élite Buddhism, impinge too little on most of the village Buddhists I knew to have provoked any formulated reaction.

Probably the most serious charge against village Buddhists is that they neither seek, nor indeed really want, nirvana: for this, the authentic goal of Buddhism, they have substituted other, less worthy, goals. This is frequently stated in the literature, though I did not recognize it in what my informants said. Since their views derive, as we have seen, in large part from books, and since also this issue is logically linked to that of meditation, I suppose that some élite Buddhists, at least, have it in mind.

This charge, or at any rate judgment, is central to Spiro's analysis in his *Buddhism and Society* (1971). Though Spiro is writing primarily about village Buddhism in Burma, he asserts explicitly that his remarks are true of Theravāda Buddhism in other countries, including Sri Lanka (ibid., pp. 16, 77). He distinguishes two major varieties of Buddhism, which he terms respectively "normative" or "nibbanic" Buddhism, and "nonnormative" or "kammatic" Buddhism (ibid., p. 12); the latter corresponds to my "village Buddhism". By "normative *Theravāda* Buddhism" he says he means "the doctrines contained in the *Theravāda* canon [of scripture], which may or may not correspond with the teachings of the historical Buddha" (ibid., pp. 6-7). Doubting that the quest for the historical Buddha has been successful, he says it is irrelevant to his inquiry since for Buddhists themselves the canonical doctrines are the Buddha's teaching. "Hence, when I refer to nonnormative beliefs and practices, I do not mean those which diverge from "what the Buddha taught", but those which diverge from canonical doctrine" (ibid., p. 7).

In Spiro's "normative" or "nibbanic" Buddhism, life — ordinary worldly life — is characterized as suffering (*dukkha*); and ordinary man is doomed to endless suffering, since rebirth delivers one from death into further life. There is only one escape from the suffering of life and from the wheel of rebirth, and this is nirvana: this must be sought single-mindedly.

> ... Physical retreat from the world is not sufficient... Salvation can only be achieved by a total and radical rejection of the world in all its aspects. Nibbanic Buddhism... demands no less.... For nibbanic Buddhism, then, the true Buddhist is the world-renouncing monk... [they] alone are sons of the Buddha (ibid., pp. 65, 64).

In popular Buddhism, however, "the religion of an unsophisticated peasantry" (ibid., p. 66), i.e. "nonnormative" or "kammatic" Buddhism, the goal has changed. Its followers seek not the cessation of rebirth but a better rebirth, for they believe that life can be happy (ibid., p. 67). "... the Burmese do not aspire to nirvana" (ibid., p. 78), but feeling guilty about this they say that they do want it eventually. "They have not rejected nirvana, they merely — like St. Augustine in the matter of celibacy — wish to defer it" (ibid., p. 79).

"The Burmese, of course, are not the only *Theravāda* Buddhists for whom a pleasurable rebirth is preferable to nirvana. All our evidence indicates that this preference obtains throughout the *Theravāda* world" (ibid., p. 77). Spiro cites several other writers who have reported the same preference. He did not of course cite Gomrich, whose book was published so soon after his own that neither refers to the other. Oddly though, in view of what we have seen of his assessment, Gombrich has a paragraph which reads like a paraphrase of Spiro's judgment, so closely do his words resemble his, even to the analogy with St. Augustine: "But most Sinhalese villagers do not want *nirvana* — yet. They are like St. Augustine who prayed 'Make me chaste and continent, O Lord — but not yet'" (Gombrich, 1971, pp. 16-17; St. Augustine, *Confessions*, VIII, p. 7). But Gombrich contrasts the goals and beliefs of village Buddhists with those of the Buddha himself.

On one crucial point, Spiro is definitely wrong. In his review of the book, Gombrich remarks that Spiro equates his "nibbanic Buddhism" with "normative Buddhism", defined as the doctrine of the Pali canon, and points out that he is apparently unaware that "kammatic Buddhism" is canonical too (Gombrich, 1972, p. 491). It had been a general conclusion of Gombrich's own book that the village Buddhism he had observed in Sri Lanka was "surprisingly orthodox" (Gombrich, 1971, p. 40). By "orthodox" he meant "that the doctrines of the villagers would have been approved by Buddhaghosa [the definitive compiler and most orthodox expounder of the Canon] and that most of their religious practices would have been familiar to him and his contemporaries" (ibid., pp. 45, 43);

"surprisingly" because of the frequent statements that village Buddhism is corrupt, his assessment of which we have reviewed. ". . . the Buddhism we can observe today is like the Buddhism of the Pali Canon. . ." (ibid., p. 56).

As an eminent Orientalist, Gombrich may be presumed to know what the canonical scriptures actually say: and he tells us that they endorse both of two kinds of Buddhism which both he and Spiro perceive as radically different. There is no one canonical doctrine. Tambiah goes further when he writes:

> . . . it must be stated at the outset that the canonical texts of Buddhism (just as the Bible of Christianity or the core texts of any other religion) are complex and rich in meaning, full of redundancies and variations, and by the same token paradoxical, ambiguous, and capable of different levels of interpretation at various points. . . any perspective that naively assumes that there are certain unambiguous prescriptions and value orientations in Buddhism from which can be deduced behavioral correlates that bear an intrinsic and inherent relation to the religion is inaccurate, usually misguided, and sometimes pernicious (Tambiah, 1976, p. 402).

It is not necessary to read much of the scriptures, without bias, to see that this is so; it is not necessary to read any to see that it must be so. If one attends to the circumstances in which, and the purposes for which, scriptures are produced, it is evident that they are composed, by a mixture of selection from legendary traditions and pious invention, to legitimate the religious views and practices of those who write them and those for whom they are written.[3] When a religion has been adopted by a civilization, these views and practices will be as various as the conditions of its members, and will demand either an equal variety of scriptures, or else a scripture which can be as variously interpreted; and every group or category which the Church cannot afford to lose will have its legitimating scriptures canonized. If the scriptures are composed exclusively by an élite category, as the Buddhist scriptures were by monastic clergy, they may be biased towards an élitist form of religion; but if the masses are needed to support the élite, their ways will not be left without legitimation.

Though not wrong, Spiro's description of the scriptural canon as "normative" seems to me misleading. In talking about Buddhism, village clergy frequently, and laymen occasionally, will remark "as Lord Buddha said" or "as scripture says", and usually the reference seemed vaguely familiar to me.[4] Except in formal sermons, however, they seem never to quote (or rather translate) verbatim, nor was I ever given chapter and verse. Only once, when I directly challenged a cleric for his authority for an odd-sounding statement, was I even given the title of a book, and that was commentarial not canonical. I often argued with clerics, and sometimes demanded their authority for odd-seeming views or practices: their references to scripture were usually vague, and sometimes hardly appropriate. On one controversial matter, I know a scriptural passage which warrants their practice far more clearly than what they actually alluded to. Village clergy have read scriptures during their training, and surely sometimes read them after ordination; but they do not possess, indeed could not possess, more than a small part of the voluminous canon. My impressions correspond closely with what Malalasekera wrote:

> Even today great respect is shown to the man who carries all his learning in his head... And the person who trusts to books for reference is contemptuously referred to as "he who has a big book at home, but does not know a thing". Anyone visiting a village monastery in Ceylon at the present time will find the ... books... wrapped up in... cloths and packed in... bookcases, that the faithful devotees may offer to them flowers and incense and thus pay honour to the Buddha's word. The monk is expected to carry all his learning in his head. (Malalasekera, 1928, pp. 45-6; quoted in Ling, 1973, p. 176)

Certainly the scriptures are revered and are drawn upon in learning and teaching Buddhism; but, except in esoteric and inconclusive controversies among the more erudite monks (cf. Malalgoda, 1976, especially chapter IV), and in sermons, they are drawn upon for authority in only the most general, even cursory, manner. It is Spiro, not ordinary Buddhists (at least in Sri Lanka), who regards the scriptures as normative in a discriminating sense; and their attitude appears more prudent than his.

But if the scriptures say too much, and the Buddha, for all we can really know, too little, it is not to be denied — and no village Buddhist does deny it — that nirvana is the proper goal of Buddhist striving. It certainly appeared to me, as it did to Spiro, Gombrich, and many others, that village Buddhists show little real interest in attaining nirvana, but very much more in achieving a better rebirth. The most learned of the village clergy whom I knew well once remarked to my wife "I am not in any hurry to attain nirvana":[5] in which he only made explicit what is more or less evidently implicit in the attitudes of all village Buddhists. Are they not justly compared to St. Augustine in his insincere prayer for chastity? In fact this is not the case: we see that St. Augustine was insincere because he knew that he might have chastity without delay if he really wanted it. But this is not the case with village Buddhists and nirvana: they know, or at least they say, that nirvana cannot be attained without delay, not in fact until the coming of the next Buddha, Maitrī, in the very remote future. We, of course, who know that nirvana can be attained quite soon, may infer that they only say this *because* they do not want it. Or is this tendentious?

The issue relates to a basic, and I think unique, doctrinal difference between the two varieties of Buddhism. Elite Buddhists often say, and seem regularly to assume, that nirvana can actually be attained. I was told by a number of them that if a man is spiritually and intellectually able, and applies himself diligently to the quest, he should be able to attain nirvana within his present lifetime; and that even people like oneself, who may be starting with spiritual or other handicaps, could expect to attain within the next two or three rebirths. Others seem to be less confident, but would certainly regard attainment after seven more births as entirely feasible. By contrast, it is standard doctrine among village Buddhists — I often heard it asserted, and never denied[6] — that no one will, or can, attain until the next Buddha comes. They further state that the last person who did attain in Sri Lanka was a monk they describe as a contemporary of a king who actually lived just over two thousand years ago.[7]

Now if this doctrine is sound, village Buddhists must be acquitted of the charge against them. If nirvana cannot be attained for thousands of births to come, it would be senseless to seek to attain it sooner; and from not so seeking there can be no inference that one does not want it. The rational course would be to seek patiently through many rebirths to improve one's condition, that when Maitri at last comes one will be qualified to be among the many who will then attain. Which is precisely what village Buddhists say they are doing, and I think they are sincere.

Similarly, if their doctrine is sound, so too is the attitude of village Buddhists to meditation. In scripture, as in everyday teaching, the way to the attainment of nirvana is the Eightfold Path. Its eight stages are commonly grouped under three heads: the first two are grouped as wisdom, the next three as morality, the remaining three as meditation (Gombrich, 1971, p. 70; Spiro, 1971, p. 44). Whether or not the stages are to be understood as sequential is a matter of debate, with learned authorities supporting both interpretations. Spiro says that scripture does not indicate any sequence, and that it was Buddhaghosa who first ordered the stages in three sequential groups (1971, p. 44). There is clearly ample authority for the sequential interpretation. If it is accepted, and if nirvana is far off, then major application to meditation is appropriate for the future; and village Buddhists are right virtually to equate, as they often do, their religion with moral understanding and practice. Conversely, the great concern of élite Buddhists with meditation implies their supposition that the attainment of nirvana is within reach.

I never asked élite Buddhists why they thought nirvana quite attainable, for the answer seemed to me perfectly obvious. The scriptures make it plain not only that the Buddha urged his hearers diligently to seek nirvana, but also that many thousands of them did attain in the same birth — some, indeed, instantaneously. But I did ask village Buddhists why they thought otherwise, and they regularly replied by citing the Buddha's prediction that after his death the spiritual capacities of his followers would steadily decline, so that Buddhism would die out altogether after 5000 years.

Gombrich remarks that this formulation derives from Buddhaghosa: canonical scripture has the Buddha forecasting the disappearance of Buddhism after only five hundred years! (Gombrich, 1971, p. 284, note 28). Thus on the crucial issue of doctrine village Buddhists have sound authority; hence they must be acquitted of improper indifference to nirvana and to meditation.

Merely to acquit, however, seems to me a travesty of justice: it is not only that village Buddhists have reason, but also that élite Buddhists are in want of it. If people can attain nirvana within one to four, or at most eight successive lifetimes (linked by rebirth); and if at most periods (especially the last two lifetimes) there have been devout monks following the vocation of the forest-dwellers; there should by now be scores, if not hundreds, of those who have attained. Where, then, are they? I found that élite Buddhists became distinctly uncomfortable, and evasive, when I asked them if they knew anyone who had attained; the most confident answer I got was from one man who said he knew one monk whom he thought, but was not sure, had attained. I must say that this hard empirical argument was never explicitly offered to me by a village Buddhist: but it may have been suggested by the clerics who, in criticizing the forest-dwelling monks, insisted it is a fact that no-one, but no-one, attains nirvana.

A similar conclusion is implicit in the criticism, which is quite explicit, that forest-dwelling monks are selfish. By Buddhists and by non-Buddhists, from the earliest times of which we have knowledge, the doctrine of *anatta* has been seen as the most distinctive feature of Buddhist thought, to which it is logically central. Nirvana is often defined as the complete realization of its truth. It says that the assumption of separate individuality is the fundamental error. Hence I reason, as many other have, that the attainment of nirvana as a separate individual is a contradiction in terms. The cleric who most forcefully criticized the forest-dwelling monks to me also said in a sermon that Lord Buddha could have attained nirvana thousand of births before he did, but chose instead to wait until he could bring others with him. Even the most sober of the canonical scriptures report that, for the same reason, he postponed his complete attainment until death overtook him. It is understandable that élite persons, who in general are not best known for their concern to share their benefits with the masses, should find it hard to grasp this basic point.

Less abstrusely, élite Buddhists seem to have stumbled over a naive confusion. In large part the scriptures characterize the Buddha — Gotama — as a superhuman being (*mahāpurisa*); in part they characterize him as a gifted but essentially normal human being. The historical Buddha — Gotama who actually lived in north India — was, of course, a normal human being. Misled by Max Müller and the like, élite Buddhists have identified the historical Buddha, of whom we know next to nothing, with the Buddha (or rather one of the Buddhas) of scripture, and have reasoned that since with him nirvana was readily attainable, so too it is with us. It is like arguing, in another religious tradition, that since the founding ancestors were incestuous, so too should we be. The stories that thousands attained nirvana in his lifetime belong not to history but to the superhuman myth. As a Buddha is a supernormal being, 88 cubits tall, flying through the air, and so on and so on, so too is the period of his lifetime a supernormal period. That thousands attained nirvana in the lifetime of Gotama Buddha, as thousands will in the lifetime of Maitri Buddha, was written not to show that we too, living in normal time, can attain, but just the opposite. As in other religious traditions, the perfection of holiness, which for Buddhists is nirvana, is not of time but of eternity. The point of myths that it entered time, like the Christian myths of the Creation and the Incarnation, is not to tell secular history, but sacred: it is to say that the holy is immanent in the world, not to deny that it is transcendent. In "the religion of an unsophisticated peasantry" (Spiro, 1971, p. 66) this is not misunderstood.

We see then that where village Buddhism actually does differ from élite Buddhism, it is at least equally sound by the criterion of canonical orthodoxy, and by every other criterion far more sound. The élite Buddhism of today is not the true Buddhism, but itself a corruption of Buddhism, which village Buddhism does not appear to be. What of the past, before European scholars corrupted Buddhism?

One thing at least seems clear: that the evaluation of forest-dwelling monks which I found among villagers has been standard through most of Buddhist history. Rahula, a learned Sinhalese cleric, tells us that after the decisions of a conference of Sinhalese clergy over two thousand years ago, two vocations for clergy came to be distinguished (Rahula, 1956, pp. 158-60). One, called the vocation of books, which denoted the learning and teaching of the doctrine, came to be closely identified with those clergy known as *grāmavāsi*, i.e. dwelling in villages and towns; the other, known as the vocation of meditation, came to be closely identified with the *araññavāsi*, the forest-dwelling monks (ibid., pp. 159, 196, 197 n.1). ". . . of the two vocations, [that of learning and teaching] was regarded as more important than [that of meditation]. . . almost all able and intelligent monks applied themselves to [the former] while elderly monks of weak intellect and feeble physique. . . devoted themselves to [the latter]" (ibid., p. 160). Rahula opines that this evaluation "is in keeping with the spirit of the Master [*sc.* Buddha]" (ibid., p. 193). Dutt tells us that at the earliest period to which the scriptures bear clear witness, the settlements of monks were normally located in towns and villages (Dutt, 1962, p. 54); and that while there was a minority of monks known as "forest-dwellers", ". . . they are not regarded in [scripture] as necessarily the best specimens of monkhood" (ibid., p. 161). He relates this to the basic charter of Buddhist monachism, attributed by scripture to the Buddha himself: who, we are told, enjoined his disciples to go out and teach the common people (ibid., pp. 22, 35), and to depend on their alms for support, being forbidden otherwise to support themselves. There was thus a profound difference from Christian monasticism: "Isolation from society was never the cue of Buddhist monachism" (ibid., pp. 25-6). I should add that my village clergy explicitly identified themselves as following the "vocation of books", i.e. of learning and teaching, and contrasted it with the "vocation of meditation".

In traditional Sinhalese society, as in other Buddhist societies, there certainly was an élite, or élites, both secular and religious — the clergy, more especially those of the major monasteries supported by royalty. Whether its members were in the habit of disparaging the common people, as is not uncommon among élites everywhere, I cannot say: for I have not felt it my business to study the large body of literature they have left. I think it unlikely that the religious élite was in the habit of actively disparaging the religious commonality. For village Buddhism was the product of the village clergy, themselves equally members of the egalitarian Sangha with the most eminent monks; and, if my experience and Gombrich's today are evidence, village clergy effectively kept their flocks within the extensive bounds of orthodoxy. No doubt the Buddhism exhibited in books, or some of them, was purer, and to that extent more true, than the Buddhism exhibited in practice: for this is one of the things that sacred books are for. But we can hardly suppose that clergy produced such books in order to disparage village Buddhism: had that been their aim they would hardly have produced others which legitimate it. It was the social fragmentation and cultural syncretism of colonial society that produced a middle class which was insecure enough to need to disparage the common people, and confused enough to do so in a religious idiom. I think it unlikely that similar conditions prevailed in traditional society.

Acknowledgements

I am grateful to the Social Science Research Council for a Research Grant, No. HR 2969/1, which supported the fieldwork on which this paper is based.

Notes

1. Redfield, *Peasant Society and Culture* (1956)
2. I have simplified the distinction between two élites as Roberts actually applies it. I

have identified the national élite with those who are fluent in English; he would probably categorize most of my English-speaking informants as of the "local élite". My usage reflects the perceptions of these people themselves, rather than the objective discrimination of a sociologist viewing Sinhalese society as a whole.

3. It would take another paper, not to say book, to give the grounds for this judgment. I formed it first from reading New Testament Criticism. As authorities for its application to Buddhist scriptures, I cite Thomas (1949), Frauwallner (1956) and Dutt (1962, chapters 2 and 3).

4. I had read extensive selections from the scriptures (in translation), though mostly many years earlier: so my own recollection was vague. But anything like a direct quotation would have been recognizable, if only from the stilted diction of the scriptures. I often debated points of doctrine with clerics, and was never overwhelmed by superior erudition: which may suggest that their command of scripture was as poor as my own.

5. From my knowledge of this cleric, I am sure he was deliberately trailing his coat: he often made statements which he knew would jolt the usual views of Europeans and would give him an opening to explain Buddhism as he understood it.

6. Gombrich reports that some of the clergy he interviewed were less positive, holding that to attain is possible if highly improbable; he implies that these show some influence from what I call "élite Buddhism" (1971, pp. 285-6).

7. I put it this way because both the monk — Maliyadeva — and the King — Dutugamunu — are in ordinary discourse figures of legend rather than of history; as Gombrich rightly says of Maliyadeva, "most people are very vague about when he lived" (1971, p. 285).

References

St. Augustine: *Confessions.*

Carrithers, Michael, 1980: Letter in *Man* (N.S.) **15**, 195-6.

Dutt, Sukumar, 1962: *Buddhist Monks and Monasteries of India.* London (Allen and Unwin).

Frauwallner, Erich, 1956: *The Earliest Vinaya and the Beginnings of Buddhist Literature.* Rome (Is. M.E.O.).

Gombrich, Richard F., 1971: *Precept and Practice: Traditional Buddhism in the Rural Highlands of Ceylon.* London (O.U.P.).

Gombrich, Richard F., 1972: Buddhism and society *Modern Asian Studies,* **6, 4**, 483-94.

Ling, Trevor O., 1973: *The Buddha: Buddhist Civilization in India and Ceylon.* London (Temple Smith).

Malalasekera, G.P., 1928: *The Pali Literature of Ceylon.* Colombo (M.D. Gunasena).

Malalgoda, Kitsiri, 1972: Sinhalese Buddhism: orthodox and syncretistic, traditional and modern (review article of Gombrich, 1971). *Ceylon Journal of Historical and Social Studies* n.s., **II/2**, 156-60.

Malalgoda, Kitsiri, 1976: *Buddhism in Sinhalese society, 1750-1900.* Berkeley (University of California Press).

Rahula, Walpola, 1956: *History of Buddhism in Ceylon: the Anuradhapura period, 3rd century B.C.-10th Century A.D.* Colombo (M.D. Gunasena).

Redfield, Robert, 1956: *Peasant Society and Culture.* Chicago (University of Chicago Press).

Roberts, Michael, 1974: Problems of national stratification and the demarcation of national and local elites in British Ceylon *Journal of Asian Studies* **XXXIII, 4,** 549-77.

Spiro, Melford E., 1971: *Buddhism and Society: a Great Tradition and its Burmese Vicissitudes.* London (Allen and Unwin).

Tambiah, S.J., 1976: *World Conqueror and World Renouncer.* Cambridge (Cambridge University Press).

Thomas, Edward J., 1949: *The Life of the Buddha as Legend and History* (3rd ed.). London (Routledge and Kegan Paul).

Wirz, Paul, 1954: *Exorcism and the Art of Healing in Ceylon.* Leiden (E.J. Brill).

The Attempted Reform of South Indian Temple Hinduism

C.J. Fuller

In South Indian temples dedicated to the god Śiva, rituals are in theory prescribed by one or another of a set of sacred texts known as the Āgamas, which are believed to have been dictated by Śiva himself and to contain his directives for his own worship.[1] The reform of temple Hinduism discussed in this paper centres upon an attempt to ensure that the rituals are conducted strictly in accordance with Āgamic stipulations and, to this end, that the priests and other officiants in the temples are properly versed in the texts. This may appear a straightforward and reasonable aim. But in fact it is not and I believe that the attempted reform, as my title implies, must fail. Why this is so provides the substance of this paper. I also discuss some of the reasons why the reform is being attempted, but in this short paper my discussion is necessarily incomplete.

South India, particularly the state of Tamilnadu, is renowned for its vast temples, which play a central role in the religious life of the Hindu population. Virtually all these temples are dedicated either to Śiva or to Viṣṇu, the two great gods of modern Hinduism, and their respective consorts, or to gods associated with Śiva, such as his son Murukaṉ (Skanda). My own research was carried out in one of the largest and most popular of Tamilnadu's temples, the Great Temple in the city of Madurai, which is popularly known as the Mīnākṣī temple and is dedicated to the goddess Mīnākṣī and her husband Sundareśvara. Sundareśvara is a form of Śiva and Mīnākṣī is thus a form of Devī and Śakti, the consort of Śiva.

The rituals in temples dedicated to Śaiva deities such as Murukaṉ are, like those of Śiva himself, in theory governed by the Āgamas.[2] In Vaiṣṇava temples, rituals are in theory prescribed by another body of texts, the Saṃhitās, believed to have been revealed by Viṣṇu; I shall not discuss them here, although much of my argument, *mutatis mutandis*, does, I believe, apply equally to them. In all temples, both Śaiva and Vaiṣṇava, the most vital ritual activity is worship (pūjā), which can be divided into three broad categories. First, there is the daily worship inside the temple, mainly performed before the deities' immoveable stone images. Secondly, there is the cycle of festivals (utsava), which mainly involve processions of the deities' moveable metal images. I refer to these two types of worship as "public worship"; they are said to be performed for the benefit of the world. The third type is "private worship" (referred to in the temples as arcana), performed by or on behalf of an individual devotee, who alone is intended to benefit from it.[3] Some private worship consists only of very simple offerings that can be made by devotees themselves, but all more elaborate private offerings have to be made by the priests. All public worship, without exception, can be carried out only by priests, assisted by other ritual officiants (Fuller, 1979, pp. 460-1).

In Śaiva temples, like the Mīnākṣī temple, the priests (bhaṭṭa; Tam. paṭṭar) belong to the Ādiśaiva or Śivācārya subcaste of Brahmans (ranked below all non-priestly Brahman subcastes). In any particular temple, however, only priests with hereditary rights in that temple can work there. These rights, more precisely, are rights to perform specific parts of the public worship, and different priests may have different rights, allocated by different rotas, within the one temple. However, all priests with rights of any kind in the public worship are equally entitled to perform private worship, which is how, through devotees' payments, they earn the vast majority of their income today (Fuller, 1979, pp. 462-4). In 1972, the legal basis of the priests' hereditary rights in Tamilnadu was changed by an Indian Supreme Court ruling, but this has not, so far, made any practical difference to the position of the incumbent hereditary priests (cf. Presler, 1978).

Those who have demanded that the priests be properly versed in the Āgamas, and have vigorously denounced their alleged ignorance and incompetence, have often proposed that all priests, even though they are hereditary, should be trained in the Āgamas and certified as competent before taking up their positions. Indeed, in 1964, the Tamilnadu government's Hindu Religious and Charitable Endowments Department, which now has most of the major temples in the state under its control, introduced service rules stating that priests and other officiants must have certificates from institutions for Āgamic training before they took up posts.[4] These rules, however, never seem to have been enforced and in fact it would have been impossible to do so properly, as I shall now explain.

I begin with the Āgamas themselves. There are said to be 28 fundamental Āgamas (mulāgama), the oldest of which are believed to date from the third to seventh centuries A.D., as well as some 200 secondary Āgamas (upāgama). Two fundamental Āgamas, the Kāmikāgama and the Kāraṇāgama, are generally thought (possibly incorrectly) to be authoritative in most of the South Indian Śaiva temples. All the Āgamas, fundamental and secondary, were written in Sanskrit. In addition to the commentaries upon them, there are also a number of Sanskrit manuals (*paddhati*), which deal especially with the rituals, providing instructions and explanations for them by systematizing the Āgamas' directions and eliminating some of their inconsistencies. The oldest extant manual is probably Somaśambhu's (11th century), but the most important is Aghoraśiva's (12th century). The latter depends heavily on the former, but it is much more detailed and has long been regarded as authoritative in the majority of Tamilnadu's Śaiva temples, to such an extent that in many of them, it is said that no-one now knows which Āgama is supposed to govern the ritual (Brunner-Lachaux, 1963, p. xxi).[5]

Probably the most important sociological and historical fact about the Āgamic literature — in which I include the Āgamas, their commentaries and the ritual manuals — is that it is nowadays largely unknown. It is not mentioned, let alone discussed, in many standard works on Hinduism and only in recent years has it been studied seriously, mainly by a few scholars attached to the Institut Français d'Indologie at Pondicherry, in South India. The total quantity of their work remains small, but it has revealed the general outline of Āgamic writings on ritual and this is now fairly clear.[6]

The handful of scholars with any knowledge of the Āgamas are scarcely outnumbered by traditional, indigenous experts. My informants in Madurai mentioned only three priests in the whole of southern Tamilnadu whom they considered as proficient in the Āgamas, although I am reliably informed that the competence of even these three is mainly confined to ritual method. They have little real knowledge of the Āgamas themselves, a qualification possessed by a minuscule number of priests in the region. Of the three priests mentioned by my informants, I have met two. Both are hereditary priests in Śaiva temples (one near Madurai and the other near Tiruchchirappalli) and both originally learnt much of what they do know from their fathers, from whom they also inherited quite large collections of Āgamic works. The sons of neither of them, however, have any interest in Āgamic ritual and both priests are therefore the last of a family line.

The knowledge of one of the priests is, though, being transmitted to the pupils in the school (*pāthaśālā)* of which he is the *guru*.[7] This school, in a village near Tiruchchirappalli, is run under the auspices of the Kanchipuram Śaṅkarācārya's monastery. (I return to the importance of the Śaṅkarācārya below.) All the pupils are the sons of hereditary Śaiva priests from Tamilnadu temples and there are, at any one time, about 30 boys enrolled. They come at the age of 12 or 13 to stay for a six-year, full-time course, on which they learn how to conduct the temple rituals by learning relevant passages from the Āgamic literature. This part of the course amounts to about half the curriculum and is taught by the *guru* of the school. The other half, taught by a Brahman not of the priestly subcaste, is devoted to the learning of Vedic passages and the study of various classical Sanskrit texts. A small amount of time is given over to Tamil religious works. The boys receive no education in other subjects in the school or elsewhere, and are therefore unqualified for any secular post.

The school is entirely traditional in its organization and teaching methods. The pupils mainly learn by memorizing passages exactly. The passages, whose words, pronunciation and scansion must all be memorized absolutely accurately, are learnt by listening to the teachers, not by reading books; there is, in the Hindu tradition of exact oral transmission, no substitute for a *guru*. Only when a passage has been fully memorized do the teachers explain its meaning. The *guru* defended this method forcefully, saying that no student can understand a piece properly until he has committed it fully to memory. When I visited the school, the *guru* asked his pupils, singly or in groups, to recite a number of different passages, which they mostly did with impressive ability. However, I do not know how much the pupils understood of the meaning of what they learnt, and it is certainly the case that even if they graduate as competent priests, able to recite many Sanskrit passages correctly, they remain inexpert in the Āgamic literature itself.

Even this brief description should show that traditional Āgamic ritual cannot be learnt quickly and easily. Altogether, there are a mere handful of Āgamic schools in Tamilnadu and thus there could only be, at best, a very slow increase in the number of proficient priests. Most pupils return to work in their temples at the end of the course and I doubt if many of them devote much time to further study. Only one young priest in the Mīnākṣī temple has taken the full six-year training in this school, although the son of another is now enrolled there. Of the 56 priests working more or less regularly in the temple in July 1980, apart from the one just mentioned, about a dozen have taken short courses, lasting a few months, in Āgamic ritual. On these, they have learnt the basic *mantras* (sacred chants) and ritual procedures, and a small amount of the relevant theology, but they have not, of course, acquired any real expertise. The rest, the majority, have had no training at all. In most temples, the evidence seems to suggest, the proportion of priests who have had any kind of Āgamic training tends to be lower than in the Mīnākṣī temple, and there can be no doubt that the majority of priests in Tamilnadu have had none.

It is improbable that this situation could be radically altered and it would certainly be impossible to provide all temple priests in Tamilnadu with a proper training in the rituals, let alone in the Āgamic literature itself. In the first place, there are simply not enough experts who could provide the tuition. Secondly, any programme would obviously need a great deal of financial support, which is unlikely to materialize. Further, it seems extremely unlikely that more than a minority of priests or their sons would actually be capable of following a full-time course of several years successfully and, in any case, the most intelligent and able of modern priests' sons tend to pursue an ordinary college education, in order to try to qualify themselves for a more secure, highly-paid prestigious job outside the priesthood. It is difficult to see how this trend could possibly be reversed in modern India. At the very best, the only practicable scheme would appear to be a more extended use of short courses to provide a minimal Āgamic training, but even these could hardly be arranged for all temple priests unless many more teachers could be found.

There are, however, further and ultimately even more intractable problems that arise out of the fact that neither the Āgamas nor the ritual manuals actually contain the kind of explicit liturgical instructions, that priests and others commonly suppose them to contain. I cannot demonstrate this fully in a short paper. However, the important point is that the precise form of the rituals performed in a temple is defined by a number of criteria: the identity of the images to be worshipped on different occasions, the order in which they are to be worshipped, the materials and food-offerings to be employed in their worship, the organization of the festival processions, etc. It is certainly possible that these multifarious details — some specific to one temple and some shared with all Śaiva temples — originally derived from a particular Āgama or manual. But it seems more than likely that many alterations have been made over the centuries and nowadays the details are stored in the memories of priests and other officiants; the putative original texts are not consulted. Moreover, much of the detailed description in the ritual manuals now available to us is almost completely unknown to the priests and finds no correlate in the rituals as actually performed. In the case of festivals, many have no Āgamic description known to any of the priests and the textual referents for them that are quoted mainly pertain instead to mythology.

It is worth mentioning parenthetically that this situation does not accord well with Goody's suggestions about the role of texts in religion, which, he argues, tend to have a conservative function; orthodoxy in ritual or dogma is preserved, to a considerable extent, by adherence to authoritative texts (1968, pp. 14-15). In fact, in the Tamilnadu temples, conservatism in the ritual is nowadays preserved mainly by the institution of heredity, for most of the liturgical lore of the temples is contained in the memories of untrained priests and other hereditary officiants, who pass it into their heirs. The texts, whatever their original role may have been, have now become tools in the hands of those demanding changes, as attention is drawn to the gap between practice and Āgamic precept. I would suggest that such a role is probably common for the sacred texts in literate, world religions and that they therefore frequently fail to possess the conservative function emphasized by Goody.

To return to particulars: a very high proportion of the stanzas in Diehl's summary (1956, pp. 95-148) of sections from Aghoraśiva's manual or in Somaśambhu's (which is similar to the former but is available in Brunner-Lachaux's scholarly translation (1963, 1968, 1977)) are not about the details that are seen by the priests and other temple personnel as most crucial in the temple's ritual practice.[8] Much more fully described in the manuals are the elaborate preparations to be made before worship itself is begun. These involve extensive rites of purification, before the invocation of Śiva into his *liṅga*, his phallic icon, is carried out. Only after his divine form has been properly invoked and established is worship of him performed. The ritual is completed by a series of rites of exit.[9]

This very brief summary of the manuals' instructions does not in itself show why exact adherence to them is, in any objective sense, infeasible. The first reason is practical; it is plain that the preliminary rituals prescribed would, if carried out fully, take several hours. That this is so is generally known by the priests. Worship in the Mīnākṣī temple, which is not atypical in this respect, begins at five in the morning. The officiating priests would certainly have to rise by two or three o'clock were they to complete the preliminary rituals, and it is scarcely surprising that none of them does. The second reason is theoretical and more fundamental, and has to do with the fact that, according to the texts, much of the ritual, including almost all the key parts, is accomplished mentally, exclusively or in part, and involves the transformation of immaterial substances and entities. For example, the invocation of Śiva is principally achieved through meditation upon his qualities, in which the recitation of *mantras*, the use of hand-gestures known as *mudrās* and the performance of other ritual manoeuvres, shape or support the mental act, but do not cause or delimit it. Śiva is only invoked and made present if the worshipper (in the temple, the priest), through his concentrated mental powers, succeeds in invoking and making him present.

In the Mīnākṣī temple at least, an explicit ritual of invocation is generally not carried out. This aside, however, any attempt to perform it by adhering closely to the manuals' instructions would present some severe difficulties. First, the instructions on Śiva's invocation are, by any standards, arcane and would certainly be incomprehensible to anyone lacking a reasonable knowledge of the premises upon which they rest. Secondly, given that the invocation is a process of immaterial transformation, in which the pure spirit that is the god is brought into an incorporeal "body" created through the recitation of *mantras*, and given that it is mainly carried out by mental means, it is impossible for an observer to decide whether the invocation has been accomplished and, therefore, whether the ritual has been done in accordance with textual direction.

Moreover, there are further difficulties presented by the concept of devotion (*bhakti*). In modern Tamil Hinduism, the stress placed upon devotion to the god is all-pervasive and the accurate performance of rituals is not considered sufficient to make them efficacious in the absence of adequate devotedness on the part of the worshipper. In Āgamic doctrine itself, the position is less clear-cut, for different texts reflect a variety of views on the relative importance of devotion, although ritual exactitude is always insisted upon. In one sense, however, Āgamic doctrine on this issue is irrelevant, in so far as it is generally held today that devotion is all-important, so that virtually everyone believes that priests must have true devotion in order to perform the rituals efficaciously. But this is clearly untestable, for no observer can possibly determine whether a priest has or has not performed his task with adequate devotedness. The observer might conclude, not unreasonably, that if a priest completes the preliminaries to worship in two minutes by mumbling sounds vaguely approximating to Sanskrit, he has not brought any real measure of devotion to the work in hand. But the sceptical observer cannot prove his suspicion and indeed his scepticism depends upon a false inductive procedure, in which the observable physical actions are taken to be crucial, when the whole point is that they are not.

At this stage, let me sum up my argument so far. It is that the demand that priests should be trained in the Āgamas and carry out the rituals according to their direction is effectively impossible, not only for various practical reasons, but also because the Āgamic texts do not contain detailed instructions about the rituals that are today perceived as the core of temple worship and festivals, and because they are, in many places, esoteric or inscrutable. Further, because of the emphasis placed on mental processes (and devotion), any external, objective testing of priests' real competence in the rituals, which would depend on their "inner state", is impossible. For all these reasons, the reformists' demands are misconceived.

Before considering why such a misconceived reform is being attempted, I must make it clear that many of the priests themselves, in line with Āgamic doctrine, insist upon the necessity of performing the rituals accurately according to Āgamic prescription. The two more proficient priests that I referred to above both stressed this point and both asserted that rituals "incorrectly" performed, as most are, could not work and were a waste of time. Their view was shared by many of the priests in the Mīnākṣī temple, some of whom even explained the problems of modern India as being due to the neglect of Śiva's proper worship.[10] However, all the priests were well aware that rituals in the temple were never done strictly according to Āgamic directions or, more exactly, according to what they themselves understood to be Āgamic directions.

A problem obviously arises here: why do the priests adhere to this position, but continue to perform rituals incorrectly? My priestly informants try to resolve the difficulty in the following way. In the first place, they say that they are not responsible for their errors; the fault lies with the officials of the temple administration, the Devasthanam, who continually interfere in their activities and have systematically undermined their status and authority in the temple. The officials, they claim, have made it impossible for priests to carry out their work properly, and they contrast the contemporary situation with the period before 1937, when the Mīnākṣī temple was not under governmental control.[11] In those days, claim the priests, rituals usually were carried out properly. None of the evidence, to my mind, suggests that this golden age ever existed. However, the priests like to believe that it did, because it fits with their attempt to shift the blame for their own behaviour onto the despised officials. In the second place, the priests assert that they themselves are truly devoted to Mīnākṣī and Sundareśvara, and that the god and goddess know this and know too that it is not their fault that the rituals all go wrong. Not infrequently, they say that the god and goddess will eventually punish the officials, the real malefactors. This latter line of argument, in the devotionalist rather than ritualistic stream of Hinduism, allows the priests to insist that their genuine devotion outweighs their continual ritual malpractice.

Nevertheless, the priests do not all appear fully convinced by their own arguments, and quite a few of them, when questioned, seemed to me to be worried about the gap between what they do and what they believe the Āgamas lay down. Some of the older and more pessimistic priests, in particular, express their fear that Śiva might eventually take revenge for his neglect on them as well as others. More generally, the priests think that they ought to reform themselves, not least to be better able to withstand the threats from outside to their position. These views are not peculiar to the Mīnākṣī temple priests; as others have noted before, temple priests in South India collectively display considerable demoralization and lack of self-confidence, not least because they have internalized the reformists' criticisms without managing to do anything very positive to improve themselves (Presler, 1978, p. 123; Srinivas, 1966, p. 135). Their failure in this respect provoked, from a few of my priestly informants, some bitter criticism of their colleagues, particularly those who have reacted to their situation with cynicism or indifference, and take next to no interest or care in their work. The priests, therefore, do not try to defend themselves in the way that I have implicitly suggested that they could, namely by arguing that the reformists' demands are misconceived.

I now turn to the question of why the demand for reform is being made. The answer has much to do with the history of temples and their officiants in Tamilnadu during the last 50 years or so. Over this period, governmental supervision of temples in the state has steadily expanded and most of the major temples are now under the control of the Tamilnadu government's Hindu Religious and Charitable Endowments (H.R. & C.E.) Department. There has consequently been a relentless movement towards centralized control, which has meant too that temples, to a very considerable extent, have now become bureaucratic organizations in which more and more power over finance and personnel, and in some measure ritual arrangements as well, is located in the hands of administrative officials appointed by the H.R. & C.E. Department.[12]

The desire to stamp out corruption amongst trustees and managers has been one of the most important ostensible motivations of all attempts made to control temples by elected Indian governments and legislatures in Madras and Tamilnadu, before and since Independence in 1947. Though less far-reaching, earlier measures by the British rulers of the region and by the local kings who preceded them had similar aims. However, the priests, who have never been popular with the general public and have, for centuries, been castigated for their alleged extortion, have also been in the reformists' sights. In more recent times, there has been as well a reiterated complaint that most temple priests are incompetent, the cause of which undoubtedly cannot be explained fully except in the context of all the criticisms made of the priests. In concentrating attention in this paper on the one complaint, I am therefore, even if unavoidably, somewhat misrepresenting the overall picture.

In the case of the Mīnākṣī temple, the first overt attack on the priests' competence appears to have been voiced in 1931, when the District Judge of Madurai wrote to the temple administration to complain and suggest remedies.[13] Nothing came of these at the time, but since Independence, the volume of criticism has become much greater. Presler (1978, pp. 115-6) remarks that H.R. & C.E. Department officials often defend their policies on the grounds that most priests are inept, and I have heard supporters of the temple administration say much the same thing in Madurai. The Department, since the 1950s, has turned its attention to the problem several times and, as I noted above, tried in 1964 to introduce certificates of competence for newly-appointed priests. It has also run short courses in Āgamic ritual to give some basic training to otherwise ignorant priests. It is these courses that some of the Mīnākṣī temple priests have attended.

In its efforts, the Department has been actively supported by the Śankarācārya of Kanchipuram, who is one of the successors of the Hindu philosopher Śankara (9th century) and is head of the Śaiva monastery in Kanchipuram, the holy city near Madras. At present, there are actually two Śankarācāryas, an old man and the young man appointed as his successor. The elder has probably been the most influential and respected religious figure in Tamilnadu for several decades, and he and now his successor are revered by many Tamils, particularly members of the educated elite (cf. Singer, 1972, pp. 195, 241-2). Both Śaṅkarācāryas have repeatedly insisted on the need for priests to be competent in the Āgamas, so that they can perform the rituals correctly and they have arranged the tuition on courses run by the monastery and the H.R. & C.E. Department. As mentioned above, the monastery runs a school near Tiruchchirappalli for the sons of priests and it may have one or two others as well. The young Śaṅkarācārya has announced his wish to found more such schools (*The Hindu*, 28.1.77). From time to time, he has also arranged conferences for priests to discuss their problems and to draw attention to their need for training. The priests' attitude towards the Śaṅkarācāryas is ambivalent. On the one hand, they appreciate their sympathy for their difficulties and some of them are willing to take advantage of the courses and schools run by the monastery. On the other hand, there is an ancient rivalry between priests and monks, related to the ambiguous opposition between the Brahman householder and the ascetic renouncer, a category that includes the monk (see, e.g. Biardeau, 1972, pp. 80-88; Heesterman, 1964). This is specifically referred to by the priests, who must all be married in order to be consecrated and carry out their duties, when explaining their dislike of the Śaṅkarācāryas' criticism and their resentment at alleged interference by them in temple affairs. Some of them accuse the Śaṅkarācāryas of exploiting their influence and popularity to try to gain a foothold in the temples, and they are certainly seen by many priests as a serious potential threat to their position, especially because of their cooperation with the H.R. & C.E. Department. Clearly, when a respected figure like the Śaṅkarācārya complains about priestly incompetence, it probably carries much more weight in the public's mind than do similar strictures from bureaucratic officials.

Popular attitudes and governmental policy towards the priests are greatly complicated in Tamilnadu by the strength of the anti-Brahman movement. I cannot discuss this here (cf. remarks in Fuller, unpublished data; Kennedy, 1974: 280-8; Presler, 1978), but must instead consider briefly the wider context, for developments within Tamilnadu are part of a pan-Indian movement to purify and reform Hinduism in all manner of ways, which is usually considered to have begun in Bengal in the early nineteenth century.[14] The reform of temples is one aspect of this broad and disparate movement. Modern thinking on temples is well-illustrated by the *Report* of the Indian government's Hindu Religious Endowments Commission, published in 1962. The Commission surveyed temples and other religious institutions throughout the country, and found that priestly incompetence and scriptural ignorance were almost ubiquitous. It concluded that the situation was much better in the government-controlled temples of South India than elsewhere, although no region was deemed wholly satisfactory (*Report*, 1962, pp. 47-52, 163).

The Commission's recommended remedy was that all priests should be properly trained in the Āgamas or other relevant sacred texts, before being allowed to work in the temples. It also argued that if rituals in the temples were performed accurately, they would necessarily be efficacious and therefore that they must be performed by proficient priests (*Report*, 1962, pp. 42, 45, 57-59; cf. Derrett, 1968, pp. 500-2). The emphasis on ritualism in the *Report* is striking and I find it rather surprising that the Commission apparently placed so little faith in the worshippers' devotion when considering the efficacy and purpose of ritual. As a quasi-judicial body, the Commission's legal logic was perhaps more attuned to ritualistic detail than to illimitable devotion. Be that as it may, very important in the formation of the Commission's views was, almost certainly, the influence on it of modern case-law. For the law on temples, partly owing to a number of important judgments in which they have been referred to, the Āgamas have become crucial yardsticks, despite the obscurity of their contents and the judiciary's evidently slight knowledge of them.[15] Since Independence, their significance has been further enhanced by the influence of the Indian Constitution's clauses guaranteeing freedom of religion, in the legal definition of which the content of texts (such as the Āgamas) plays a crucial, if not always determining, role.[16]

Westernization and Christianity have undoubtedly been vital in the development of modern Hinduism, but it would be wrong, as Derrett for example notes, to deny the extent to which modern reformism is, in many ways, thoroughly traditional (1968, pp. 458, 481). However, there are important new factors, particularly the emergence of educated, partly-Westernized elites at the national and state levels, which are conscious of what they see as the "public interest", and which are hostile to so-called superstition and parasitism upon the true religion that alone receives Constitutional protection. That the most vigorous reformers, members of these elites, do not really represent the views of the masses, who display little evident interest in reform, seems overwhelmingly clear (Derrett, 1968, p. 483). Dumont notes the tendency of modern Hindu reformers to perceive popular Hinduism as a degraded form of a superior religion (1970, p. 10) and Derrett remarks upon the "paternalistic interference with the religion of others" by the Hindu upper classes, whose

> relatively intolerant Hinduism ... derives from two sources, their own westernization which has imparted to their outlook a discrimination which previously was not felt, and their consciousness that in due course the example which they themselves set as the prestige-holding class should draw the others to their point of view. (1968, p. 62)

In other words, the modern elites which have emerged wish to eliminate the "impurities" from the religion and apparently expect that they will eventually persuade the masses of the necessity and benefit of such a reform. This aspect of modern Hinduism, which I do not suggest characterizes the religion as a whole, does seem apparent in the attempts to bring the major religious institutions under governmental and judicial control, so that corruption and incompetence amongst the officiants and trustees, which are believed to damage the religion itself, may be minimized. For the major Tamilnadu temples, as I have noted above and explained in more detail elsewhere, this has resulted in a steady expansion of centralized control (Fuller, unpublished data). We can now see, however, that this process is not occurring only at the organizational level; it is also proceeding — or is rather being attempted — at the liturgical level. A uniform liturgical system is sought to be imposed by endeavouring to bring the ritual of all the Śaiva temples in the region into line with the directions of the Āgamas, the only true standards for ritual practice because they alone embody Śiva's commands. Ritual centralization, hand in hand with organizational centralization, is therefore the means to the purification of temple Hinduism.[17]

In this paper, I have tried to show that the demand for ritual reform, as it has been expressed, is replete with illogicalities. But these are not apparent to most of the reformers themselves, because they lack any real critical knowledge of the Āgamic texts. Their attitude is close to that characterized by Geertz as "scripturalist" (1970, pp. 60-61), for they insist on the unqualified truth of the Āgamas *per se*, not on the truth of the Āgamas' real contents, of which they know little. The net result is not so much religious reform as a chimerical reformism, whose most marked social consequence to date, at least within the temples themselves, appears to have been the progressive demoralization of the hereditary priests. Most of what I know about Tamil temples I have learnt from the priests of the Mīnākṣī temple and this paper is certainly not meant to be read as yet another attack on them. In the final analysis, it is probably true that the priests have a much less complete ignorance of the texts than most of those who are so critical of them.

Acknowledgements

Field research in the Mīnākṣī temple was conducted for 12 months in 1976-77 (supported by the Social Science Research Council) and for another 2 months in 1980 (supported by the British Academy Small Grants Research Fund in the Humanities). I thank both organizations for their financial support; I also thank my informants and assistants in Madurai, participants at the A.S.A. conference for their comments, and two Āgamic experts, Mr N.R. Bhatt and Mme Hélène Brunner, for invaluable information provided in personal correspondence from them. All errors of fact and interpretation remain, however, entirely my own reponsibility.

Notes

1. Names of gods, titles of texts and ritual terms are nearly all transliterated from their Sanskrit forms. (Tam. = Tamil.)
2. "Śaiva" and "Vaisnava": of or pertaining to Śiva and Visnu respectively.
3. This "private worship" is not to be confused with the personal or private worship performed at home, the *ātmārthapūjā* classically contrasted with the public worship (*parārthapūjā*) of the temples (cf. Brunner-Lachaux, 1963, p. xxii, note 10).
4. Referred to in *Seshammal* v. *State of Tamil Nadu*, (1972) 3 S.C.R. 815, p. 819. Such certificates are, in terms of Āgamic doctrine, an absurdity, for a man should not be consecrated as a priest by his *guru* unless he has learnt the Āgamas properly. However, no such qualification is actually demanded before consecration in modern temples.
5. In the Mīnāksi temple, the ritual is said to be governed by the Kāmikāgama, with some reference to the Kāranāgama, and Aghoraśiva's manual is treated as authoritative.
6. On the Āgamas, see particularly Brunner (1975-6) and also Brunner-Lachaux (1963, pp. i-ix, xx-xxiii).
7. This school is very similar to the schools teaching only the Vedas described by Subramaniam (1974, pp. 54-67). Some of the Vedic schools are also supported by the Śankarācārya's monastery.
8. Somaśambhu's manual covers the *ātmārthapūjā*, not the *parārthapūjā* (see note 3 above; Brunner-Lachaux, 1968, p. ii). However, the fundamental structure of the two types of worship is similar and the differences between them are unimportant when discussing the matter as broadly as I do in this paper.
9. Brunner-Lachaux (1963, pp. xxvi-xxviii) summarizes, in rather more detail, the main stages of Śiva's worship as described in Somaśambhu's manual.
10. The preservation and prosperity of the kingdom is, in the Śaiva tradition, dependent on the grace of Śiva, the fruit of his proper worship in the temples. The king is the patron of the worship and the protector of the temples, and uncorrected errors in the rituals will, according to Āgamic doctrine, endanger the king, the priests and the people in general (cf. Brunner-Lachaux, 1968, p. 254, note 1).
11. In 1937, the Mīnāksi temple was placed under the control of an Executive Officer appointed by the Hindu Religious Endowments Board, established by the then Madras government. It has remained under the control of Executive Officers to this day, although since 1951 they have been appointed by the state government's Hindu Religious and Charitable Endowments Department, the Board's more powerful successor. For more details, see Fuller (unpublished data).
12. The modern history of governmental control over the Mīnāksi temple, and its consequences, are discussed in Fuller (unpublished data). For more general discussion of the relation between temples and the government in Tamilnadu, see Appadurai and Breckenridge (1976), Baker (1975; 1976, pp. 58-63) and Mudaliyar (1976).

13. Referred to in the judgment in *Sri Meenakshi Sundareswarar Devasthanam* v. *M. Subramania Bhattar*, O.S. 6 of 1947, Madurai District Court.
14. For very general, modern surveys of Hinduism and its reform in the last two centuries, see, e.g., Gonda (1965, pp. 358-406) and Zaehner (1966, pp. 147-92).
15. The most important cases in this respect are: *Sankaralinga Nadan* v. *Rajeswara Dorai*, (1908) I.L.R. 31 Mad. 236; *Gopala Muppanar* v. *Dharmakarta Subramania Aiyar*, (1914) M.L.J. (Rpts.) 27, 253; *Sri Venkataramana Devaru* v. *State of Mysore*, (1958) S.C.R. 895; *Seshammal* v. *State of Tamil Nadu*, (1972) 3 S.C.R. 815. The apparent learning of the judgment in Gopala Muppanar's case, cited as authoritative in Sri Venkataramana Devaru's and Seshammal's cases, is questionable; the Āgamic manual quoted, the Nirvacanapaddhati, is certainly not "frequently referred to" as the judge stated and is unknown to contemporary Āgamic scholars.
16. On religion and the Constitution, see Derrett (1968: chapter 13) and Mukherjea (1970: chapter 8).
17. In Tamilnadu, it has even been suggested that centralization should be taken to the point of establishing an "ecclesiastical organization", which would provide all prospective priests with a proper training (Presler, 1978, pp. 108-9). No organization of this kind has ever existed in Hinduism and it is to be doubted whether it will ever come to pass, but its very suggestion testifies to the thinking of at least some reformers. I should note here that governmental control over temples is firmest in South India, whereas in some areas of North India it scarcely exists at all. My concluding arguments are meant to apply only to Tamilnadu, although I believe that they may be pertinent for some other parts of India as well.

References

Appadurai, A. and Breckenridge, C.A. 1976: The South Indian temple: authority, honour and redistribution. *Contributions to Indian Sociology* (N.S.) **10**, 187-211.
Baker, C.J., 1975: Temples and political development. In *South India: Political Institutions and Political Change 1880-1940* (by C.J. Baker and D.A. Washbrook). Delhi (Macmillan).
Baker, C.J., 1976: *The Politics of South India 1920-1947.* Cambridge (Cambridge University Press).
Biardeau, M., 1972: *Clefs pour la pensée hindoue.* Paris (Seghers).
Brunner-Lachaux. H., 1963: *Somaśambhupaddhati, pt. I: Le rituel quotidien.* Pondicherry (Institut Français d'Indologie).
Brunner-Lachaux, H., 1968: *Somaśambhupaddhati, pt. 2: Rituels occasionnels I.* Pondicherry (Institut Français d'Indologie).
Brunner, H., 1975-6: Importance de la littérature Āgamique pour l'étude des religions vivantes de l'Inde. *Indologica Taurinensia* **3-4**, 107-24.
Brunner-Lachaux, H., 1977: *Somaśambhupaddhati, pt. 3: Rituels occasionnels II.* Pondicherry (Institut Français d'Indologie).
Derrett, J.D.M., 1968: *Religion, Law and the State in India.* London (Faber & Faber).
Diehl, C.G., 1956: *Instrument and Purpose: Studies on Rites and Rituals in South India.* Lund (Gleerup).

Dumont, L., 1970: *Religion, Politics and History in India.* Paris (Mouton).

Fuller, C.J., 1979: Gods, priests and purity: on the relation between Hinduism and the caste system. *Man* (N.S.) **14**, 459-76.

Fuller, C.J., unpublished data. The government and the temple: the Madurai Mīnākṣī temple priests 1937-1980. Paper for 7th European Conference on Modern South Asian Studies, London, July 1981.

Geertz, C., 1970: *Islam Observed.* Chicago (University Press).

Gonda, J., 1965: *Les Religions de l'Inde,* vol. 2. Paris (Payot).

Goody, J., 1968: Introduction. In *Literacy in Traditional Societies* (J. Goody, ed.) Cambridge (Cambridge University Press).

Heesterman, J.C., 1964: Brahmin, ritual and renouncer. *Wiener Zeitschrift für die Kunde Süd- und Ostasiens* **8**, 1-31.

Hindu, The. Madras daily newspaper.

Kennedy, R., 1974: Status and control of temples in Tamil Nadu. *Indian Economic and Social History Review* **11**, 260-90.

Mudaliyar, C., 1976: *State and Religious Endowments in Madras.* Madras (University Press).

Mukherjea, B.K., 1970: *The Hindu Law of Religious and Charitable Trusts* (3rd ed.). Calcutta (Eastern Law House).

Presler, F.A., 1978: The legitimation of religious policy in Tamil Nadu. In *Religion and the legitimation of power in South Asia* (B.L. Smith, ed.) Leiden (Brill).

Report of the Hindu Religious Endowments Commission (1960-2). 1962. New Delhi (Government of India).

Singer, M., 1972: *When a Great Tradition Modernizes.* London (Pall Mall Press).

Srinivas, M.N., 1966: *Social Change in Modern India.* Berkeley (University of California Press).

Subramaniam, K., 1974: *Brahmin Priest of Tamil Nadu.* New Delhi (Wiley Eastern).

Zaehner, R.C., 1966: *Hinduism.* London (Oxford University Press).

Authority and Enthusiasm:
the organization of religious experience in Zulu Zionist churches

Jim Kiernan

Writers on the Independent Church movement in Southern Africa have drawn attention to the proliferation of offices in these churches, a development which is particularly noticeable in those churches which are styled Zionist, and have suggested that the emergence of elaborate hierarchies serves the purpose of maximizing opportunities for the exercise of leadership, thus compensating "for the loss of such leadership opportunities in the political and administrative spheres" (Pauw, 1960, p. 77). Sundkler observed that in each church there is "a definite system of rank, with well-defined tasks assigned to the subordinate in respect of his immediate superior and of the higher ranks in the hierarchy" (1961, p. 138). In his survey of churches in Soweto, Johannesburg, West points to the variety in leadership hierarchies and provides a number of typical hierarchies in tabular form, for example, Archbishop, President, Vice-President, Ministers, Deacons, Evangelists, Preachers (1975, p. 70). By his own admission, such hierarchies are incomplete, for he mentions (ibid., p. 69) "the office of *umgosa* or Steward (sometimes referred to in English as 'Doorman' or 'Porter') which is not usually listed in the ecclesiastical hierarchy". Though less specific, Sundkler is much nearer the mark when he contends that 'even between each minister and his little flock, there stands a more or less elaborate system of office-bearers, who have to be controlled, and through whom the minister must control his flock" (1961, p. 139). It was at this level of the congregational unit under a minister that I studied Zulu Zionists in KwaMashu, Durban, in the late 1960s. There were 22 of these groups, each with a membership ranging from seven to 34, in which women were at least twice as numerous as men. The offices of minister, deacon, evangelist, preacher and steward were all to be found in these groups and, since all these offices were held by men, it was not unusual to

169

find that all the men of a congregation or band were office-holders. To be added to and accommodated somewhere within this hierarchy was the office of *umkhokheli* or "class leader" (of which there were two or more per band[1]) which could be held by women. Furthermore, the wives of office-holders were ordained along with their husbands and, at mid-weekly meetings at which no men were present, were entitled to wield the authority appropriate to their husband's position. From all of which it is quite clear that more than adequate provision was being made for the exercise of leadership and authority.

Yet Zionist churches essentially profess and exhibit a religion of the "spirit", a term which in its Zulu rendering (*umoya*) connotes breath, air and wind. And the "spirit", in its various manifestations, is inspirational and random in its choice of vehicle and promotes freedom of expression on the part of the individual adherent. The "spirit" of itself is not restrained or contained. The experience of a typical small group gathering fulsomely exhibits this freedom of expression in prophetic proclamations and denunciations, in trance, visions and glossalalia, in witnessing, in vigorous dancing and other exuberant, even violent, forms of movement, in deafening and raucous sound. The quality of this entire experience is best described as enthusiasm; throughout the meeting there is a release and expenditure of tremendous energy so that at the end participants are drained and completely spent. Moreover, they conduct themselves as people possessed, in the sense of being taken up and wholly preoccupied by some commitment greater than themselves which eventually squeezes them dry. It is surprising that nowhere in the literature on the African Independent Churches is the term enthusiasm employed to characterize the religious experience. The most that some writers concede to it is the designation "emotionalism". But on the basis of being repeatedly enveloped by the Zionist religious experience, though without surrendering myself to it, I would claim that there is more than mere emotionalism involved and that Zionism is experienced as an enthusiastic abandonment of self-control.

We are now faced with the paradox that a religion, whose fundamental expression lies in free and uninhibited sensory experience, utterance and movement, should be overstaffed with officials whose function it is to order, arrange, manage and control various aspects of that experience. That Zionism should exhibit such a curious blend of authority and enthusiasm is no great mystery. It can be accounted for by historical precedents. A Dutch Reformed minister in a little-known village situated about halfway between Durban and Johannesburg was attracted to Pentecostalism which he attempted to graft on to the Dutch Reformed religion. When the White Afrikaners of his parish rejected this innovation he introduced it to his Zulu parishioners who immediately embraced it and subsequently developed it in their own way (Sundkler, 1976, 13ff.). This first Zulu Zion was established in 1904 and, since all the Zionist groups of my study traced connections in one way or another back to the leading men of this new departure, it will be clear that from its inception up to the present Zionism combined elements of Dutch Reformed authoritariaism with the freedom in the Spirit so characteristic of Pentecostalism. However, awareness of how this organizational paradox arose historically does not significantly advance our understanding of it, particularly since Weber was strongly of the opinion that authority and rationality were at enmity with the enthusiastic and the charismatic. "Charisma is opposed to all institutional routines, those of tradition and those subject to rational management" (Gerth and Mills, 1967, p. 52). How then can such apparently contradictory strands as authority and enthusiasm co-exist within the same religious organization and be part of the same religious experience? For there is no doubt that enthusiastic experience and authoritative control do cohabit, on a basis that can only be described as harmonious, within these small Zionist bands. And in analysing the consequences of this odd combination, one is forced to the conclusion that, far from being at enmity, these two features complement one another in a manner so mutually accommodating as to impart to Zulu Zionism a character all its own.

There are two different organizational levels on which Zionists encounter religious experience; at the weekly meeting of the small group or band, held usually in the home of its minister, and at more infrequent and irregular larger gatherings at which a number of bands of the same and of different denominations combine in extended overnight sessions and for which the venue is not fixed. As will be seen, these occasions produce different forms of religious experience and, therefore, require separate treatment.

At meetings which are the concern of a single band, there is a partial separation of the spheres of authority and enthusiasm, so that the meeting is divided into two quite distinctive parts, with a definite break between them. The first part is a prayer and Bible service under the direct control of the leader of the group, usually a minister or occasionally a preacher. The latter part of the meeting is given over to a healing session, of which a prophet takes charge or, in the absence of a prophet, some other healing specialist. This arrangement ensures that, as far as possible, neither the minister nor the prophet transgresses upon the competence of the other.

A prophet is a charismatic person who in his or her[2] personal capacity has become a medium of the power of the spirit, which in these groups is acknowledged to be the universalist Holy Spirit of Christian tradition. By means of this power, the prophet is enabled to divine the source of an illness and to treat it and prophets are further empowered to detect hidden personal faults, which may have a bearing on an illness, and to interpret glossalalia. They are believed, therefore, to have insight into the moral and physical condition of those who come into their presence and, since there is an acknowledged connection between moral transgression and physical affliction, they are particularly well equipped to assume the leading role in healing. In this they are assisted by other grades in the healing ministry, those with the gift of tongues, who can provide inchoate clues as to the nature of an illness, and those who can engage in healing simply by praying over the afflicted. All of these healing specialists are to some degree infused with the power of the spirit which they endeavour to transmit to the sick.

The prophet conducts and directs these efforts and the collective fervour and enthusiasm which inspires them, by channelling it towards afflicted individuals in different ways, depending on how he has diagnosed and prescribed for their ailments. Having been examined and treated by the prophet in charge, they move from one healing specialist to the next, in the course of which they are vigorously pressed, or even briskly pummelled, particularly on the head, shoulders and arms by the hands and staves of their wellwishers. Now much of this enthusiasm, which is released in healing activity, has been generated in the earlier part of the meeting, that is, through the prayer and preaching of the minister. The prophet merely brings it to its peak and directs it towards a goal. Hence both minister and prophet contribute in different ways to the sequence of arousing and disposing of enthusiasm.

Moreover, both prophet and minister are also involved in different ways in the control of enthusiastic expression. Yet among their fellow Zionists, prophets are not noted for their self-restraint and are freely likened to children for their irresponsibility. As instruments of the spirit they act under compulsion and without respect for the sensitivities of others. Because prophets are unpredictable as to the timing and extent of their revelations of human foibles, other Zionists regard them with a measure of respect compounded by fear. All the more reason, therefore, for institutional checks on the exercise of their powers, since in an excess of enthusiasm they are capable of estranging members and potential members from the group. It is the minister who is entrusted with the task of controlling the prophet or prophets of his group; this is simply part of his general mandate to exercise discipline over his followers, except that in the case of a prophet, the minister is prevented from interfering directly in prophetic work because of the separation of spheres of competence. However, much of a prophet's success depends on the implementation of his recommendations for the patients who consult him and, in many cases, this calls for the subsequent active cooperation of the minister (Kiernan, 1976a, p. 358). A determined minister can bring an over-zealous prophet back into line by denying him this cooperation or by simply withholding it temporarily. The minister will almost certainly exercise this disciplinary measure when membership and group interests are at stake. There are still other ways in which the minister directly controls the ebb and flow of group enthusiasm during the earlier phases of a meeting but which do not concern the prophetic function (cf. Kiernan, 1976b).

On the other hand, prophets are not unaware of the sanctions which the minister can employ against them and are capable of registering collective dissatisfaction at their own performance. To the extent that they internalize these limitations on what they may or may not do, they exercise a degree of self-control over the eruption of their own enthusiasm and thus contribute to the regulation of group enthusiasm. Time and again, prophets have assured me that, even at the height of their inspiration, they lose neither their self-possession nor their awareness of their surroundings. A particular implication is that they remain sensitive to the manner in which patients respond to their probings and ministrations so that, if necessary, an explosive confrontation which would damage group harmony can be averted. Similarly, prophets are equally capable of detecting any flagging of group enthusiasm for the direction they wish to take in healing. Of course, prophets are not all equally adept at orchestrating an acceptable level of group enthusiasm to fit the requirements of a sensitive patient. But the effort to keep the expression of enthusiasm within acceptable bounds and to tailor those limits to the tolerance of the individual patient is most clearly displayed where inexperienced prophets are being trained by an older more reputable one. The mere fact that in some of these groups prophets undergo training or, at the very least, learn from the example of more experienced exponents, is evidence in itself that constraints upon the outbreak of enthusiasm are supplied from within the prophetic function. Thus in the course of the healing rite, the prophet Mt., a man of considerable reputation, would steer his younger colleagues away from extravagant and damaging interpretations of a patient's condition and advise them to try again — all of them, himself included, being under inspiration the meanwhile. Mt. was not averse on occasion to declaring that the cause of a complaint was "a private matter", i.e. private to the patient and therefore off-limits to enthusiastic scrutiny and group concern (Kiernan, 1979, p. 101).

These observations indicate that, obviating the possible intervention of minister or preacher, prophets themselves exercise a fairly close control over the expression of enthusiasm. Prophets do not entirely conform to the idea that Zionists have of them as being wayward, impulsive mavericks but, in practice and within their own domain of competence, they employ the kind of restraint that more properly belongs to the authoritative role of minister. The real differences between prophet and minister in this respect are that, firstly, ministerial control proceeds from an institutional endowment of the spirit acquired by rite of ordination from the acknowledged head of the church, while prophetic power is a personal infusion of the same spirit without human mediation, and secondly, the ultimate control is vested in the institutional authority of the minister. Nevertheless, there is a definite fusion and interpenetration of the roles of minister and prophet and to that extent a blurring of the distinction between the spheres of authority and enthusiasm in Zionist religious experience at the band level. This blurring effect is further compounded in those instances in which the minister and leading prophet were one and the same person (Kiernan, 1976a, p. 364). Here the same individual stepped from one role to the other and back again and, in the course of doing so, combined the exercise of both sets of control in the management of the religious experience. Only a small minority of the groups studied exhibited this specific feature but, in addition, the prophet Mt. for example, though not the leader of his group, was an ordained preacher and thus belonged to the authoritative structure of the band.

Whereas the operation of prophets and healers is provided for and demanded within the framework of a single-band meeting, it is quite disallowed at intergroup gatherings. The assembly of local bands, which could bring together as many as two hundred Zionists on occasion, has a much more fragile unity than the single cohesive band. Although members of the several bands mix together to form an audience which is divided only according to sex, these bands assert their separate identity again and again during the meeting and vie with one another in a competitive form of fund-raising. Also characteristic of the assembly is a period of witnessing, which is an informal contest in oratory indulged in mainly by ministers and others prominent in the authority structure of bands (Kiernan, 1980). The assembly is called into existence by one band and its leader offering by invitation to host the others. The host minister assumes control of proceedings but is careful to assign a prestigious task to each of the visiting ministers. Having no legitimate function in the assembly, the prophets who are present are expected to remain quiescent throughout the meeting. Yet from time to time, the prophetic impulse does erupt even in these discouraging circumstances. When it does, it is condemned as disruption and, if possible, unceremoniously quashed. But occasionally, prophecy refuses to be subdued and bursts through these restraining barriers.

I have witnessed two such occasions on which prophets got "out of hand". The first was at an annual Church Conference during the course of an ordination service. Some prophets raised a commotion near the entrance but, since they were thus capable of being confined to the periphery of the meeting, they were not able to seriously disrupt proceedings and they were no more than a momentary nuisance to the ministers and bishops involved in the ceremony. They were ushered outside where their protest eventually petered out for lack of an audience. What these prophets were protesting about never became clear; their interjection did not develop beyond the inchoate stage of glossalalia before being stifled. Of its nature, this was not an interchurch gathering, although groups representing other denominations were present as invited guests and observers, to further legitimate what was taking place.

A fuller account can be provided of the second occasion. The assembly was concerned with conducting an *ukuBuyisa* ceremony, which Zulu custom demands at the end of the mourning period in order to lay the ghost of a deceased man to rest. His children are prayed over by the healers to shield them from danger and to separate them from the possibly disturbing influence of their father. The minister of the dead man, Rev. L., took charge of the assembly.

At the appropriate moment, L. called for the children of the deceased to come forward to be prayed over. While this was going on, Deacon MK. (who had his own congregation but was technically subordinate to L.) interrupted to say: "We should have prayed for these young boys earlier, before beginning the meeting. When we prayed at home, the 'Spirit' said something will befall the boys". A prophet announced: "I had a headache to signify that something will happen to these boys. Something has gone wrong with Masuku (the dead man) himself". Masuku's brother described the difficulties he had experienced in procuring the beast for the occasion and added: "On our return we saw an accident. That is why Deacon MK. spoke as he did. There have been prayers over the sick before coming here to see us and they prophesied about a mishap which will befall the boys. Latecomers shoud be careful not to interrupt proceedings since they knew when they were to come here". L. then asked that the ministers should pray in order to avert the danger.

A second prophet opposed this. "The healers should pray again. I see an opening of danger. Let us pray again so that God gives mercy". A younger prophet added: "I have sorrow at heart and feel like going out. Let the ministers pray over water and sprinkle the premises". A woman prophet exclaimed: "What has happened to the liver of the beast?" A series of scriptural readings then followed, emphasizing divine protection and mercy and culminated in the description of the reception given to the Prodigal Son by his father (Luke 15, 21ff.). The area was sprinkled with blessed water. Masuku's brother-in-law then rose to speak: "I have been sent by my family to purify my sister by giving her a ring and the sons a blanket each, a handkerchief for my mother-in-law and one for each son, and one rand. I bring pinafore material for those attending Mrs. Masuku during her illness (mourning confinement)." This was the signal for cash collections to be made for the widow which realized a total of 116-30 rands.

At this point, just when the proper order was being peaceably restored, a fresh wave of inspiration swept through the assembled prophets. L. tried to stem it: "I thought we would go on singing and praying so as to push the late man up to heaven. Remember there is individual and general judgement. Won't we preach and send him to heaven, as it is said 'All knees in heaven and on earth should fall down to Christ'. Won't we have the witnessing?" Another minister, D., spoke up: "We appreciate all that has been done. I just want to point out one thing. The Word of God is the foundation of all. All should follow the Word. When we started it was prophesied that there was impending danger. I have had experience of such things. [He related some such experiences.] I think we should pray and heal the prophesied danger. Otherwise, the prophets will blame us one day that the ministers prevented them from redressing the situation after they had foreseen it. Let us remember that Deacon MK. saw this and asked for the boys to be prayed over. We should think of the Word of God read in Luke. Some may be coming here merely to test others. The Word says 'Let us get him clean robes, a ring and kill a fat cow'. It is certain that many are called but few are chosen. What do you want? What are you short of? We want no bickering and petty quarrelling here. . . Let us put aside all spite and hatred. May the Lord cleanse my heart. Remember the envy of the son who had not left his father's house, how he complained. You must be happy that you are here to thank the Lord".

Rev. B. announced: "I am happy to be here. Children who worship God, my heart is sore if we leave off that which has been prophesied about Masuku's sons". Rev. S. added: 'I ask the assembly not to leave off. The ministers have given you the chance to pray about the prophecy. In my mind, we should stand and sing and allow the spirit to work". Free rein was given to the prophets and a noisy disorderly scene followed. At its height, a prophet shouted out that there was something between Masuku and his minister, L. The prophet kept hammering away at this theme until L. stepped in and admitted that he had refused Masuku a letter of removal (i.e. permission to join another band within the same denomination, that of Deacon MK., as it transpired). This was because of some misunderstanding which had arisen many years before through malicious gossip which had aimed at harming Masuku by driving him away from L. Since then there had been continual backbiting aimed at Masuku, who had complained that he had served his church well and did not merit such treatment.

While L. sympathized with Masuku's problem, he claimed that it would have been wrong to issue him a document of release while the old scores (unspecified) had not been settled amicably between them. Many had tried to persuade him to issue the document for the peace and edification of the church, but he resolutely refused, for he considered he would be committing an irregularity. His view had been that Masuku should first settle the quarrel with him, so that he could leave a clear record behind him. If that would not happen, then there could be no point in creating a situation for which he (L.) would be answerable before God.

L. remained adamant that it was a matter between himself and Masuku and succeeded in ruling no competence on the part of the assembly to take further steps, but sufficient had already been achieved. The prophets had succeeded in bringing the issue into the open and in delivering a stinging public rebuke to L. for exceeding his ministerial authority. This had been achieved by stages, at any of which the complaint might have been killed, but the prophetic tide was strong enough to carry it to the point of denunciation. First of all, danger in the form of an impending affliction was diagnosed, without any specific cause or source being alluded to. Secondly, the prescribed remedy, the cooling purifying rite of sprinkling the premises with blessed water, was administered. The assembly for a time resumed its appointed course but the third stage was reached when the source of the danger was finally laid bare with the pronouncement that there was bad feeling between the dead man and his minister, who was now conducting the assembly.

Although there was more than a suggestion that, since Deacon MK. was the leader of the dead man's choice and therefore rightfully responsible for matters pertaining to his religious welfare, it was he and not L. who should have had charge of the assembly, the more fundamental issue was ministerial malpractice on the part of L. amounting to an abuse of his authority. That a man could not transfer from one band to another, without the written testimony of his minister that he was a member in good standing, was a means of discouraging wholesale "sheep-stealing" between groups. Understandably, it was a very sensitive issue among ministers. Yet none of his colleagues would openly accuse L. although they must have known the facts and that L. had unreasonably exceeded his authority, by persistently withholding a certificate of removal. However, a number of them were instrumental in keeping the door open for prophecy to pin the blame on L. Significantly, it was the conductors of enthusiasm who forced the issue and ultimately censured the abuse of authority. Under certain circumstances, therefore, general dissatisfaction with the conduct of persons in authority can well up and find an outlet in enthusiastic condemnation. If authority is the legitimate regulator of enthusiastic expression, enthusiasm is equally the "watchdog" which restrains immoderate authority.

One further aspect of the relation between authority and enthusiasm requires clarification, namely, the alleged proliferation of authoritative positions. That there is a multiplicity of titles and officials in these churches is beyond dispute. What is not so certain is whether they all carry title to authority as such. A great deal of confusion can be eliminated by clearly distinguishing two different kinds of "authority", namely, jurisdictional and functional. Both are to be found in Zionist churches. Jurisdictional authority is what is normally meant by authority, i.e. a legitimate right to make decisions on behalf of others. It also involves being responsible to some degree for the wellbeing and behaviour of those over whom the authority is exercised. The Zionist Bishop-President, the minister and the preacher all possess this kind of authority. It gives them the right to control all aspects of the lives of followers and subjects and makes them responsible for the conduct and quality of their lives as Zionists. The preacher exercises this authority and control in relation to a small number of individuals, i.e. a cell within a band, or occasionally he has charge of a band which is a satellite outpost of a congregation with a minister and which is allowed to meet at a distance from the minister's home. The preacher thus exercises his authority in subordination to a minister, who has a jurisdiction of greater span and who is virtually autonomous at the local level in the day-to-day running of Zionist affairs. Once or twice a year the minister meets with other ministers at the headquarters of the denomination, at which point the Bishop-President's responsibility for providing overall leadership of the church is collectively acknowledged. But apart from the very occasional visit, the leader leaves his local minister to make his own decisions. Although, ideally, all decisions at whatever level should be reached in consultation with followers, in practice ministers simply impose their authority when necessary and take compliance to be approval.

Stewards, Evangelists and Deacons have but functional authority, that is, they are entrusted and empowered to carry out specific recurring tasks or functions. Of course, Evangelists and Deacons are already Preachers and are invested with jurisdictional authority in that capacity. But that authority over the lives of subordinates is not thereby increased when they are elevated in rank to Evangelist or Deacon. What is added is the acquisition of a privilege, the right to perform baptisms and to administer communion respectively. The exercise of these functions bring fellow Zionists under their control very rarely and irregularly; their powers lack the continuity and all-purposive character of jurisdictional authority. The Steward has no jurisdictional authority whatever, and is merely appointed to carry out tasks at the behest of the minister such as will ensure the smooth running of a band meeting.

Despite appearances to the contrary, the hierarchy of real authority is an eminently simple one, proceeding from Preacher to Minister to Bishop. The very simplicity of the chain of authority facilitates the intertwining and mutual exchange between authority and enthusiasm. Since the minister is the pivot of the authority system, it is at this level that the strands of merging are thickest. Here there is a complex overlapping of the functions of authority and enthusiasm which is expressed in a complementary interdependence. At band level, enthusiasm is not allowed to run unchecked but is submitted to the rein of authority which is applied in a quiet, even and continuous manner. In interband association, enthusiasm is occasionally employed to control rampant authority, by slipping the reins and erupting in a highly visible and spectacular fashion.

It seems to me that, by overtly isolating authority from enthusiasm and thereby claiming to have eliminated conflict between them, Zionists presuppose potential conflict in the relationship. In practice, however, authority and enthusiasm are neither insulated one from the other nor are they damaging in their relationship each to the other. Quite the contrary. The complex traffic across the imposed boundaries between authority and enthusiasm renders them mutually compatible and indispensable to one another within the organization of Zionist religious experience.

Notes

1. This term is a free translation of the Zulu word *ibandla* (originally, a gathering of men) which Zionists themselves employ to refer to a congregation.
2. Although female prophets are more numerous in Zionism than their male counterparts, they tend to play subdued, secondary and supportive roles, when male prophets are present to take over leadership in healing sessions.

References

Gerth, H. and Mills, C.W., 1967: *From Max Weber*. London (Routledge & Kegan Paul).

Kiernan, J.P., 1976a: Prophet and preacher: an essential partnership in the work of zion. *Man* **11(3)**, 356-66.

Kiernan, J.P., 1976b: The work of zion: an analysis of an african zionist ritual. *Africa* **46**, 340-56.

Kiernan, J.P., 1979: Spouses and partners: marriage and career among urban zulu zionists. *Urban Anthropology* **8(1)**, 95-110.

Kiernan, J.P., 1980: Zionist communion. *Journal of Religion in Africa* **11(2)**. 124-136.

Pauw, B.A., 1960: *Religion in a Tswana Chiefdom*. London (Oxford University Press).

Sundkler, B.G.M., 1961: *Bantu Prophets in South Africa* (2nd. ed.). London (Oxford University Press).

Sundkler, B.G.M., 1976: *Zulu Zion and Some Swazi Zionists*. London (Oxford University Press).

West, Martin, 1975: *Bishops and Prophets in a Black City: African Independent Churches in Soweto, Johannesburg*. Cap Town (David Phillip).

Freedom and Constraint among Shona Spirit Mediums

M.F.C. Bourdillon

This paper arises out of a misconception in Shona ethnography. Peter Fry (1976, pp. 54-60) has typified Korekore (northern Shona) spirit mediums as "bureaucratic" in contrast with the "charismatic" Zezuru (central Shona mediums), a contrast that has been accepted in modified ways by I.M. Lewis (1971, pp. 136-40), G.K. Garbett (1977, p. 91) and R.P. Werbner (1977a, p. xxxiii).

Elsewhere (Bourdillon, in press) I argue against this contrast. The connotations of rigidity and control, together with the systematic rationalization that the word bureaucratic carries, are so far removed from the free and fluid independence of traditional mediums, that the term is patently out of place in this context: quite simply, Fry misunderstood and misrepresented the Korekore data. I further argue that a detailed examination of the ethnography shows only very minor differences between Korekore and Zezuru mediumship.

To say that Fry misrepresented the data raises further questions about the data, and about methodology in social anthropology. To some extent Fry was reflecting the way the Korekore think about their mediumship cults: that is, the anthropologist was reflecting Korekore perception of the cults (and in this sense, Korekore experience), which, however does not conform with cult practices. In this paper I wish to pursue the relationship between the cognitive model of Korekore cults, and Korekore cultic practices.

First, I need to summarize the ethnographic argument.

The ethnography[1]

The Korekore are the northern Shona peoples who originated in the 15th and 16th century migrations from the Zimbabwe State in the South. Many of the Korekore chiefdoms came under the influence of the Mutapa state at various times in the subsequent centuries (Beach, 1980, pp. 113-51). As a result, the cult of Mutota, the founder of the Mutapa dynasty, acquired a certain pre-eminence for the Northern and eastern Korekore peoples. Today, the Korekore occupy a stretch of land in the North of Zimbabwe, an area which has received relatively few of the economic and technological benefits which the settler economy has brought.

G.K. Garbett did anthropological fieldwork in 1960-1 and 1963-4 among the Vally Korekore in the Mount Darwin and Sipolilo Districts. The chiefs of the area he worked in claimed to be direct descendents of Mutota. From the religious point of view, the area was dominated by George Kupara, the medium of Mutota for over 50 years until his death in 1975. Garbett's fieldwork was thus conducted in the domain of a well-established senior medium, and in the relative political calm prior to the Rhodesian Government's Unilateral Declaration of Independence in 1965.

The Valley Korekore have a variety of religious cults, the most important of which comprises a system of "lion" spirits and their mediums. Garbett presented this system as based on a genealogy which placed the spirits in a recognized hierarchy, and a set of territorial domains assigned to the various spirits: the spirit mediums thus appeared to be ranked in accordance with the genealogical hierarchy. He described how junior mediums were initiated and served a kind of apprenticeship under senior mediums, after which they could conduct seances and other rituals at their own shrines. Garbett also argued that in political matters and in the settlement of disputes, "lion" spirit mediums could do no more than crystallize and reinforce public opinion, notwithstanding their supposed authority (Garbett, 1963, 1966, 1969).

On the high land plateau in central Shona country is a cluster of heterogeneous chiefdoms commonly called Zezuru. Like the Korekore, the Zezuru have a variety of religious cults: personal cults of spirits of strangers, ancestral cults which are the concern of family groups, cults of chiefly spirits and associated spirits which are instituted as territorial guardians. Unlike the Korekore, the Zezuru never came under a single political system, and have no paramount spirit like Mutota at the apex of their spiritual hierarchy. The Zezuru do, however, have cults of certain hero-spirits that are not localized, in that they are not associated with any particular territory or group, and whose mediums attract clienteles across chiefly boundaries.[2] Certain of these heroes, like Chaminhuka and Nehanda, have attracted such widespread fame, particularly in wars against the invading Ndebele and the settling whites, as to be clearly at the apex of most Zezuru spirit hierarchies (cf. Gelfand, 1959, pp. 13-15).

In 1965-7, Peter Fry did fieldwork among the Zezuru of Chiota. This was a time of intense nationalist feeling and political suppression, and Fry's data were collected in a situation of hostility and suspicion. They consisted largely of the case studies of a few mediums whose prestige was rising rapidly in the unstable situation, and whose careers he was able to describe in sensitive detail. Fry observed that in Chiota, a growing number of persons were taking up careers as spirit mediums, and that mediums competed for clienteles. The status of a particular spirit depended on the medium's ability to attract a large clientele, and not on any pre-established hierarchy. Fry's observations refuted the Zezuru supposition, accepted by Gelfand (ibid.), that their spirits operated in ordered hierarchical relations, and that mediums simply allowed this order to express itself.

Fry went on to contrast the situation he found in Chiota with Garbett's data on the Korekore, arguing on a number of grounds that in contrast to the charismatic character of Zezuru mediums, Korekore mediums operated a "bureaucratic" system. Here I merely summarize the conclusions of my argument against Fry, since the details appear elsewhere (Bourdillon, in press).

Firstly, Fry stated that spirit mediumship amongst the Korekore was confined to the long dead, whereas among the Zezuru all spirits, ranging from the most junior ancestors to ancient heroes, could possess mediums. In fact Fry was wrong concerning the Korekore: a wide range of spirits, similar to that of the Zezuru, are possessed by Korekore mediums, although it is true that the Korekore both in theory and practice keep the cults of junor and senior spirits clearly apart.

Secondly, Fry argued that, unlike the Zezuru spirits, Korekore spirits were rigidly structured according to their fixed genealogical connections. In practice this contrast is largely illusory. Although the most senior Korekore spirits, such as Mutota, are widely accepted as being senior (as are the most senior Zezuru spirits), the relative statuses of other spirits is not fixed, nor are there any clear criteria according to which persons in chiefly or commoner genealogies come out as spirits. Moreover, oral genealogies are subject to variation according to political exigencies. Even the territorial associations are subject to variation according to the needs and stratagems of particular mediums.

Thirdly, Fry pointed out that in Chiota the backing of a senior medium may be worthless outside the sphere of the medium, and that a new medium required a following for his legitimation, acquiring his authority "from below". He suggested that for Korekore mediums, the backing of a senior medium is both necessary and sufficient for legitimation, and that accordingly Korekore mediums acquire legitimation "from above". This suggestion corresponds to Korekore belief (as it does to Zezuru belief); people say that recognition by a senior medium is an infallible assurance of the legitimacy of a new medium, but in practice a medium must acquire the confidence of the people if he is to exercise any authoritative influence.

Fry also pointed to rivalry between Zezuru mediums, and the possibility of upward mobility, in contrast to the Korekore mediums whose relative domains and statuses are fixed by their historical genealogy. In fact the limits on mobility and rivalry placed on Korekore mediums by genealogies appear not to differ in any fundamental way from the limits placed on Zezuru mediums by the generally accepted hierarchies mentioned earlier.

Finally, Fry points to the contrast between the growth of mediumship cults in Chiota, and the fact that a number of Korekore spirits have no living mediums, and he argues that mediumship among the Korekore has become ossified. In practice, new mediums proliferate in Korekore country when they are likely to become influential, as when succession to a vacant chiefship is likely to be widely disputed by various houses of the chiefly dynasty.

My argument against Fry's typology is laid out in more detail elsewhere. Here I simply refer to Garbett's more recent paper (1977) which makes it clear that even among the Valley Korekore the cult of a particular spirit can wax and wane, and in which it becomes clear that the hierarchical and territorial structure of the cult does not eliminate the possibility of rivalry between mediums. Indeed, the intermingling between Zezuru and Korekore cults described in this paper suggests a similarity in organization between them. My own experience is that Shona people often take part in both Korekore and Zezuru cults without noticing minor differences that may exist. Also, my own field work among the more eastern Korekore, performed in 1969–71 (immediately prior to the outbreak of the guerrilla war), showed that spirit mediumship was neither dying, nor rigidly structured among the Korekore (Bourdillon, 1972a, pp. 169-75. Data on the fluidity of this structure is brought together in Bourdillon, in press).

It could be argued that Fry was simply offering a typology, and that it is too harsh to demand exact conformity with all field data. The models of a scientist are devices to clarify and to control a mass of diverse facts cognitively, and we expect to have to modify any model as data accumulate. In this case, however, I argue that the model so controls the data as to conceal, rather than to clarify, social operations. The question remains as to how we are to account for Fry's typology, if it is so clearly contradicted by field data.

Doctrine and practice

One answer is that Fry was comparing different types of data. In the Korekore case, Fry was using official doctrine: what the Korekore say is the case. Korekore people say that the mediums are controlled by their spirits; that these are spirits of persons who lived in the past; that they care for their living descendants; that their relationships are determined by history, particularly as expressed in the commonly accepted genealogy; that senior spirits could never make a mistake in the recognition of a new medium; that each spirit was assigned its territory by an ancient Mutapa in the unchangeable past, and so on. Statements such as these form part of Korekore belief and of Korekore experience, in the sense that they are simply taken for granted by most of the people. Discussion of mediums revolves round these beliefs — how to explain current events in terms of them. Although the Korekore readily suspect a medium who autocratically contradicts the wishes and expectations of the people within his domain, they explain this in terms of the belief system: a spirit always cares for his people and would not wish to hurt them in any way, and some mediums only pretend to be possessed, putting forward their own words as the words of the spirit. The Korekore do not explicitly think of their mediums as acquiring authority "from below".

Such a system of beliefs then, forms the cognitive structure by means of which the Korekore put their cultic practices into a controllable mental arrangement. The system also provided the field-worker with a basic structure, into which much of his data fitted, and from which he was able to describe and explain deviations.

One aspect of the cognitive structure is that the order is supposed to be dependent on the past, and consequently to be unchangeable. In practice, even written history can be re-interpreted and re-written in the light of contemporary values. Oral history has much greater scope for change and manipulation. Korekore legends and myths, like legends and myths in most societies, are frequently adjusted to suit present political purposes (cf. Bourdillon, 1972b). That the Korekore system of mediums is based on Korekore history allows it to be experienced as unchangeable; that the history is oral rather than written allows for a fluid organization.

The organization based on a mythical past is not a constraining bureaucratic structure. Since the mediums are official custodians of the past, history becomes a tool they can manipulate in their stratagems to obtain status and power. When Mutota was forced by the white government to move from his traditional domain, and settled in that of Chihwahwa, the medium of Chihwahwa cited the tradition that the medium of a senior spirit should not settle in the territory of a junior spirit, while Mutota pointed to his traditional seniority and claimed to own all the land; in the end, Chihwahwa found refuge in a newly revealed "tradition" that he had a sacred grove in the domain of another spirit, allowing him to settle in a vacant domain (Garbett, 1977, pp. 61, 66). When a new medium of Nyanhehwe, a senior spirit who was supposed to rule over all the Korekore, tried to settle in the easternmost Korekore chiefdom (citing conflict with Portuguese officials as his reason for moving from the spirit's traditional territorial domain in Mozambique), the local senior spirits rejected him, citng a tradition of incest as their reason; in this case, the medium of Nyanhehwe was not sufficiently established to use the traditional seniority of his spirit to enforce his wishes, and it was the more senior medium that had to move elsewhere. When a new medium tried to associate himself with the anti-white traditions of the famous spirit, Dzivaguru, he went too far against the convenience of the lay public in trying to ban schools and stores; to the effect that he became discredited.[3] Oral traditions can be taken up, dropped, modified, and even created to suit convenience.

I have argued that the stable structure of Korekore mediums, based on the unchanging past, is a cognitive construct which does not accurately reflect Korekore practice and organization.

In the case of the Zezuru, a similar (though not identical) cognitive structure exists, and had been described by Michael Gelfand (1959, pp. 13-15). Indeed Fry comments that the Chiota people *think* of their spirits in "stable hierarchical terms", and that "there is a certain stability of authority relations between spirit mediums" (1976, pp. 44, cf. also 59). Fry recognizes, however, in his Chiota material that the organization of spirit mediums in practice diverges from the cognitive perception of the local people concerning them. But Fry then went on to contrast the actual organization of the Zezuru cults with the cognitive structure of the Korekore: the practice of the Zezuru with the formal doctrine of the Korekore.

This is not the whole answer to the methodological problem. If there were no differences between Fry's and Garbett's data, the error would be too elementary to be credible. Indeed, Garbett implied a difference when he suggested that Zezuru mediums allying themselves to Mutota (the senior Korekore spirit) were looking for a stability which their own system did not provide, and indeed which is incompatible with the "non-hierarchical nature of Zezuru mediumship" (1977, 90f.). Garbett appears not to have noticed Fry's confusion of the cognitive with the practical. This leads us to a further point: the danger of confusing situational factors with the fundamental characteristics of social structure.

Situational factors

Both Fry and Garbett acknowledged the importance of George Kupara, the long established medium of Mutota, on whom depened the structure of Korekore mediumship as Garbett described it.

Fry quoted Garbett as noting "that many Korekore spirit-guardians are no longer represented by mediums and that the whole structure may well collapse with the death of the present Mutota medium" (1976, p. 60). The implication is that Kupara fitted into an established system which was slowly collapsing, and for which he was the last reliable support.

Garbett's data did suggest that the contemporary status of the Mutota cult was largely of Kupara's making (1977, pp. 74-80). He commented on the decline of the chthonic cults shortly after Kupara became a medium in 1919. In at least one case (that of Karuva and Dzivaguru) this can be partly attributed to government interference; but as Garbett noted, the cult remained significant outside Mutota's realm of influence (Bourdillon, 1972b; 1979a). It is only among the Valley Korekore, who came immediately under Kupara's sphere of influence, that the chthonic cults became almost totally overshadowed. Kupara's fame as a medium also allowed him to incorporate into his sphere of influence a number of Zezuru cults.

A man who held such a dominant position in the religious life of his people for over half a century cannot be dismissed as contingent to the religious organization of that people. How the system is affected by Kupara's death remains to be seen,[4] but it does appear that he was primarily responsible for giving a certain stability to the cults of the Valley Korekore, and that Fry's explanations in terms of the ancient history of the Mutapa "empire"[5] and of the remoteness of the Korekore from centres of European contact (1976, pp. 62-7) are not called for. Eastern Korekore communities, which share the history of the Mutapa state, and which are equally remote from centres of European contact, do not have the stability of religious organization which Kupara was able to give to the Valley Korekore.

A case in point is the chiefdom of Diwa, which according to most informants was under the control of the spirit of Nyahuwi, a woman and the first chief of Diwa, from whom all subsequent chiefs, and most of the spirits, were descended. In 1970, Nyahuwi had an aged woman as her long-established medium. At that time the succession to the vacant chiefship was coming up for settlement, a responsibility of the senior spirits who, according to popular belief, should consult together before the medium of the senior spirit makes the appointment at a common and public seance. When I started my fieldwork, it was widely acknowledged that the appointment was primarily the responsibility of Nyahuwi, but it soon became clear that at least two of the supposedly junior mediums had no intention of simply deferring to Nyahuwi's wishes on the matter. One of these, only recently initiated, began (with the support of lay members of the chiefly house to which the spirit was genealogically related) to defy Nyahuwi's authority in ritual matters immediately after her initiation: at the same time certain elders began to mutter that the country could not be ruled by a woman (Bourdillon, in press; see also the comments on Kotswa and Nemuru of Chiruja). The authority structure of the Diwa mediums suddenly appeared very fragile when the medium of Nyahuwi was no longer able to command the respect of the chiefdom as a whole.

The second stituational factor which needs to be noted involves the circumstances in which fieldwork took place. I have mentioned that Garbett's fieldwork took place in the relative calm of the early 1960s, while Fry did fieldwork amid the political unrest of the middle 1960s, at a time in which many new mediums were arising and competing to establish themselves. A comparison between Fry's data, obtained with great difficulty at a time when suspicion was rife and the people were politically unsettled, and Garbett's data, obtained over a longer period in a more settled fieldwork situation, is not so much a comparison between two peoples (the Zezuru and the Korekore) as a comparison between two situations (cf. Murphree, in press).

In situations of relative stability, there is little challenge to any established order, which gives the appearance of an established hierarchy of senior mediums exercising control over subordinates. In such situations, we expect to find ideologies which are widely accepted, and which contain symbols capable of exerting considerable social pressure. In stable situations, we can expect to find an emphasis on an ideal hierarchy supposedly established in mythical time. On the other hand, in situations which are unsettled, such as the tense situation in Chiota in the mid-1960s or the forthcoming dispute over chiefly succession in Diwa, religious authorities are shown to be able to exercise little power in practice. Ideologies are seen to operate in favour of some against others, and the symbols they contain lose their moral force. In such situations, mediums exercise little control, and are able to acquire status only as symbols of use to their clienteles. Accordingly, in such situations a successful medium must assess and express the ideals and values of the people who follow him. In more stable situations, the ideals and values of the people are easier to assess, and include an emphasis on stability and order, which successful mediums must accordingly symbolize.

These comments are relevant to Garbett's explanation of the interpenetration of the Korekore and Zezuru cults (1977, 90 f.). He suggests that Zezuru mediums allying themselves with Mutota were looking for a stability which their own system did not provide, and indeed which is incompatible with the alleged non-hierarchical nature of Zezuru mediumship. But it might be truer to say that the stability of the idealized system of Korekore mediumship is incompatible with the contemporary Shona situation, in which a variety of economic, political, educational and even religious opportunities allow for continual manoeuvering for status (cf. Garbett, 1967, for an example of such manoeuvering among the Valley Korekore). Garbett comments that it is meaningful to speak of strategy only in limited local arenas, and that the interpenetration of Korekore and Zezuru cults cannot be understood in terms of a grand strategy either on the part of Mutota or of the Zezuru mediums. Perhaps the key word is "grand": there is no evidence of an overall plan on the part of the mediums to combine the cults, and there is no evidence of scheming between mediums. But the interpenetration of the Korekore and Zezuru cults can still be explained in terms of strategems for status. Mutota's medium clearly gained in prestige from Zezuru mediums incorporated into the Mutota genealogy. Each time he gave recognition to a Zezuru medium as being possessed by a child of Mutota, Kupara's status was enhanced. Garbett points out that Kupara's behaviour can be interpreted in terms of a series of tactics which had among their objectives the increase in status, and in the sphere of influence, of his spirit in relation to other spirits (1977, p. 78). On the part of the Zezuru mediums, it was surely not stability for its own sake that they were seeking, but rather stable support for their own positions. The backing of so famous a medium as Kupara was clearly an aid against any who might challenge their authority. One can speculate that were there an equally long established medium of Chaminhuka available to provide this support, there would have been no incentive for the Zezuru mediums to seek validation in Korekore country. There is no evidence to suggest that they were seeking a supposed stability in the Korekore system rather than the support of the tactically most useful person.

Since fieldwork ideally involves a sharing by an anthropologist of the experience of the people he is studying, it is not surprising that the contrasting situations are reflected in contrasting perceptions of religious organization. Garbett accepted the dominant stable structure which was expressed by the Valley Korekore at the time, and which was never seriously challenged. This could form a useful base for the anthropologist's descriptions and analyses. In Fry's case, although a formal structure received verbal acknowledgement, it received little emphasis in practice as the mediums struggled for power by attempting to create and establish new traditions about their spirits (cf. Fry, 1976, p. 47).

Questions of authority

We come now to consider the status of the conceptual hierarchies of spirits and their mediums. I have argued that a Korekore medium does not, and cannot, rely simply on the genealogical position of his spirit for the status he is to be accorded by the lay public. Fry showed from his Zezuru data that religious authority is not located where superficially it appears: that is, mediums can rarely exercise coercive authority. I argue that the same applies to the Korekore data: the apparent hierarchical structure of mediumship does not in itself determine a ranking of power or coercive authority.

Yet Korekore and Zezuru people believe in their hierarchies of religious authorities in at least two senses. Firstly, people verbally rank these authorities — not always consistently, but they do assert a ranked order. Secondly, they assert and appeal to such hierarchical authorities in order to justify actions or points of view that they appear to support. For example, in the succession dispute regarding the Diwa chiefship, members of the house supported by Nyahuwi asserted, with a degree of emotional commitment, that Nyahuwi was the senior spirit and controlled the chiefship. Other houses asserted, with equal emotional commitment, that the chiefdom could not be ruled by a woman, and that other (male) spirits should have the last word in the appointment of a new chief. I have pointed out elsewhere how Korekore people appeal to the oracles of their spirit mediums primarily to support judgements made on other grounds, that is, to evoke among others a moral response in favour of a particular point of view (Bourdillon, 1979b). In these senses, both Korekore and Zezuru believe in their religious hierarchies.[6]

From the point of view of the mediums, they must obtain some authority from traditional beliefs about the spirits, or these traditions would be useless as a tactical tool. Mediums accept some of the constraints of the system in the expectation of gaining status through the system. The traditions which support Korekore mediums provide a language, the rules of the game, within which and through which mediums can operate. The traditions surrounding mediums are the symbols which communicate and make sacred the identity that a medium acquires, a stable niche of high status in society (cf. Mol, 1976). They are symbols in the sense that they evoke a response, rather than describe the world (cf. Sperber, 1975). They carry a moral force, although this force is strong only when a relatively stable structure is widely accepted.

So it is in their stratagems to obtain status that people sometimes accept limitations on what they may do. The old medium of Mutota became a symbol of the power and authority of spirit mediumship. As a result, mediums, both Korekore and Zezuru, could gain in status by submitting themselves to his authority: in this way they reinforced the authority of the senior medium, and by implication their own as less senior mediums. By accepting taboos imposed on mediums, including territorial restrictions, Korekore mediums reinforced their traditional elite status. Such symbols can, however, be reinforced only if sufficient numbers of people wish to use them. The major constraint on mediums from both ethnic groups is the opinions of their prospective clienteles.

To understand traditions as language or symbols,[7] is to take into account both the stability they provide, and the way in which they provide for movement and change. A symbol, to work as such, must be widely accepted: symbols cannot be arbitrarily created nor arbitrarily changed. The accepted pool of symbols in a society circumscribes communications that can be conveyed. Choices within this pool provide the possibility of communication, and the possibility of developing new ideas and new symbols. Similarly, traditions circumscribe behaviour without thereby preventing change.

A good example of the symbolic use of traditions about spirits and their mediums is the case of Nehanda. In Zezuru country, Nehanda is a hero spirit of particular renown, so much so that often there are a number of simultaneous pretenders to her mediumship, each commanding acknowledgement in a particular locality. Nehanda was prominent in the 1896–7 war against white settlers, and remains a nationalist figure today (cf. Ranger, 1979, pp. 384-5; 392-4). In the Zambezi Valley, Nehanda is known as the daughter of Mutota, a spirit with a medium and a territorial domain of her own. The Korekore identify their Nehanda with the spirit of the same name on the Zezuru plateau, even though they acknowledge that there are two distinct and genuine mediums — a rare exception to the belief that two persons cannot at the same time be true mediums of a single spirit. Garbett (1977, pp. 86-8) comments on how one of the pretenders to the mediumship of Nehanda in Zezuru country incorporated herself into the Mutota cult, presumably in a bid for status and recognition *vis-à-vis* a rival. In the course of the recent war, nationalist guerrillas associated the medium of Nehanda in the Valley with the Nehanda of the 1896–7 war, and took her across the border to Mozambique for protection. Neither the medium active in the 1896–7 war nor the daughter of Mutota are fixed historical facts: rather they are undefined ideas which can be conjured up and fused in the symbol of the name, Nehanda, to be used as the occasion demands — by the medium of Mutota to emphasize the pre-eminent status of his spirit; by the medium of the Zezuru Nehanda to validate her claims; by guerrillas fighting a nationalist war, to obtain courage and unity from a symbol of the glorious past and hopes for a glorious future.

The symbolic nature of the traditions concerning spirits and their mediums was generally indicated in the roles of mediums in the recent war, when they were widely respected and consulted by nationalist guerrillas. Spirit mediums had little say in initiating and planning the war as a whole. In one case I came across, the senior medium told guerrillas who had come to pay their respects that he wanted no bloodshed in his country, and was roundly told that his demands were absurd: he subsequently worked in close liaison with the guerrillas, and it is said that an army vehicle overturned where one of his charms was placed by the road. The mediums acquired authority, to be consulted in in times of fear and uncertainty, particularly when life was threatened, as a result of their symbolic status which represented a radical contrast to the power and culture of the whites. The traditions surrounding mediumship were used symbolically by forces advocating radical social change. Religion, which can act as a conservative force, can also provide a medium for change.

I have argued that the believed hierarchy of Korekore religious authorities is a symbol of power rather than a source of power. Like most symbols, it can be manipulated, and restructured, to evoke various responses, sometimes conservative and sometimes radical, according to the stratagems of those who use them. Like any symbol, it can evoke a strong moral reaction, provided that it serves the interests of a sufficiently wide section of the community. Since the hierarchy is a symbol, it can be manipulated and modified to support various stratagems: it should not be mistaken as simply reflecting a fixed and rigid social organization.

Acknowledgements

I gratefully acknowledge helpful criticism of earlier drafts of this paper by my colleague in the University of Zimbabwe, Dr. Angela Cheater.

Notes

1. For a general account of the religion of the Shona, including the ethnography of Shona spirit mediumship, see Bourdillon (1982).
2. Professor Ranger (1967) argued that the cults of such heroes, under the direction of the High God cult in the south, served to unite diverse political units in the rebellion against the whites of 1896-7. His argument has, however, been challenged by Cobbing (1977), who denied the organizational influence of the high god cult on other cults; by Werbner (1977b, pp. 207-14), who pointed out the High God cult was not altogether behind the rebellion; and, with particular relevance to the present essay, by Beach (1979), who argued that the mediums were able to exert little, if any, political pressure. The argument presented in this essay that mediumship is a symbol rather than a source of power, would appear to resolve some of the disputed questions.
3. It is relevant to note that Dzivaguru appears to have actively supported early rebellions against white governments (cf. Ranger, 1963). Considering that preparations for the impending guerrilla war appear to have been in progress in the valley at the time in question, one might have expected that the time was ripe for the emergence of a medium of Dzivaguru with strongly anti-white attitudes.
4. David Lan is currently doing fieldwork among the valley Korekore, and is collecting data on the present organization of the "lion" spirit cult. Preliminary reports suggest that the spirit of Mutota is losing something of his pre-eminent status.
5. The Korekore did come under the influence of the Mutapa polity, which at times had a vast area of influence just south of the Zambezi River, although the relations between successive Mutapas and outlying chiefdoms appear to have been fluid (cf. Beach, 1980, pp. 113-51), and Fry's characterization of the Mutapa state as an "empire" (which is by no means unique to Fry) seems exaggerated.

6. In the same way, I suggest that we can conclude from Christopher Fuller's data in this volume, that the Indians he was studying believed in the ritual authority of the *Agamas*, notwithstanding the contradictions which such a belief implied.
7. I do not claim that this approach is new, Abner Cohen (1974, pp. 132-4) has shown how customs, and religious practices in particular, can serve as symbols through which a community can maintain its coherence and its economic advantage against outsiders: religious rites can also provide a locus for struggles for power and for rebellion. David Parkin (1978, pp. 296-311) has elaborated on the relationship between symbol and custom, and has discussed in the context of change the symbolism of verbalized roles and their relationship to ideology (Parkin, 1976). The data on Shona spirit mediums provide variations of the theme (see also Bucher, 1980).

References

Abraham, D.P., 1966: The roles of "Chaminuka" and the mhondoro cults in Shona political history. In *The Zambezian Past* (E. Stokes and R. Brown, eds) Manchester (Manchester University Press).

Beach, D.N., 1979: Chimurenga: the Shona rising of 1896-97. *Journal of African History* **20**, 395-420.

Beach, D.N., 1980: *The Shona and Zimbabwe, 900-1850.* Gwelo (Mambo Press).

Bourdillon, M.F.C., 1972a: *Some Aspects of the Religion of the Eastern Korekore.* Unpublished D. Phil. thesis, Oxford University.

Bourdillon M.F.C., 1972b: The manipulation of myth in a Tavara chiefdom. *Africa* **42**, 112-21.

Bourdillon M.F.C., 1979a: The cults of Dzivaguru and Karuva amongst the north-eastern Shona peoples. In *Guardians of the Land* (M. Schoffeleers, ed.) Gwelo (Mambo Press).

Bourdillon, M.F.C., 1979b: Religion and ethics in Korekore society. *Journal for Religion in Africa* **10**, 81-94.

Bourdillon, M.F.C., 1982: *Shona Peoples.* (2nd. ed.) Gwelo (Mambo Press).

Bourdillon, M.F.C., in press: Suggestions of bureaucracy in Korekore religion: putting the ethnography straight. Zambezia.

Bucher, H., 1980: *Spirits and Power: an analysis of Shona cosmology.* Cape Town (Oxford University Press).

Cobbing, J., 1977: The absent priesthood: another look at the Rhodesian risings of 1896-1897. *Journal of African History* **18**, 61-84.

Cohen, A., 1974: *Two-Dimensional Man: an essay on the anthropology of power and symbolism in complex society.* London (Routledge & Kegan Paul).

Fry, p., 1976: *Spirits of Protest: Spirit-mediums and the articulation of consensus among the Zezuru of Southern Rhodesia (Zimbabwe).* Cambridge (Cambridge University Press).

Garbett, G.K., 1963: *The political system of a central african tribe with particular reference to the role of spirit mediums.* Unpublished Ph.D. thesis, University of Manchester.

Garbett, G.K., 1966: Religious aspects of political succession among the Valley Korekore. In *The Zambezian Past* (E. Stokes and R. Brown, eds). Manchester (Manchester University Press).

Garbett, G.K., 1967: Prestige, status and power in a modern Valley Korekore chiefdom, Rhodesia. *Africa* **37**, 307-26.

Garbett, G.K., 1969: Spirit mediums as mediators in Korekore society. In *Spirit Mediumship and Society in Africa* (J. Beattie and J. Middleton, eds). London (Routledge & Kegan Paul).

Garbett, G.K., 1977: Disparate regional cults and unitary ritual fields in Zimbabwe. In *Regional Cults* (ASA Monograph 16) (R.P. Werbner, ed.) London and New York (Academic Press).

Gelfand, M., 1959: *Shona Ritual with Special Reference to the Chaminuka Cult*. Cape Town (Juta and Co.).

Lewis, I.M., 1971: *Ecstatic Religion*. Harmondworth (Penguin Books).

Mol, H., 1976: *Identity and the Sacred*. Oxford (Basil Blackwell).

Murphree, M.W., in press: The study of religion in Central Africa (Essay Review). *Zambezia*.

Parkin, D., 1976: Exchanging words. In *Transaction and Meaning* (B. Kapferer, ed.). Philadelphia (Institute for the Study of Human Issues).

Parkin, D., 1978: *The Cultural Definition of Political Response*. London and New York (Academic Press).

Ranger, T.O., 1963: The last days of the Empire of the Mwene Mutapa, 1898-1917. Paper presented to the Conference on the History of the Central African Peoples, Lusaka.

Ranger, T.O., 1967: *Revolt in Southern Rhodesia, 1896-7*. London (Heinemann).

Sperber, D., 1975: *Rethinking Symbolism*. Cambridge (Cambridge University Press).

Werbner, R.P., 1977a: Introduction. In *Regional Cults* (ASA Monograph *16*) (R.P. Werbner, ed.) London and New York (Academic Press).

Werbner, R.P., 1979b: Continuity and policy in Southern Africa's High God Cult. In *Regional Cults* (ASA Monograph *16*) (R.P. Werbner, ed.) London and New York (Academic Press).

Dimensions of Meaning:
western music and the anthropological study of symbolism

J.S. Eades

In many cultures musical experience and religious experience are seen as closely related. European culture is no exception. The view of music as a manifestation of divine harmony and order has been a commonplace in philosophy since Phythagoras, while religion has nearly always involved music in ritual as one of the main means of heightening religious awareness. Many of the finest products of European music, as well as many of its forms and performance traditions, have a basis in the liturgy, which has provided inspiration (and employment) for an unbroken line of musicians up to the present. The religious experience and the musical experience have long been used as metaphors for each other, and the powerful, though often indefinite, nature of both seems to lead naturally to these parallels. The main assumption of this paper is that music and religion both involve the use of highly evolved systems of symbols, and that the exploration of the way in which musical symbolism is experienced may yield insights into the nature of symbolism in general and of religious symbols in particular. This involves examining not only the nature of western musical symbolism, but also the circumstances under which it might be seen as conveying intellectual or emotional content, and the social context in which this takes place. This chapter falls into three sections. The first deals with the problems of interpreting symbols and the cognitive and social processes to be taken into account. The second deals with the ways in which different permutations of pitch, dynamics, timbre and durational variation are conventionally "decoded", while the third discusses the parallels between the interpretation of musical and religious symbolism, and the implications of the musical analogue for the anthropology of religion.

I

A large but scattered literature on the meaning of music exists in a number of different fields — aesthetics and semiotics, musicology, ethnomusicology and the sociology of knowledge. Western "serious" music is a literate tradition: the notation system has made it possible to study texts in isolation and with little reference to the social context in which music is created and performed. Similarly, consideration of musical meaning has often underemphasized the complexity of the act of cognition. The assumption here is that three levels of analysis have to be taken into account in order to explain how meaning is attributed to music:

(1) The act of cognition, and the mechanisms through which an individual listener constructs a "meaning" of the music for himself.

(2) The mechanisms through which shared understandings of meaning are generated, shared and controlled.

(3) The "grammar" of the musical system itself, its potentiality for mapping and communicating content, and changes in this potentiality over time.

It is arguable that many of the difficulties and much of the debate in the literature stem from discussion of one of these levels in isolation from the others, and although sociologists and ethnomusicologists generally avoid these pitfalls nowadays, even quite recent work by some writers on music and aesthetics does not. Thus writers like Hoaglund (1980) and Leahy (1976) are still largely dealing with the same issues as Deryck Cooke (1959) and Suzanne Langer (1957) a generation ago — issues about meaning which are impossible to resolve outside a social context. One way out of this impasse seems to be to discuss the questions of cognition and social communication before that of meaning. Some of the recent literature from anthropology and semiotics appears to be relevant here.

For Dan Sperber (1975, 1980) symbolic interpretation is not a matter of decoding a language, but of the individual and idiosyncratic improvisation of meanings. He sees cognition as consisting of three analytically separable processes: perception, conceptualization and symbolization.[1] Many perceptions are dealt with on a routine basis, interpreted by being assimilated to one or more of the categories involved in conceptualization. The question is, therefore, which stimuli are subjected to symbolization and when does this occur? Sperber argues that when the conceptual mechanism cannot reach a satisfactory result on the basis of information derived from perception on the one hand and direct access to the memory on the other, a non-sequential search is made in the long-term memory for "additional premises" by which the perception might be evaluated, and the result is an "evocation". Information is likely to be processed in this way when it challenges the basic assumptions of a cognitive system, or when the degree of intellectual alertness is low and the conceptual mechanism easily overloaded. There is also a feedback mechanism whereby the information symbolically evoked is fed into the conceptual mechanism and used as the basis for further evaluation of stimuli.

This analysis is useful in describing how a listener might improvise his own meaning from a piece of music, but it has to be supplemented: first, with an account of the units of perception involved in the process and, second, with an account of its social dimensions, through which a particular interpretation comes to be shared and standardized. Eco (1976) gives some insight into both of these problems. His position can be summarized as follows. Signs exist only in the act of interpretation, on the basis of a decision by the the person to whom they are addressed and the creation of a social convention. Codes — systems of relationships between signs onto which meaning is mapped by agreement — are similarly the product of convention, with no reality outside the minds and shared ideas of the listeners. Conventions arise through repeated consistent interpretation within a group or society. All the same, it is possible for an individual to "interpret" a new piece of music, even if it comes from an exotic culture, through the process of "undercoding". Various elements are abstracted and assumed to be the pertinent units, whether they are or not. Through a similar undercoding process, a single meaning may be assigned to a large portion of musical text or a whole piece. As Eco puts it:

> Everyone has experienced how a given musical composition that has for many years been enjoyed as a complex text, with all its features subjected to intense scrutiny, is at a certain point (as one's taste becomes accustomed to the musical object in question) simply conceived as an unanalysed form that means approximately "Fifth Symphony" or quite simply "Romanticism" or "Music" (1976, pp. 239-40)

The process of undercoding is involved both in the response of the individual to music, and in the establishment of conventions within a social group.

Eco thus arrives at a position similar to that of the social scientists involved with music from Schutz (1971) to Blacking (1976), Shepherd *et al.* (1977) and Wright (1975), for whom the significance of music must necessarily be located in the commonly agreed meanings of the group or society in which the music is created. Asocial views of music are inherently problematic. However, there is in western society a considerable variation in the ways in which music is produced, perceived and evaluated, and widely differing musical cultures exist. A person's musical culture consists of a stock of musical experiences derived from a complex web of past and present social relationships, and transmitted through his family, teachers, peers, the mass media, and so on (Wright, 1975, pp. 422-3). The patterning of social relations reflects other major cleavages in society: thus it is likely that in class societies, differences in reaction to music have much to do with class divisions, the distribution of power and the operations of the market. Distinctions, largely arbitrary in origin, between different musical traditions — for instance as between "art" music, "pop" music and "serious" jazz or rock become part of the symbolism of class or ethnic differentiation, and are reinforced by the media and the structure of subsidy and finance (cf. Wishart in Shepherd *et al.*, 1977; Frith, 1978).

The third level of analysis is that of the musical elements themselves and their relationships, and the meaning which can be attached to them. A useful distinction which can be made at the outset is that between congeneric and extrageneric meaning (Coker, 1973, p. 61; Wright, 1975, pp. 419-20). While congeneric meaning lies exclusively within the realm of musical sounds and the relationship between them, extrageneric meaning refers to non-musical concepts, emotional states etc. The two are not mutually exclusive: Beethoven's Pastoral Symphony is at once both a statement about the combinatory and development potential of a series of musical motifs and an evocation of aspects of nature. Most of the discussion of musical meaning has concerned extrageneric meaning, and writers have tended to adopt one of three positions. The first is well represented by Stravinsky's comment: "I consider that music is, by its very nature, powerless to *express* anything at all, whether a feeling, an attitude of mind, a psychological need a phenomenon of nature etc..." (cited in Cooke, 1959, p. 11). Similar views are expressed by writers from Hanslick (1891) to Leahy (1976). An intermediate position is represented by Langer, for whom music communicates powerfully, though the communication is ambiguous and imprecise and fixed meanings are absent. However, music can reveal the nature of feelings with a detail and truth which language cannot approach by sharing formal properties of the inner life it symbolises — motion, rest, tension etc. (1957, p. 228).

The third viewpoint is that of Deryck Cooke, that music is a language with fairly fixed meanings and that a phrase-book can be written with which to translate it. Cooke (1959) deals with the basic elements of musical construction — pitch, rhythm, timbre etc, but his main emphasis is on harmony and melody. He argues that particular pitch intervals and a melodic succession of them can convey a complex emotional message.

To a large extent this is a non-issue. If it is conventionally agreed that certain melodic motifs, timbres, rhythms etc have fairly precise extrageneric meaning, then this meaning will be constructed by those with the requisite musical culture. Cultures change: we do not and cannot hear the music of the Baroque with the ears of Bach or Handel. Subtle conventions which were significant for them such as key or number symbolism, well-illustrated by Mellers' account of the B Minor Mass (1980, pp. 178, 211-3), largely escape our notice, while our own perception of their music is influenced by later conventions and performance techniques.

It may be possible to bring all the processes I have discussed in this section into a single model. Three preliminary points can be made. First, no musical listener is completely naive: everyone has a musical culture and, when faced with unfamiliar music, will approach it in terms of categories already internalized through a feedback process. Second, in this model, the processes I term formal and semantic evaluation largely correspond to the search for congeneric and extrageneric meaning respectively. Third, a search for formal or semantic significance is not necessarily involved in listening to music. "Background music" is simply used to blot out more random noise and provide a more homogeneous sound environment for other activities. The model involves the following components.

(a) Perception. This involves not simply passive reception of stimuli, but the active "filtering" of what are considered to be significant musical elements as opposed to "noise", according to a set of internalized criteria. Listeners have a considerable capacity for ignoring quite substantial noise such as the hiss of old records. In addition, the filtered stream of music is subjected to undercoding — division into motifs and phrases, rhythmic patterns etc., which form the basis for formal and semantic evaluation.

(b) Formal evaluation involves relating units of sound to others heard previously and evaluating the relationship in terms of a repertoire of previously encountered musical forms. Thus a lyrical passage in a new key somewhere near the start of a sonata-form movement will probably be perceived as "second subject" by a listener aware of the conventions of the form. Some insight into the actual processes of, for instance, perception of key and metre may be gained from the work of Longuet-Higgins and Steedman on computer transcription of Bach fugue subjects (Longuet-Higgins, 1976; Steedman, 1977). Their main concern has been the amount of information the computer needs in order to be able to establish the key and time signature of a performance of a subject. There is, of course, a feedback relationship between the processes of perception, undercoding and formal evaluation. Once the listener has decided that a piece of music is in 3/4 time, this will affect his perception of the rhythm of the rest of it, and composers such as Haydn regularly exploit this by starting a movement with a subject of deliberate metrical ambiguity.

Semantic evaluation, on the other hand, may consist of one or both of two processes. The first involves relating the sound units to categories of meaning previously assigned to similar material by oneself or others and stored in the conscious memory — for instance interpreting a falling chromatic motif in a Mozart movement as "melancholy". The second entails the idiosyncratic improvization of a meaning along the lines indicated by Sperber. The two processes can take place at the same time: the fallng motif in Mozart may evoke *both* melancholy *and* a picture of the aunt who used to play it in one's childhood.

(c) As it is difficult to assimilate and remember an entire movement, the question arises, what will be remembered of it in the conscious memory after it is over? The answer is usually a broad formal categorization such as "sonata" or "fugue", possibly a melodic phrase or two, and a general impression of the main mood. Further processes of undercoding simplify the reality of the performance and create stereotypes which are then remembered. This is in part an idiosyncratic process, but it is often conditioned by what others think, or have written, about the same piece.

Processes of formal and semantic evaluation involve the comparison of sound units with previously abstracted formal models. In the case of classical music of the 18th century, these models may well broadly correspond to the "programmes" or "paradigms" (p-structures)[2] that the composer was working with, in terms of key relationships and thematic material. Much of the interest of this music, indeed, lies in the way in which the notes fail to fit the well-known conventions. The increasingly free use of chromatic harmony, changes of metre and varied instrumentation in the 19th century made it increasingly difficult for the listener to predict the exact direction in which the music would develop. With much modern music, the listener is more likely to be in the position of a "cryptanalyst" rather than a "decoder",[3] attempting to infer the "programme" from the output rather than knowing it in advance. But the internalization of musical models is largely influenced by social interaction patterns. Groups of performers may modify their interpretation of a piece through discussion with each other, or because of a leader or conductor, while listeners may modify, or even form, their impressions in the light of what others think, or what the music critics think. A large critical industry exists, including the BBC, the press and the writers of record blurb, disseminating pre-packaged interpretations, as well as determining to a great extent which music is likely to be heard. The next section considers the ways in which conventions of meaning may be established, and the dimensions of musical expression which may be invested with significance by the listener.

II

As implied in the previous section, not all music need be semantically evaluated: much of Bach's Art of Fugue or the Musical Offering will be evaluated mainly in formal terms. All the same, most music is invested by its listeners with semantic significance as well. These meanings fall into two broad categories. First there are references to the self — particularly to emotonal or physiological states.[4] Secondly, there are references to the outside world, to both concrete objects and abstract concepts, both of which can have musical motifs or phrases conventionally associated with them. There are no completely naive listeners, and most approach much of the music they hear with a clear notion of the sorts of meanings they might extract from it, owing to one or more of the following:

(a) The music is a setting of a text with a clear meaning and established connotations.

(b) The meaning may be inferred from the context, as with much sacred or ceremonial music.

(c) Semantic content is indicated by the composer's directions in the score: tempi indications such as *largo appassionato, allegro agitato* are also normally recorded in programme notes or record blurb.

(d) Content may also be implied by composers' statements of intent, either in the score itself or in their other writings. The programmes of the symphonic works of Berlioz or Strauss are extreme examples of this.

(e) Use of compositional conventions of a given period can convey a good deal to anyone familiar with them — as for instance with the use of key symbolism during the Baroque.

(f) Timbres imported from other areas of cultural life are significant: the association of brass instruments with state ceremonial or warfare, woodwind with pastoral settings, etc. is long-established. More extreme naturalism comes with the use of cow bells by Strauss, anvils by Wagner and a cow horn by Britten. Folk instruments from elsewhere are imported to add local colour — the use of castanets in "Spanish" pieces being one of the most obvious.

(g) A final rich vein of meaning arises from the quotation of other music which the audience is likely to know. An early ironic example is Mozart quoting *Figaro* in *Don Giovanni*. Wagner took the process to its furthest extreme in the *Ring* cycle, while the quotations used by Strauss in *Heldenleben* were explicitly autobiographical.

The impact of all these devices is reinforced by the fact that many people for much of the time listen only to music which they already know well. The conservative commercial policies of the record companies and concert promoters are the major influence on repetoire. The infrequent programming of contemporary music and the small audiences which it attracts are cited as causes for concern, particularly for its composers. In general, the occasions on which one has to face an unfamiliar work without either a record sleeve, programme notes or a BBC introducton are few and far between. However, when music is encountered without semantic packaging, the question arises of how a meaning for it might be constructed.

The starting point must be the basic parameters of musical expression: pitch, dynamics, timbre, harmony and rhythm, together with their various combinations. Even single notes may be meaningful for some, but normally it is a sequence of notes which will be seen as significant: the greater the number of parameters whose values change during the course of the sequence, the more complex the meaning evoked is likely to be.

The significance of melody has been dealt with in great detail by Cooke (1959). Much of his analysis revolves around the use of particular intervals — especially the major and minor thirds, and the "bright" or "dark" harmonies which they imply. One might also stress two other sources of possible semantic significance. One is spatial metaphor, using the juxtaposition of high and low tones. The words *et resurrexit* and *et ascendit* are often set to rising scales or motifs in mass settings, and similar motifs have become common in music with sentiments of the *per ardua ad astra* type. Similarly, falling motifs are usually associated with grief or rest. The other is onomatopeia which is often implied in melodic motifs conventionally associated with particular instruments. A good example is the fairly consistent equation made by composers from Bach to Strauss of melodies based on the harmonic series with horn calls and, by extension, hunting, chivalry and heroism. This originated in the period when the only notes the horn could play were the natural harmonics.

Dynamics are conventionally interpreted in a similar way. There is a conventional association between repose and quiet dynamics, and between activity and loud dynamics. Changes in dynamics can similarly be interpreted as "dying away" (*diminuendo*) or "gaining strength" (*crescendo*). Rhythmic pulses, which are at root rapid dynamic changes, can easily be associated with heart-beat, other physiological or emotional states, or physical activity, such as dance, with all the cultural overtones which different dance metres imply.

The final parameters are those of harmony and texture. In western tonal music, the basic principles are usually seen as the resolution of discords into concords, and tonal movement away from and back to a tonic key. Together these provide many of the cues by which the listener is able to break down a stream of sound into phrases, paragraphs and episodes as well as evoking a range of emotional connotations. Texture can also be seen as highly expressive. Polyphonic textures usually imply a greater degree of harmonic and rhythmic complexity than homophonic textures, and they are often used (as by Beethoven) with connotations of "struggle" or "conflict" in development sections and the like. On the other hand, polyphony can also bring together a diversity of thematic material with a sense of "culmination", as, for instance, at the end of the Jupiter Symphony or Bruckner's Eighth Symphony.

A different level at which meaning can be inferred is not intrinsic to the music, but lies in the context of performance. For many, music carries highly personal associations deriving from the contexts in which it was previously heard. Second, in stage and television performances, a major sources of cues for semantic evaluation lies in the dress, gestures and facial expressions of the performers, particularly the conductor and/or soloist. These are often idiosyncratic, but are circumscribed by broad conventions and are highly ritualized, from the moment of entry on to the platform to the final bows and bouquets at the end.

In a sense, this sort of ritualized repetition of the familiar is similar to the types of formalized discourse discussed by Bloch (1974). His argument is that much of the formalized speech, song and dance in ritual cannot be understood as conveying a message primarily. The restrictions on what is actually expressed make it impossible to communicate argument or meaning. As Bloch puts it, "you cannot argue with a song." The implication is that formalized ritual is conservative and supportive of the *status quo*.

This argument is of interest in the case of the ritualized performance of familiar music. Radical innovation in "art" music in the 20th century has usually been commercially unpopular, and new modes of symbolic expression (atonal music is the classic example) are unlikely to be generally accepted until a consensus has emerged as to the appropriate undercoding systems to be applied to them. Early European music or Indian classical music are at present much more popular than 20th century "art" music of the avant garde, precisely because a large proportion of the elements of which they are composed (such as scales and rhythmic repetition) are open to established procedures of undercoding. It is easier to be accepted by reworking the past than by fundamentally changing the rules. Liturgical conservatism in the churches (instanced by the debate over the Catholic Latin Rite or the various versions of the Anglican prayer book) illustrate similar processes. There is security in familiarity and the individual elaborations of meaning which result from the repetition of archaic forms to which we have, in effect, programmed ourselves to respond. In the ritualized western musical performance of familiar music, what Bloch calls the "illocutionary force" is important: it is not only what you play but how you play it that counts.

All the same, the musical examples suggest two qualifications of Bloch's account. First, the paradigms of musical composition do change, if slowly, and many composers (and their interpreters) do think of their role as having something new to communicate. In other societies, even if the actors insist that their performances of ritual are "traditional" it is open to question whether any compositional or performance tradition is completely static and impervious to outside influence or musical innovation. Second, illocutionary force is itself multi-dimensional, and through this means alone a variety of meanings can be conveyed. Third, there has been a tradition of parody and satire in European artistic performance from the Greek dramatists to the present, and the performance of formalized ritual in an innappropriate style can undermine the status quo and expose it to ridicule as well as uphold it.

III

Two sets of implications arise from this rather sketchy survey. The first is that of the implications of anthropological theories of symbolism for musicology and music criticism, particularly theories dealing with the individual improvization of meaning and the generation of shared meanings within a social group. These theories raise questions about some of the basic assumptions underlying a great deal of music criticism: that music constitutes a code which can be objectively deciphered through a careful reading of the "text" In the final analysis many of the insights of even the most socially aware critics such as Cooke and Mellers must be evaluated in the same way as those of, say, Turner's informant Muchona (Turner, 1967): they are the insights of skilled ritual practitioners whose views are more elaborated but as idiosyncratically constituted as those of anyone else, and they need not necessarily tell us much about the processes of appreciation going on in the mind of the average listener.

The other implications are for the study of ritual and symbolism in general. At the level of individual cognition, the distinction between formal and semantic evaluation made here may have parallels in the analysis of other symbolic systems. The discussion of music has also drawn attention to three other sets of factors which create problems in the analysis of symbols. The first is to do with undercoding and the perception of units — a process which can vary from person to person. The second is the distinction between conceptualization and symbolization. Sperber is correct to distinguish between the two and to point to the idiosyncratic nature of the latter. What the musical analogy suggests is that in most cases the two processes occur simultaneously. The third is the multidimensional nature of symbolic systems. In music, the dimensions of pitch, rhythm, timbre, etc. are analytically separable, and in some cases they convey different messages as well. These dimensions are largely independent of each other, and where each can take a separate loading the symbol will tend to be interpreted either ambiguously or differently by different actors, as they differ over which dimension they see as important. Parallel dimensional distinctions can be made in the cases of other symbolic systems and they frequently make the assignation of a single "meaning" to a unit of symbolic material problematic, unless the process of undercoding by the observer corresponds closely to that of the actors themselves.

A number of issues relate to the relationship between individual performance and text. Since the advant of recording, we have evidence of the quite dramatic changes in performing tastes and techniques, for instance in the string playing of the 1930s compared with the present, even when it is the same performers involved. Much that is actually played is not notated in the text — indeed the older the music (or the more recent in the case of John Cage and others) the more that is left to the discretion of the performer.

A third set of issues relates to social processes. Different evaluations of the content, meaning and quality of symbolic objects can arise, and these are likely to be disseminated within social groups along existing lines of cleavage. Schisms have been common both in ecclesiastical and musical history — the best known musical example being the conflict between the supporters of Wagner and Brahms in the late 19th century, but there are plenty of other cases in which some of the most sensitive critics have come to what are now considered hilariously wrong judgements about their greatest contemporaries (Slonimsky, 1965). As paradigms on which evaluation is based change, this polarization often gives way to a consensus, but, as with some religious denominations or the division between "serious" and "pop" music, the boundaries between different schools of thought may be perpetuated and reinforced by the activities of other agents: in music these include the media men, commercial interests and other funding agencies, and one suspects similar processes to be at work in certain of the media-conscious religious denominations. Both artistic performance and religious ritual may become symbolic expressions of solidarities which can be used for political ends, and thus the state may also have an interest in their control. The papers by Christian and Ruel in this volume show how individual belief and the expression of emotion have been carefully controlled in different periods. However, belief and emotion have, largely, been made private concerns, particularly in the Protestant tradition, and the emotional catharsis which characterized Spanish Christianity has been transposed from religion to the pop concert or the football terraces. This may seem a far cry from the sort of terrain usually inhabited by the anthropologist of religion and symbolism, but it is not necessarily so. The growth of literacy and the mass media may mean that we have to rely increasingly on the sorts of insights which can be generated from looking at a highly complex and literate symbolic system like western music to understand what is happening in a range of other ritual and symbolic systems.

Acknowledgements

This is a shortened and revised version of the paper presented at the Sussex conference. I would like to thank John Blacking and David Reason, along with the conference participants, for their extensive comments on the first draft: many of the issues they raised will have to be taken up elsewhere. As the idea for the paper stemmed from a practical interest in the performance of music of a particular tradition, it deals mainly with European "art" music as opposed to music in general.

Notes

1. My terminology differs slightly from that of Sperber's two accounts, which, in turn, differ from each other. The process I describe as conceptualization is what he calls "the conceptual mechanism" (1975) and "the rational device" (1980).
2. I use these terms in the sense suggested by Ardener (1971). For an alternative usage (on which the first draft of this paper relied more heavily) cf. Laughlin and Stephens (1980).
3. Ardener (1971, p. 453) citing Jakobson and Halle. The essential distinction is that the cryptanalyst lacks the code book and has to work out a set of rules for himself.
4. For an interesting discussion of the physiological bases of emotion and their relationship with musical expression, see Clynes (1977, chapter 8).

References

Ardener, E., 1971: The new anthropology and its critics. *Man,* **6(3)** 449-467.
Blacking, J., 1976: *How Musical is Man?* London (Faber and Faber).
Bloch, M., 1974: Symbols, song, dance and features of articulation. *European Journal of Sociology,* **15** 55-81.
Clynes, M., 1977: *Sentics: The Touch of Emotion.* London (Souvenir Press).
Coker, W., 1973: *Music and Meaning.* London (Collier-Macmillan).
Cooke, D., 1959: *The Language of Music.* London (Oxford University Press).
Eco, U., 1976: *A Theory of Semiotics.* Bloomington (Indiana University Press).
Frith, S., 1978: *The Sociology of Rock.* London (Constable).
Hanslick, E., 1891: *The Beautiful in Music.* London (Novello).
Hoaglund, J., 1980: Music as expressive. *British Journal of Aesthetics* **20(4)**, 340-348.
Laughlin, C.D., Jr., and Stephens, C.D., 1980: Symbolism, canalization and p-structure. In *Symbol and Sense.* (M.LeC. Foster and S.H. Brandes, eds.). New York and London (Academic Press).
Langer, S., 1957: *Philosophy in a New Key* (3rd edn.). Cambridge, Mass. (Harvard University Press).
Leahy, M.T.P., 1976: The vacuity of musical expressionism. *British Journal of Aesthetics* **16(2)**, 144-156.
Longuet-Higgins, H.C., 1976: Perception of melodies. *Nature* **263**, 646-653.
Mellers, W., 1980: *Bach and the Dance of God.* London (Faber and Faber).
Schutz, A., 1971: Making music together. *Collected Works,* Vol. 2. The Hague (Mouton).
Shepherd, J., Virden, D., Vulliamy, G. and Wishart, T. 1977: *Whose Music? A Sociology of Musical Languages.* London (Latimer).

Slonimsky, N., 1965: *Lexicon of Musical Invective.* Seattle (University of Washington Press).

Sperber, D., 1975: *Rethinking Symbolism.* Cambridge (Cambridge University Press).

Sperber, D., 1980: Is symbolic thought prerational? In *Symbol as Sense* (M.LeC. Foster and S.H. Brandes, eds.). New York and London (Academic Press).

Steedman, M., 1977: The perception of musical rhythm and metre. *Perception* **6**, 555-569.

Turner, V.W., 1967: *The Forest of Symbols.* Ithaca (Cornell University Press).

Wright, D.F., 1975: Musical meaning and its social determinants. *Sociology* **9**, 419-435.

Author Index

Subject Index